RECOVERING
ABUNDANCE

RECOVERING ABUNDANCE

TWELVE PRACTICES FOR SMALL-TOWN LEADERS

ANDY STANTON-HENRY

FORTRESS PRESS
Minneapolis

To the ordinary leaders who are doing the hidden
but holy work of renewing their small towns
and rural regions

"What we need is here."

—Wendell Berry, "The Wild Geese"

CONTENTS

Acknowledgments xi

Introduction 1

Chapter 1: The Practice of Retreat 11

Chapter 2: The Practice of Discernment 32

Chapter 3: The Practice of Stability 56

Chapter 4: The Practice of Inventory 77

Chapter 5: The Practice of Imagination 97

Chapter 6: The Practice of Organizing 118

Chapter 7: The Practice of Hospitality 137

Chapter 8: The Practice of Grounding 159

Chapter 9: The Practice of Gratitude 179

Chapter 10: The Practice of Generosity 198

Chapter 11: The Practice of Solidarity 217

Chapter 12: The Practice of Memory 239

Notes 265

Recommended Reading 279

ACKNOWLEDGMENTS

APPRECIATION TO MY EDITOR, BETH Gaede. You were the midwife for birthing my first book.

Much obliged to Ben Brazil and the gang at Earlham School of Religion. You believed in this project from the beginning and always insisted that writing is ministry.

Much gratitude to my parents, who always encouraged me in reading, 'riting, and 'rithmetic. You always celebrated my affinity toward the first two and loved me when I was bad at the third.

Many thanks to my long-suffering and ever-encouraging spouse, Ashlyn. This book is one of the many things I wouldn't, and couldn't, have done without you.

I WOKE UP ON NOVEMBER 9, 2016, and gazed out the window at what looked like another cool and crisp autumn day in central Ohio. But it wasn't just another day. It was the day after election day in a presidential election year. I had been following the campaigns closely and watched the results as they came in the night before, but I fell asleep at about two o'clock in the morning. The small television in my room stayed on after I fell asleep, so it was still on when I awoke. I didn't have to wait long before learning the election had been decided.

Donald Trump was going to be our next president.

I stood shocked, holding the remote loosely in my hand and watching the news a little longer to make sure I hadn't heard incorrectly. All the models and predictions had agreed that Hillary Rodham Clinton was going to win, possibly with a historic margin. How did this happen? How did we not see this coming? Where did this surge of support come from, and what did it mean?

Of course, I wasn't the only one taken by surprise at Trump's victory. My friends processed their shock on social media. Scrolling through my Facebook newsfeed, I witnessed posts ranging from elation to devastation. Whether they were protesting or partying, almost all agreed that they hadn't seen it coming.

The following weeks inspired commentary from a host of political pundits doing their best to make sense of this anomaly. Before long, a consensus emerged. We were told that the surprising success of Donald Trump's campaign could be attributed to a particular demographic of Americans who have long felt left out and left behind in America's social and economic transformation. This disaffected population was known as the "white working class."

The white working class label was broadly applied but generally referred to white folks without a college degree who worked in blue-collar jobs. They could be found across the rust belt of the Midwest, the small towns of Appalachia, and rural regions across the country. They were typically resistant to social change and had been victimized by automation and bad trade deals.

This cacophony of commentary converged into a national narrative. According to this common story, the white working class, largely made up of rural voters, were the antagonists. Economically disenfranchised and resentful of social change, they made their voices heard through the "strong man leader" named Donald Trump. He would stand up for them and set things right. He would toss aside elitism and political correctness and make America great again.

Eager to capitalize on the media attention, some advocates for rural revitalization confirmed the story, emphasizing the cultural breakdown and spiritual poverty of rural communities. At the time, the story made sense to me, and I adopted it as my interpretive lens for understanding what was going on with my rural neighbors and fellow citizens.

I had only recently moved back to my hometown in rural Ohio, and I was trying to reacquaint myself with the people and places that so shaped the first two decades of my life. I was completing my seminary program and was eager to integrate all the things I had studied about social justice and spiritual formation with what I was experiencing in my rural context. It seemed like all the resources about social justice were directed to people in urban settings. And it seemed like the spiritual formation resources were directed to people living a suburban lifestyle.

After the election I listened intently to proponents of this national narrative, and I read relentlessly about rural issues. I learned about the economic, cultural, and moral breakdown experienced by many rural communities and small towns. I saw the patterns of decline and devastation that brought suffering to rural Americans and seemed to foster a spirit of resentment and despair. I read books like *Hillbilly Elegy*, in which J. D. Vance offered a critique of working-class folks from his Kentucky childhood and ultimately concluded: "There is a cultural movement in the white working class to blame problems on society or the government, and that movement gains adherents by the day."[1] And I read articles like one in the *Wall Street Journal* that outlined troubling trends in rural communities across America, declaring them the "new inner city." I didn't believe President Trump would be their savior, but I had empathy for rural and rust belt folks who voted "against their interests" because they were in pain.

THE REST OF THE STORY

However, as I dug deeper into the stories of my neighbors and learned more about individuals and groups working on projects of rural renewal, I began to uncover a new story. Or at least, as Paul Harvey would say, "the rest of the story." Yes, there were indeed folks who were looking for a strong man with a big mouth to be their angry advocate. Yes, there is real prejudice and ignorance in rural communities. And yes, there is very real pain and oppression. But there are also folks who aren't waiting for an intervention from big government or big business. Instead of waiting, they are working. Working to build inclusive, thriving, local economies. Working to weave a welcoming social fabric in their region. Working to start new businesses, revive old buildings, and co-create a positive future for their small town.

Before I learned these stories, I was utterly unaware of all the projects going on across the country led by so many ordinary—yet extraordinary—people. I had no idea how much I didn't know. When

I discovered this new story, I realized how the old story, though perhaps meant to inspire empathy and aid, is actually disempowering.
It perpetuates the idea that rural folks are backwoods and backward
and can only be helped by powerful leaders from our nation's urban
centers, whether those leaders be liberal technocrats or conservative swamp-drainers. But I know that rural folks are competent and
creative, resourceful and resilient. Good public policy can go a long
way but only in partnership with the folks who are already leading
their communities and loving their neighbors in often hidden but
important ways.

AN ALTERNATIVE STORY

I realized that this new narrative was the one I needed to learn more
about and lift up as an example. After all, stories are powerful. They
don't just tell us about what happened in the past. They interpret the
present and impact the future. They influence how we direct energies and resources. The philosopher Ivan Illich argued that neither
revolution nor reformation could truly transform society without a
new, persuasive, inclusive story. "If you want to change a society," he
insisted, "then you have to tell an alternative story."[2]

Likewise, the Jewish philosopher Martin Buber tells the tale
about his grandfather who had limited mobility and spent most of
his time in a wheelchair. One day his grandfather was telling the
story about his favorite teacher, who would jump and dance when
he prayed. Buber's grandfather got so swept away in imitating his
teacher that he was cured of his disability and began jumping and
dancing. That's how you tell a story, Buber said.[3]

Indeed, stories have healing and transformative power. In her
TED Talk about "the dangers of a single story," Nigerian author
Chimamanda Ngozi Adichie insists on the importance of telling
multiple stories about places and people. "The single story creates
stereotypes," she said, "and the problem with stereotypes is not that
they are untrue, but that they are incomplete. They make one story

become the only story." This has often been true for small towns and rural communities. Sometimes those stories have been used to dismiss and dispossess rural folks, and sometimes those stories were used to attract pity and public awareness. But the old story, when told as the dominant narrative, is a single story that leaves out some really important and inspiring stories. Thankfully, the storytelling continues, and we, as ordinary leaders, have the power to shape our own stories. "Stories can break the dignity of a people," said Adichie, "but stories can also repair that broken dignity."[4]

I want to tell an alternative story about small towns and rural regions, one that helps "repair that broken dignity." Not a story about decline and desperation for outside intervention but a story about the agency and creativity of what I call "ordinary leaders" from within those communities. Not a story about scarcity and depravity but of abundance and generosity. This alternative story not only fills out the narrow narrative that is pervasive in our time, but it also shapes our intention and direction as we work to repair and renew our communities. Because we don't just tell stories, we live them. And the stories we tell become the stories we live.

THE OLD-NEW STORY

Do you know someone who tells the same stories over and over again? Maybe it's a relative with memory challenges who constantly forgets which stories they have told you and which they haven't. Maybe it's a spouse who likes holding a past failure over your head to make sure you never forget it. Or maybe it's a buddy who likes reliving the glory days by retelling stories from high school every time you get together.

Stories that matter are told and retold. They keep popping up and inserting themselves into our conversations and reflections. Interestingly enough, as I was learning about this new, alternative story about rural communities, an ancient story from the gospels kept coming up. The new story I was discovering was being shaped by this old story. Actually, it's a very old story. But also one that is somehow ever new.

This ancient-new story is sometimes called the story of Jesus feeding the multitude or, often, the feeding of the five thousand.

This gospel story about a prophetic picnic in a rural region was one of those "told and retold stories" that kept coming up in early Christian communities. Apparently, this story conveyed and mediated something important about Jesus and his kingdom way. We will unpack these themes in subsequent chapters, but suffice it to say that this story reminded early Christians of important truths that spoke to them again and again in different situations and settings. It was so meaningful to these early communities that all four gospels include a version of the story. It's actually the only miracle story that has such a claim to fame. Not even the Christmas story makes it into all four gospels. This gospel story has also stood the test of time, impacting countless lives across the centuries. And I believe this ancient story has contemporary relevance for folks seeking to tell and live a new story in rural communities.

It's a moving and inspiring story. Yet it can be tempting to read it as awe-inspiring in a reverent way but not actionable in a relevant way. We can read it as a story about a messianic leader and the miracle he performed a long, long time ago in a galaxy far, far away. But I will argue that the story's reach is much wider and deeper. Jesus transformed a situation of scarcity and decline into a story of abundance and renewal. And he did so in an instructional and invitational way. Jesus was teaching his disciples and by extension, teaching us, how to live a new story.

To get the most out of this book, I encourage you to reframe the way you read this gospel story. Read it many times at different paces, in different places, and with different people as you work your way through this book. Read it as a story about Jesus, a rural leader whose story continues to transform the world. Also read it as a parable about life and leadership in a rural setting that "speaks to your condition," as Quakers say.

The story is often called the feeding of the five thousand, putting the emphasis on Jesus's divine power and glory. That's partly true, of course. But it's also the story of Jesus feeding *with* the five thousand. Jesus initiated the miracle but invited his disciples and even the crowd to participate in the process. I believe you and I, as ordinary leaders, are invited to partner with God in making miracles within our contexts, though they may not feel quite so dramatic.

LEADING THE NEW STORY

I'll be talking a lot about the importance of ordinary leaders, so let me clarify who I mean by that. Ordinary leaders often don't consider themselves leaders. They generally avoid the spotlight and don't pursue fancy titles. But they are eager to make a difference, help their neighbors, and build a better future for their family and community. They are entrepreneurs, pastors, parents, mayors, educators, farmers, activists, and more.

Ordinary leaders have many of the qualities common among all leaders: integrity, vision, courage, and so forth. But ordinary leaders are defined by at least three specific qualities: ownership, membership, and influence.

Ordinary leaders practice *radical ownership*. They own the problems and possibilities of their community. They don't deny the diverse factors that contribute to the problems that plague their region, but neither do they wait for an outside intervention to start organizing, collaborating, and creating for positive change. They welcome fresh resources injected into their community, but instead of blaming or begging, they focus on uncovering and developing the assets already available.

Ordinary leaders also inhabit their community as *rooted members*. They are not looking for the next big thing somewhere else. They view their community as home, not a hotel. They are committed to their people and their place and are sticking with them long enough to gain invaluable local knowledge and social capital. Not only are they committed to sticking around, but they enjoy life in their town. It's not always easy, but they are motivated by a sense of love and solidarity. They understand why Wendell Berry said, "It all turns on affection."[5]

Also, ordinary leaders exercise *relational influence* rather than rely on positional authority. They may or may not hold a position of authority, but they have trust, respect, and social capital in the community. They exercise voluntary responsibility for their community's well-being and value the relationships that keep the community strong. Because of their ownership, membership, and relationships, people trust them enough to show up and join in when this ordinary leader proposes a call to action.

Does that sound like you or someone you know? Or does that sound like someone you want to become? If so, let's learn to lead together.

PRACTICING THE NEW STORY

The truth is that learning how to live the new story of abundance and renewal is going to take some practice. That's why this book is about practices. We learn by doing then reflecting on that doing as we become reflective practitioners in our context. Personal and community renewal isn't about *trying to make a difference*; it's about *training to become different* (and at the same time, more fully ourselves). We have been socialized to envision and embody the old story, so we have to be trained to walk in the ways of the new.

When I say "practices," I mean disciplines and rhythms that cultivate abundant life within us and around us. I invite you to think about practices in terms of both spiritual formation and civic virtues. Put another way, these twelve practices are ways to both form our personal wellness and wholeness (for Christians, this means "Christ-likeness") and shape our communities into just and flourishing places to live. These twelve practices help us experience, embody, and expand the abundant kind of life that Jesus modeled.

They help us learn and live the new story of abundance and renewal, even when the default story is scarcity and decline.

There's a Zen story that illustrates the value of practices. Three monks decided to meditate together beside a nearby lake. After they closed their eyes and began to concentrate, the first monk suddenly stood up and said, "I forgot my prayer mat!" Remarkably, he stepped right onto the water in front of him and crossed, striding across the lake. He grabbed his mat from the hut and walked on the water all the way back. After he returned, the three monks closed their eyes again and began to concentrate. They were just about to settle into their meditation when the second monk jumped up and said, "I also forgot my prayer mat!" Amazingly, he too stepped right onto the water, fetched his prayer mat, and returned, striding upon the water.

For the third time, the monks once again closed their eyes and prepared to meditate. The third monk decided that this must be some kind of test, so he was eager to learn and even more eager to prove himself. He stood up, rushed to the water's edge, and stepped in confidently. He abruptly sank and found himself in water over his head. Determined and frustrated, the monk dragged himself out of the water and tried again. He sank. He tried again; no miracle. After watching this for a time, the first monk turned to the second and said, "Do you think we should tell him where the stones are?"

Thankfully, Jesus isn't secretive or stingy with wisdom. He does not just stand back and laugh when we fall into the water. He tells us where the stones are. Jesus shows us how to use the stepping-stones of civic-spiritual practices to experience and expand abundance. In fact, he wants to teach us his ways and watch us do "even greater things" (John 14:12).

Within this gospel story, we witness twelve practices, or stepping-stones. Each helps us embody the new story that Jesus called abundant life, available for all people in all places, not least in the rural communities and villages that were close to Jesus's heart as a rural leader.

Having a clear path makes a big difference. Knowing where the stones are makes miracles possible. Yet it's not really about a formula or method. It's about an apprenticeship and partnership with the one who walked on water and walked on the earth in such a way that renewal followed his footsteps. After all, as Thich Nhat Hanh wrote, "The miracle is not to walk on water. The miracle is to walk on the green Earth in the present moment, to appreciate the peace and beauty that are available now."[6] Hanh wrote a book called *Peace Is Every Step* in which he reminded readers that we can experience and extend peace in our ordinary lives and our everyday interactions. I would like to borrow the idea and apply it to our work for renewal. Renewal is every step. Every day and every interaction provide an opportunity for renewal, and the twelve practices help us see and seize those opportunities that are given to us. May we learn to walk in such a way that renewal is every step and our lives manifest the possibilities of a new story.

Let's take the first step.

CHAPTER ONE

THE PRACTICE
OF RETREAT

Come with me by yourselves to a quiet place and get some rest.

Mark 6:31

IT ALL STARTED WITH A retreat. Before the crowd, the food, or the miracle, it was just Jesus and his disciples. In Mark's telling, the disciples had been out and about, learning how to practice what they preached and how to preach what they practiced. They were eager and excited to report back to Jesus about all they had been doing (Mark 6:30). And they had been doing a lot. We are told that there was so much "coming and going" that they "had no leisure even to eat" (v. 32). These companions of Jesus were hungry and weary.

Have you ever been so caught up in "coming and going" that you didn't have "leisure even to eat"?

My first job was working for a landscaping company in Marion, Ohio. It was hard and hot work. The days were long; sometimes we would be digging, planting, weeding, mowing, and mulching from dawn to dusk. Sometimes we were working so hard that we skipped our lunch break and worked right through midwestern dinner time. I will never forget how good it felt to come home after a long, hot day outside. Food never tasted so good. Showers never felt so refreshing.

Sleep never embraced me so sweetly. There is nothing quite like the feeling of entering the solitude of one's room—showered, full, and in the luxurious air conditioning after a long, hot day of manual labor and cranky clients.

Sometimes, though, our weariness has nothing to do with manual labor. It has to do with the emotional labor of raising kids, shepherding souls, or managing a business. Ordinary leaders have all manner of "labors of love" that occupy their minds, break their hearts, and demand their energy. Yes, even in small towns and rural regions.

It's tempting to believe that living in a rural region affords a simple life by default. Indeed, the rhythms and landscapes of rural life have a way of inviting us into a more simple and peaceful way of life. But the truth is, no matter where we live, we are about as busy as we want to be. City folks would be amazed at how quickly our lives and calendars fill up, despite there being "nothing to do."

C. S. Lewis observed in the first half of the twentieth century that "we live, in fact, in a world starved for solitude, silence, and private: and therefore starved for meditation and true friendship."[1] Still very true. And unfortunately, just as true in rural regions.

Ordinary leaders grow weary from all the "coming and going." Paradoxically, we also get lonely. Rural life can be lonely. Rural leadership can be lonely. We work on a project we believe in, but it feels like there aren't enough people or resources to make it happen. We work for change when it feels like everyone else is content with the way things are. Or we seek like-minded friendships but feel like the black sheep of our community. Solitude can turn into loneliness. Room to breathe can turn into isolation.

With these risks of isolation and burnout, as well as the mental health challenges faced by most folks, it's important that we develop rhythms of regular renewal. As Jesus's example confirms, retreats are an important part of those rhythms.

Some of my small-town friends see retreats as something of a luxury, mostly for wealthy, self-obsessed city folks. They imagine a highfalutin character from Hollywood or Silicon Valley taking a week off to sit at the feet of a guru and practice yoga poses on the beach. It's an expense they can't afford, and besides, they don't get into all that touchy-feely find-yourself stuff. They try to live a godly and grounded life; maybe they go to church to feed their souls and go on an occasional vacation to rest their bodies. In their minds, that's enough "retreating" to sustain them.

We all have different needs and walk our own unique paths. But I find that rural folks are like most other folks in that they often have an unnamed hunger and weariness that they carry through their lives. It lives just beneath the surface of the life they share with the world. They hide a hunger for unconditional love when childhood traumas resurface following a painful divorce. They hide a hunger to be held, to release uncried tears after having cared for a cranky, confused parent for the last five years before their passing. They hide a weariness from decades of factory work to provide for their family. The aches and pains reveal a price paid for being a provider, for "manning up" day after day for so long. Or they feel the profound exhaustion of being a "good housewife" for their husband and children and community and country and God and . . .

Jesus was no stranger to this kind of deep hunger and weariness. It came to him after times of intense, intimate ministry, and it came to him after times of public opposition and difficult discernment. Jesus knew he needed time away for rest, prayer, grief, and discernment. The author of Luke's gospel tells us that "Jesus *often* withdrew to lonely places and prayed" (Luke 5:16). Practicing this life-giving rhythm enabled Jesus to minister with energy and authority. It centered him in the divine presence, so that he was able to invite others into the rest of God.

Attentive to the weariness of the disciples, Jesus knew what they needed most. It wasn't to talk about all the cool stuff the disciples had been doing, though debriefing is important. What they needed most was a renewing retreat. So, Jesus offered a clear, liberating invitation: "Come away to a quiet place by yourselves and rest a while" (Mark 6:31).

How life-giving Jesus's invitation must have been. How life-giving it is today, when the Present Teacher invites us to come away with him to a place of peace and quiet where our souls and bodies can be renewed. I have found that the practice of retreat is essential to my own health and growth, so much so that I've committed to taking some kind of retreat at least four times a year, one for each season. It's central to my spiritual practice. But it hasn't always been so.

BULLS AND BUSHES

The first time I really learned about the importance of taking retreats was in college. Since I was a child, I have been aware of how refreshing it is to take solitary walks in the woods—meandering, imagining, praying. And I had taken a number of youth retreats where we stayed up late, ate junk food, and had emotional worship sessions. All kinds of things pass for "retreats" these days, events offered by churches, gurus, and corporations. Each has its place. But my college professor, Dave, told us about something else. He was talking about getting away for a day, a weekend, or a week to intentionally seek God's presence and rest our whole self. He was talking about carving out time and space in which we make what Emilie Griffin calls "a generous commitment to our friendship with God."

We have "generous commitments" to many things, so retreats sometimes seem implausible, if not a little indulgent. But Dave said we cannot wait until the timing is perfect and the opportunity is convenient. Emilie Griffin agrees: "Times come when we yearn for more of God than our schedules will allow. We are tired, we are crushed, we are crowded by friends and acquaintances, commitments and obligations. The life of grace is abounding, but we are too busy for it. Even good obligations begin to hem us in."[2] When we feel we least have time for it is probably when a retreat is most needed.

I think about it this way: if Jesus needed retreats, how can I argue that I don't? Dave's oft-repeated axiom reminds me of this truth: "Even the Messiah didn't have a messiah complex." Jesus knew he had limits. He knew he needed to practice a sustainable, life-renewing rhythm. And he invited disciples and seekers to learn it for themselves. Eugene Peterson's paraphrase of Jesus's invitation in *The Message* says it well: "Are you tired? Worn out? Burned out on religion? Come to me. Get away with me and you'll recover your life. I'll show you how to take a real rest. Walk with me and work with me—watch how I do it. Learn the unforced rhythms of grace. I won't lay anything heavy or ill-fitting on you. Keep company with me and you'll learn to live freely and lightly" (Matt 11:28–30 MSG).

Dave found this invitation compelling. He was convinced that if we are to recover abundant life for others, we have to get away with Christ to recover our own life and learn those rhythms of grace. The risks, he argued, were great: leaders and families and souls damaged with ripple effects across our congregations and communities. He agreed with Dallas Willard's warning: "If you don't come apart for a while, you will come apart after a while."[3] I was convinced and ready to learn. And it just so happened that taking a retreat was an assignment for Dave's class.

I was excited to try out this spiritual retreat thing, but there was one problem. I was living in Kansas. The college I attended was a small Quaker college in western Kansas. It was extremely rural. I grew up in rural Ohio, but the Kansas landscape and culture made me feel like I was from the big city. Most of the surrounding area was made up of enormous wheat farms and ranches. Tumbleweed literally blew through town. Don't get me wrong, Kansas has its own forms of beauty: stunning sunsets, earth-shaking thunderstorms you can watch roll in from miles away, and a general feeling of what Belden Lane calls the "solace of fierce landscapes."[4] But I had no idea where I could go to rest, reflect, picnic, and take a couple of contemplative walks.

Then it came to me: state parks. I always enjoyed hiking in Ohio state parks. They always had plentiful shelters, restrooms, and kiosks with helpful information. So I googled Kansas state parks and found one about an hour away. It looked like it had a lake and a couple of trails, and the website even boasted seven "modern pit toilets." Sounds good!

So off I went in my Chevy Cavalier, ready for a day full of serenity and theophany. After an uneventful drive, I was excited to see the weathered sign that informed me I had arrived at the park. The "park," however, was not what I expected. I saw no shelters, trails, kiosks, or modern pit toilets. I saw only gravel roads, rugged pasture marked off by barbed wire fences, and cows. Many cows. Judgmental cows who paused their grazing to look up and stare at me as if to say, "What are you doing in my house?"

Nevertheless, I was determined to find this quaint, lovely park, so I kept driving, ignoring the No Trespassing signs (at a public park?), assuming they were only there for setting the mood or maybe to keep away cow tippers. My journey was suddenly halted when I turned a corner and found the way blocked by a cow. A bull, actually. A bull I didn't intend to upset. I wasn't sure if my car insurance covered bull brawls. So I waited. Not wishing to waste time, I pulled out my journal and began to write earnestly. The bull wasn't budging and seemed content to stare threateningly as the judgmental cows gathered around on each side. I decided to ignore them and turn inward, journaling about college life, God, girls, politics. After a while, they decided to move on, so the way was opened for my unconventional retreat to continue. As I drove over the stinky gift the bull left me on the road, I took a breath and told myself I would find evidence of the park soon. Rejuvenation and revelation were sure to come.

The gravel turned to dirt, and the barbed wire fencing turned into open pasture. After a few more miles and no signs of direction, I decided it was time to fish or cut bait. I pulled over the car, parked it, and forged my own path on foot. Over yonder there was evidence of a small stream and a couple of trees, so I headed that direction. After twisting my ankle and conquering the brush, I reached the pitiful stream. It seemed like as good a place as any to sit and contemplate, but I couldn't find a place that wasn't inhibited by prickly-pear cacti. Nor could I find space in my mind that wasn't filled with anxiety about getting injured so far from cell service or colliding with livestock, getting sunburned, and failing my assignment. I walked back to the car and cut my losses. I felt like a failure. And even worse, I felt like a city slicker.

It probably comes as no surprise to you that my first experience with the practice of retreat didn't endear the discipline to me. The reflection paper was difficult; I played around with the bull as a metaphor and the dirt roads as pilgrim paths, but it felt forced. I told a few people about my experience but mostly kept it to myself—partly out of embarrassment and partly because I loved the idea of retreat and didn't want to believe my bull-dodging expedition was "as good as it gets." Thankfully, I worked up the courage to try again.

PRAIRIE AND PILGRIMAGE

About a year later, I was driving across the Kansas plains for a retreat once again. But this time, it was different. First, I was going to a specific retreat center at a specific location. Second, I was going with a group of people for a structured weekend. And third, I would be leading it. Well, not leading it exactly. Dave was leading it, but he invited me to come along as an assistant. (Had he not read my paper?)

The first evening began with a hearty dinner and a lovely time of worship and sharing with clergy from the surrounding region. The next morning, I explored the retreat house a bit further. Oasis Ranch and Retreat Center sits on a working ranch and 320 acres of Kansas countryside. The website gives the rationale for the name: "Oasis is about life; it is about a refuge from the desert and the mirages that appear to bring life but lead to nowhere. An oasis brings hope and life to the desperate desert surrounding it. Finding an oasis is always good news for the weary."[5] I now read those words as a great mission for a great ministry enterprise in rural renewal. At the time, though,

I heard the words with hopeful anticipation. Maybe this time, this retreat could be an oasis in the wilderness of my life—a life-giving weekend for me and for the hard-working clergy who were there with me.

The next afternoon, the group had free time. Dave didn't need me for anything, so I decided to go out to the old chapel that the hosts told us about. The little country church was over a century old. The original pews and pulpit remained in the building, but the congregants also added some comfy couches in the back and installed a large screen on the front wall. There weren't enough people to pay a pastor in their remote location, so they got creative and gathered together every Sunday for small group fellowship and a satellite sermon.

I could see the chapel from the retreat house, but there was no clear path. The hosts said we could cut through the pasture. Nervous but desiring a contemplative walk, I set out, following a faint footpath. After about ten minutes, I found myself hopping over barbed-wire fences, avoiding herds of meandering cattle, and pushing through prickly-bush patches. "Oh, sweet Lord," I said out loud. "Cows, unclear paths, prickly bushes, and stressful strides across the prairie—it's exactly like my last retreat!"

Nevertheless, I persevered. I was almost there, and I could savor the shelter and quiet solitude of the sanctuary. Finally, I arrived at the doorstep of the chapel and pulled the handle. But it didn't move. It was locked. Okay, maybe there's a back door. I walked around the building, peeking through the windows and seeking a hidden door. Nothing.

Frustrated and feeling defeated, I sat down on the doorstep. The wind howled across the pasture and wacked my face. Unable to make the retreat a life-changing spiritual encounter, I simply surrendered. I sank into the solitude of the plains. In weariness, I emptied my mind and consented to the spiritual force of the landscape.

In that moment, I had a spiritual experience that shaped me for years to come. I won't try to explain the exact nature of the experience, but I will tell you that I felt addressed by the divine in a very real way. I experienced the Spirit opening to me the experience of marginalized communities, particularly the LGBTQ community, who are "locked out" of the church. They do not have an easy, clear path to get there in the first place, and when they arrive, they are not welcomed. The doors are closed and locked. They are left to face the brutality and perplexity of life on their own. But they need the sanctuary of the church and the wisdom of the church; they need the supportive community and sustaining sacraments of the church. And the church needs them. She needs their stories and testimony, their laughter, tears, and voices.

Sitting there on the steps of this rural chapel, I was addressed by the Present Teacher. I remembered how Saint Francis stood amid the ruins of San Damiano's chapel and heard Christ say: "Francis, go and rebuild my church which, as you see, is falling down." I'm no Saint Francis, to be sure, but on those steps, before that chapel, surrounded by that pasture, I heard the same Spirit of Christ: "Andy, go and unlock the doors of my church which, as you see, are being closed off to my beloveds."

It would be more relaxing if retreats always went as planned, but the truth is that they rarely go as planned. And yet, somehow, if we are open, they will give us what we need. I could not have planned or predicted that chapel encounter.

Many of my retreats have been both relaxing and renewing. But sometimes, like my Oasis retreat, the retreat is disruptive and renewing. Spiritual writer Philip Zaleski observes this pattern with retreats in his book *The Recollected Heart*: "While any given retreat may start out as a joyride—a few days away from spouse, kids, or job, a chance to spread one's wings, loosen one's belt, kick up one's heels—it always winds up as a pilgrimage."[6] I wish you nothing but "serenity now" when you practice retreat, but don't be surprised if you go on retreat for a joyride and it ends up being a pilgrimage.

When we read the gospel stories of the New Testament, it seems like retreating with Jesus resulted in all kinds of renewing pilgrimages—sometimes relaxing but often surprising, disruptive, transformative, and life-changing. In the ensuing chapters, we will find out just how wild and wonderful a pilgrimage the disciples will experience when their retreat is redirected. We can expect surprises too, but we can trust that if Christ is the one who offers the invitation, he is also the one who prepares the time and space. Yes, we are responsible for clearing our calendars, booking the room, getting directions, even opening up our hearts and minds, but Christ, the Wise Host, is the one who "prepares a table" (Ps 23) for us with what we need most.

If retreats so often turn into pilgrimages, are there any common benefits we can expect for rural leaders and helpers who are interested in practicing retreat? Yes, and I will offer three.

REORIENTING: OUTSIDE THE VILLAGE

First of all, as my prairie pilgrimage at Oasis demonstrates, retreats *reorient* us. They awaken vision and imagination; they open our eyes to see things we weren't able to see before. While I'm not typically one for formulas, Pastor Mark Batterson provides one I find helpful: a change of place + a change of pace = a change of perspective.[7] I have found this to be true. It amazes me how just a weekend (sometimes even a day or evening) away can help me reframe my life and work.

One of my favorite gospel stories is found in Mark 8, where a vision-impaired man in a fishing town called Bethsaida was brought to Jesus for healing. Instead of immediately laying on hands or speaking a healing command, Jesus took him on a little retreat. He took the man by the hand and led him "outside the village" (v. 23). In that set-apart space, Jesus prayed for him and then asked, "Do you see anything?" When the man replied that he could see partially but not fully, Jesus touched him and prayed with him again. The man "looked intently," and "his sight was restored" until he "saw everything clearly" (v. 25).

This story is a great illustration of Jesus's wisdom and the wisdom of retreat. First, it conveys the power of getting "outside the village"—initiating a change of place and pace, so that we are able to see things in a new way. Sometimes the fullness of vision can come only when we get away from the roles, responsibilities, and systems that define us in everyday life. We can get insulated and isolated in our rural communities. We become dominated by the predominant worldview and expectations of the village. So it's important to detach from time to time.

Ordinary leaders need to stand back and step outside of our community (geographically, emotionally, spiritually) so that we can get a better sense of the landscape. Leadership guides Ronald Heifetz and Marty Linsky call this process "going to the balcony."[8] We all need that balcony time where we step away from our daily work to take a longer look and wider view. Otherwise, our vision is limited to the status quo, which isn't good for us and keeps us from leading the community to new places with new visions.

Sometimes it's helpful to literally get distance during a retreat, like actually scaling a mountain, staying in a hillside lodge, or finding some kind of "balcony" to inhabit for a time. But it's also important to temporarily create some emotional distance from your community.

In rural communities, it's easy to get stuck in what psychologist and rabbi Edwin Friedman called "imaginative gridlock."[9] When we are stuck in imaginative gridlock, we can't see beyond our own system. So, when we see a problem, we turn to the same old techniques, which get us nowhere new. Friedman writes that emotional differentiation and a sense of adventure are essential to reaching a breakthrough from this gridlock: "Any renaissance, anywhere, whether in a marriage or a business, depends primarily not only on new data and techniques, but on the capacity of leaders to separate themselves from the surrounding emotional climate so that they can break through the barriers that are keeping everyone from 'going the other way.'"[10] I believe the same principle is true for the renaissance, or renewal, of communities. In order to recover abundance in our rural communities, ordinary leaders need time away where they can regain perspective and glimpse new visions.

The second lesson in the gospel story is that new perspective and vision require attention and intention. Jesus had to touch the man twice and pray with him twice. The new vision was partial and in process the first time. And even after the second touch, the man still needed to focus his energies on what was happening. He "looked intently." Sometimes new vision will come unsolicited, in a moment of epiphany and revelation. But often it requires energy and effort. We have to focus our attention and intention to look closely at a situation and see it with new eyes.

In his teaching about prayer, Jesus instructs his disciples to "go into your room and shut the door" (Matt 6:6). Closing the doors on distractions, inward and outward, is essential to renewing our minds and seeing new sights. This requires what author Cal Newport calls "deep work."[11] Deep work requires shutting out distractions, disconnecting from social media, and dedicating intentional mental energy to learning and creating. While balcony time helps break through tunnel vision, deep work helps clarify vague vision.

Newport quotes David Brooks, who says great creative minds "think like artists but work like accountants."[12] In other words, they are open to fresh ideas and visions, but they don't wait for inspiration to strike. They plan particular times for doing deep work and use rituals to enter an imaginative space with intentionality. Retreats create an environment for ordinary leaders to practice both deep prayer and deep work.

Another way that retreats reorient us is that they "right-size" us. When we think we are all alone in the world and nothing good is happening in our rural context, time away will remind us that God has many other friends and partners at work in the world. As Elijah was reminded on his broom tree retreat, God has "reserved 7,000 in Israel" (1 Kings 19:18). It reminds us that though our work may seem small and simple, in the divine process of growth and multiplication, a great and secret work is taking place behind the scenes. We can trust in the slow work of God.

The author Madeleine L'Engle writes: "Every so often, I need OUT; something will throw me into total disproportion, and I have to get away from everybody—away from all these people I love most in the world—in order to regain a sense of proportion."[13] Have you ever found yourself having a disproportionate reaction to someone's comment or behavior? Or maybe you find yourself thinking that you are absolutely indispensable to some project or person?

Between the busyness of life and the bumps and bruises of relationships, it's easy to lose our sense of proportion. But it's in those moments when we are reminded to "be still and know" that God is God, and we are not. We are important and irreplaceable, to be sure. But we are not the lone bearers of the world's burdens. We are not the saviors of our rural communities.

RENEWAL: IN THE BOAT

Second, retreats *renew* us. I have a secret. I don't tell many people about it, but I feel like I can trust you. You see, I like . . . country music. I also like NPR, so I'm a little complicated. I'm not really ashamed, but not everyone gets it. When I confess my affection for country music, they look at me with a face that communicates both pity and perplexity, as if to say, "You poor, poor country boy." I can handle it. But maybe country music has gotten an undeserved bad rap. People say all the songs are sad laments about the singer losing their dog, their truck, or their woman, with a few patriotic songs thrown in for good measure. I say these people are wrong. There are also a lot of songs about boats. From Jimmy Buffett's boozy, tropical cruises to Craig Morgan's "Redneck Yacht Club," there are a lot of boats in country music. It turns out that this is one thing the Bible and country music have in common.

The Bible is full of boats. Think of the story of Jonah or Noah's Ark. As it turns out, boat stories are a kind of literary genre. Think of *Moby Dick* and *Voyage of the Dawn Treader* or movies like *Life of Pi*, *Titanic*, and *The Perfect Storm*. There's something archetypal and

spiritual about boats and how they take us on a psychological journey, whether that's from the workaday world to an island vacation
or from safe harbor to a life-changing, man-versus-nature encounter with a storm.

No wonder boats show up so often in the gospels. However,
most of the sermons and teachings you hear about boats in the gospels are about getting *out* of the boat. Probably the most famous
gospel story of this genre is when Peter walks on water after Jesus
invites him to step out of the boat and into the water (Matt 14). It's
a powerful story that teaches us the truth of author John Ortberg's
book title: *If You Want to Walk on Water, You've Got to Get Out of the
Boat.*

Though I've never heard a sermon about it, there are just as
many gospel stories about getting *into* the boat. Not to mention the
ones about Jesus getting into the boat. It was a common practice
for Jesus to get into a boat with his companions, where they could
have more candid and intimate dialogues about what was going on.
Sometimes it was a working retreat, and other times they were taking a much-needed break. Jesus himself wasn't opposed to a good
nap (Mark 4:38), maybe the easiest way for many of us to practice
the imitation of Christ. Sometimes it was the only way to escape
from noisy and needy people who constantly pressed in upon their
lives and leadership.

In our gospel story, the vehicle for Jesus's retreat was a boat: "So
they went away by themselves in a boat to a solitary place" (Mark
6:32). It was a space of renewal. Often, when Jesus became aware
that he and his companions needed to be renewed, he would invite
them to step into a boat with him and head off into the water.
During their times together in the boat, the disciples experienced
renewal of their bodies through rest. They experienced renewal of
their minds through timely teaching. They experienced renewal of
their callings through Jesus's words of affirmation, challenge, and
commission. Apparently, a lot can happen when you consent to get
in a boat with Jesus—or when you let him get in your boat.

The presence of Jesus can make any place into sacred space, but there is also something soothing and centering about simply being on the water. The water itself has a renewing quality. It's not surprising that we are drawn to boats and the beach and the poolside or riverside. Marine biologist and author Wallace J. Nichols explores this dynamic in his book *Blue Mind: The Surprising Science That Shows How Being Near, In, On, or Under Water Can Make You Happier, Healthier, More Connected, and Better at What You Do*. He notes the common quality of modern life that neuroscientists have called "Red Mind," described as an "edgy high, characterized by stress, anxiety, fear, and maybe even a little bit of anger and despair."[14] When experienced occasionally, Red Mind can be helpful as we face challenges and accomplish tasks, but experienced as a continuous state, it has a number of harmful side effects.

Nichols believes, in harmony with several scientific studies, that an important way we counter the risks of Red Mind is through the experience of "Blue Mind." Blue Mind is what happens to us when we are near, in, on, or under water: "a mildly meditative state characterized by peacefulness, unity, and a sense of general happiness and satisfaction with life in the moment."[15]

I bet you can easily recall a vivid memory of a special time you spent near water. Maybe it's a childhood memory of traveling to the beach with your family. Maybe it's fishing in the creek with a buddy. Maybe it's kayaking on a placid lake during some much-needed alone time. Or maybe you prefer simply soaking in a bathtub or relaxing by the pool. We crave, and need, those times of Blue Mind in which we are renewed.

Of course, most of us can't live a waterfront life. And there are many other ways we can get renewed, in nature and elsewhere. But we all need that "boat time" in which it is said of us: "they went away by themselves on a boat to a solitary place." Whether or not it's literally on a boat, ordinary leaders can't afford to neglect this practice. We can only sustain our work if we have regular rhythms of retreat. We need dedicated times and spaces where we lay down our work, leave behind the crowds, and get on our boat to be renewed and spend time with the one who calms the storms.

RESTORATION: ON THE BEACH

Third, retreats *restore* us. They provide a safe and sacred space in which we can process our thoughts and emotions. Life is always happening. We are constantly experiencing events, absorbing hurts, and facing new challenges. In addition to the usual wear and tear of life, ordinary leaders in small towns and rural regions are often targets for sabotage and criticism because their efforts for change represent a threat to cherished systems and structures.

Sometimes, regular quality conversations with a close friend, spiritual director, or therapist are enough to help us stay well. Spiritual practices, faith community, medication, and counseling can go a long way. But there are some hurts, habits, and hang-ups that need more. We need space to become aware of complex feelings and bring them into the Light. We need space to let healing and wisdom arise.

On retreats, we remember that "Jesus wept," and we aren't ashamed to imitate our Teacher. We release what we've been holding and hiding; we receive the gift of tears. We let out and lift up the "sighs too deep for words" (Rom 8:26). As author and spiritual director, Beth Booram likes to say, feelings make terrible masters but important messengers.[16] Retreats offer a safe and sacred space where we can welcome those messengers and listen for how God may be guiding us through them. God knows what we need, even when we don't, and will provide the tools and experiences we need to find direction and wholeness.

There is a beautiful story at the end of John's gospel (John 21) about how Jesus and his disciples found healing through a retreat. The disciples had just been through the intense drama and trauma of their master's crucifixion. They faced fear for their own safety and immense grief at the loss of political hope and the personal intimacy they had known through their relationship with Jesus. Not knowing what to do with their pain and confusion, they went fishing. A fine rural thing to do, and a throwback to their previous professions. As the saying goes, when we don't know what to do, we do what we've always done. Maybe it was a regression to previous patterns of life or maybe they were simply practicing that "boat time" we talked about.

Kindly and creatively, the risen Jesus met them right in the middle of their working and grieving. When they caught nothing, he showed up and told them where to find fish. When they landed again and brought back their catch, they found that the familiar stranger had prepared a picnic. He had started a charcoal fire over which he was cooking fish, with some bread ready on the side.

Seeing this food and feeling this presence, they didn't even have to ask—"they knew it was the Lord" (v. 12). As he had done many times before, Jesus offered them a clear, kind, and life-giving invitation. It wasn't "come and follow me," the invitation that transformed the meaning and direction of their lives years ago. It wasn't "come with me and get some rest," the invitation that led to their reorientation and renewal many times before. No, the life-giving invitation they heard from Christ was "come and have breakfast" (v. 12).

An ordinary, simple invitation. But the one that the disciples needed.

So, they sat down around Jesus, with all their grief and confusion (and latent power and possibility), and let Jesus host them. "Jesus came and took the bread and gave it to them, and did the same with the fish" (v. 13).

After they were done eating, Jesus turned to Peter. Jesus knew that he needed particular attention and direction. Peter had publicly betrayed Jesus three times during the chaos of the crucifixion. So, Jesus used this beachside retreat to restore him. He asked Peter to reaffirm his love and loyalty three times—three times to match the three denials. In this exchange, Jesus restored Peter's spirit, reconciled their relationship, and reinstated his calling to apostolic leadership. Peter would go on to be a major force in the Jesus movement.

It is also worth noting that before Jesus gave Peter the call of "feed my sheep," he gave him the invitation of "come and have breakfast." Before Jesus calls us to feed his sheep, he makes sure to feed his shepherds. We cannot give to others what we have not tasted.

When retreats are hosted and held well, they have the capacity to restore the spirit of wounded leaders and redirect the pathway of lost leaders. I wonder what would have happened if Peter and those early disciples—and the many who followed after them—had said no to the invitation. What would their life or leadership have been like if they had decided they didn't have time for a retreat or that it was only for the privileged and super spiritual? I also wonder what rural communities could be like if leaders would set aside the time and space in which Christ could come to heal deep hurts, provide life-giving bread, speak empowering words, and reveal compelling visions.

My personal ministry is focused on renewing rural leaders through retreats. I am passionate about creating space for rural leaders to be renewed and restored. Why do I care so much? Well, because I care about ordinary leaders as individuals. It's also because renewed leaders renew communities. Specifically, renewed rural leaders renew rural communities. Never underestimate the power of one restored leader.

Unfortunately, while renewed leaders renew communities, it's also true that wounded leaders wound communities. Wounded leaders may still have charisma and passion. People may like them and look up to them. But the unaddressed hurts, unconfessed failures, and unacknowledged longings influence the leader's behavior in subtle ways. Out of a need to please people, they don't have the courage to call people beyond their comfort and gridlock, saying only what they want to hear. Out of a need for validation, they unconsciously use their helping profession to cultivate codependent relationships. Maybe when feelings develop into inappropriate advances, these leaders will let them go on just a little bit longer because those encounters provide both the power and affirmation that they crave.

Richard Rohr says it succinctly: "If we don't transform our pain, we will transmit it in some form."[17] Indeed, what we don't reveal and heal, we pass on. What we don't get from healthy relationships we steal from people through unhealthy ones. Taking a retreat won't fix all dysfunction, solve all problems, or heal all wounds. But the safe and sacred space of retreat creates the conditions for an experience that brings repair and redirection in a decisive way.

Like Peter, I had my own restorative retreat on a beach. We don't often think of the coast as being a rural place, but between the occasional booming urban clusters are miles and miles of rural coastline. The piece of rural coastline I retreated to was a beach in northern Oregon. Understand, beaches in Oregon are not like the beaches in Florida that I visited as a kid. On those beloved Florida vacations, I could play in the warm ocean waves, design castles sitting shirtless in the sand, and sunbathe under the hot sun while smothered in tropical-smelling sunblock. Oregon is much different. It is typically cool and often windy; the waves roar ferociously (yet soothingly).

I was not on a Florida vacation; I was on an Oregon retreat. It was a lightly programmed weekend called "Sabbath by the Sea," and I spent much of my time walking along the beach. The nice thing about the Oregon coast is that the noise created by the waves allows a person to speak out loud, even holler, without being heard. I was doing a fair bit of that over the weekend.

I was devastated, exhausted, and angry. I had moved to Oregon with my wife three years before for graduate school. The transition wasn't easy, but life rose wonderfully like a wave as things came together. Soon, however, my life crashed violently. As I walked, the waves crashing in front of me were a metaphor. After a bout of deep depression and unsuccessful couples' counseling, my marriage had ended. In order to tend to my mental health, I had to resign from my pastoral position at a church I loved. My mentor died. A friend betrayed me. A list of other disrupting and disturbing events had taken place over the year that led up to my beachside retreat. Maybe the most disorienting part of the whole deal was that I had no felt sense of God's presence and no strong evidence of God's supposedly sovereign activity.

One of the few spiritual practices that still held meaning for me during that time was walking a prayer labyrinth, so I decided to make one on the beach. Locating a long, weathered stick, I strategically and mindfully outlined the labyrinthine design. After I completed the outline, the labyrinth was ready for me to walk. But I wasn't quite ready. In a moment of inspiration, I decided to fill in the lines with items from along the beach. I gathered up all the stones, seaweed, sticks, and trash I could find within about fifty yards of my labyrinth. After filling in the labyrinth lines with all those bits and pieces, I stood back to witness my creation.

I looked upon it with a sense of pride, and a spiritual sensation arose within me. It was strangely beautiful in its brokenness and randomness. In the midst of this realization, I heard an inner voice speak piercingly into the moment: "This labyrinth is like your life. I have taken all the random and broken pieces of your life and created a design that is beautiful, meaningful, and useful."

Already full of awe at the moment, I wanted to seal the experience with a walk. As I walked my labyrinth, I turned on my iPod to enhance the moment. Turning it on shuffle, I was serenaded by the eclectic mix that is my taste in music. After two upbeat songs, a song came on that literally stopped me in my tracks. You see, it was the song that two friends had sung at my wedding. The wedding where I was full of innocence and optimism; it was five years ago, but it seemed like ages ago, in a different world with different people. But it was still very real, real enough that the song awakened a flood of memories and emotions that washed over me. I began to weep as I was overwhelmed by feelings of grief over past love and gratitude for the current reality of Eternal Love—a Love that flows into my life as wave upon wave. Remember, I was looking out at the Pacific

Ocean while I walked this labyrinth and listened to this song—this song with a chorus describing the end as "oceans and oceans of love and love again."

The presence and activity of God was more real to me than it had been for a long time. And the experience of that beachside retreat set in motion a process of healing and restoration that set my life in a transformed trajectory. Of course, I continued to struggle and grieve. But I became more resilient than I imagined possible and began to believe that maybe I could be a healthy, creative leader once again. By the end of the year, I had decided to return to Ohio, reconnect with my family, complete my seminary studies, root myself in a particular place, and cultivate the seed of an idea for a ministry of rural renewal.

I have experienced the good, the bad, the frustrating, and the transformative possibilities of retreats. Jesus offered the life-shaping invitation to those early ordinary leaders, and the invitation is extended to us today. When we answer it, we practice becoming the kinds of leaders our small towns and rural regions truly need. And we practice becoming the kinds of persons capable of experiencing and embodying abundant life.

CHAPTER TWO

THE PRACTICE OF DISCERNMENT

When Jesus landed and saw a large crowd, he had compassion on them.

Mark 6:34

I HAVE TAKEN MANY RETREATS. But last fall I tried something different; I took a *silent* retreat. And not just for a day. For a week. A family friend had gifted me a weeklong retreat at the Abbey of Gethsemani in rural Kentucky. She figured I was exhausted after pushing through to finally graduate from seminary. She was right. And she figured I would benefit from a retreat where my spiritual hero Thomas Merton used to live. She was right again.

Having never been on a silent retreat, especially not for a week, I was a bit nervous. I wondered how I would handle being disconnected from social media and regular creature comforts like television, coffee shops, and pizza delivery. I've never been a purist about my own retreats. I typically book a hotel or bed-and-breakfast just to have a space where I can rest and reflect for the weekend. I set aside intentional time to journal, sleep, pray, and plan, and I make myself mostly unavailable during that time. However, I may occasionally venture out for a hike, get some good food, or take in a movie. There would be none of that at the monastery, though the monks did sell some excellent bourbon fudge.

Nevertheless, being practiced at retreat and being both a Quaker and an introvert, I didn't fret about it much. Besides, I was tired. Deeply tired. More tired than I had been in years. I had been pressing and pushing to reach the finish line of seminary. I had been working extra hours to pay off some lingering bills. And I had been traveling from Ohio to Tennessee weekend after weekend, as my partner's father battled cancer.

When I arrived at the retreat center and found my room, I literally collapsed onto the bed, stretching out my arms and legs across the carefully made bed and smashing my face against the pillow. I immediately took a three-hour nap. When I woke up, I joined the monks and guests for the afternoon prayers and walked peacefully to dinner, where our meal was enjoyed in silence. I ate slowly and mindfully, not worrying about whether I should ask the person beside me if they had any kids or what they did for a living. It was glorious.

By the end of the second night, I had adjusted to the environment. The cares and concerns that were so big just a couple of days ago began to look small. As I soaked in the silence and savored the solitude, I was feeling more aligned with the monastic rhythm and peace of the land. By the third evening, I was like Jim Carrey in *Ace Ventura*, meditating serenely with birds perched peacefully around me, moments away from achieving "omnipresent, supergalactic oneness."

Then I got a phone call.

My phone had been turned off, so I was quite surprised to hear the ringtone breaking the silence. But I had turned it on about an hour before to look up a quote for my journal then apparently left it on. I walked across the room to see who it was that dared to defy my mystical union. It was my fiancée (now wife), Ashlyn. This instantly alerted me that something was wrong, because she would not be calling me unless there was a really good reason. So I answered.

Ashlyn told me that things were deteriorating down in Knoxville. Her dad had been suffering for almost a year, recovering and declining, but the situation was getting worse as some family members struggled to cope in a healthy way. Ashlyn felt strongly that she needed to go down and help her family for a week, maybe two. She did not ask me to go, but of course I was considering it. If I were not on a retreat, I would call my employer, pack a little bag, and hit the road. But I was on a retreat that had been planned for almost a year and was just recovering from a profound weariness of body and soul. While trying to listen to her as she processed her fears and frustrations, in the back of my mind I was wrestling with what my response should be.

Should I stay or should I go?

If I stayed, would I be betraying my partner and her family?

If I went, would I be neglecting my own self-care that makes other-care possible?

Would my being there even be helpful to Ashlyn and her family? Or would I end up being one more exhausted, emotionally volcanic person in the mix?

Before I knew it, this retreat for rest and renewal had turned into a retreat for discernment. I had to exercise some spiritual and mental muscles that I had been letting rest. A decision had to be made that involved the well-being of precious people and important relationships, including myself, my partner, and her family. So much for omnipresent supergalactic oneness.

In our gospel story, Jesus and the disciples were also on a retreat intended as a time for rest and renewal. They had hopped in a boat and taken off for some good old-fashioned R and R. But about the time they entered the Blue Mind zone, something happened. Mark informs us of this disruption by using that great and terrible conjunction: *but*. "So they went away by themselves in a boat to a solitary place," we are told. "*But* many who saw them leaving recognized them and ran on foot from all the towns and got there ahead of them" (6:33).

As they approach the shore, Jesus sees the people and recognizes their needs. He has to decide how to respond. At that point, the retreat intended for rest and relaxation is turned into a retreat for discernment. Should he avoid or engage the crowd? Would he protect their retreat or open it to the people calling upon their time and energy?

So much for omnipresent supergalactic oneness.

Though we may not recognize it as such, we face similar dilemmas regularly, even daily. You get up in the morning, and about the time a warm shower or cup of hot coffee wakes you up, you become aware of all that needs to be done for the day. There are kids who need rides, bills that need to be paid, grass that needs to be cut, a pile of reports that need to be filed at work. Not to mention the ever-present "shoulds" that follow us around: I *should* be doing more volunteering or exercising or protesting or praying or essential oil-ing.

Disregarding these voices as you continue to awake from the night of insufficiently restful sleep, you grab the remote and turn on the television as you toast a bagel. It doesn't matter whether it's Fox News or CNN, five minutes watching the news is sure to drain whatever remnant of optimism is still alive in your heart. The news anchor tells you about school shootings, political scandals, corporate domination, famine in the developing world, hurricanes in the First World, and always wars and rumors of wars. By the first commercial break, you desperately need a break from the negativity. So you pick up your phone and get on Facebook.

Social media reminds you of your "shoulds" as you see the seemingly perfect lifestyle of smiling moms with honor students and the brilliant, lay social analysts who post their commentary on current events with a dollop of shame that your slacktivism is insufficient. As you scroll, you see reminders from your favorite local businesses and nonprofits that you support for fundraisers or community events coming up. Going to that chili cook-off is one thing you would really like to do, but it also feels like one more thing.

Filled to the brim with shame and sadness and feeling a little sick, it's time to go to work! You're exhausted before you even leave the house. You peer down at your last gulp of coffee and wish it were filled with something stronger.

So much to do and so many things we should be doing. How do we know how to respond? How do we decide which activities and people to prioritize?

THE PARADOX OF RURAL LIFE

Some of us moved to a rural community (or chose to stay in one) to escape the worries of the world and the social problems of the cities. We hoped that the mountains, mesas, or cornfields would absorb the bad news from the cities before it could reach us. We wanted to live a simple life focused on faith, family, and farming. Maybe with just a few acres of land in the country we could get off the grid and have space to find ourselves and find God or raise a family in a safe community or get back to the land for a saner and more sustainable lifestyle. While bad wireless service and stubborn nonconformity may work for a time, we ultimately become like the boy holding back the dam with his thumb in the hole. You can run from the world and its brokenness, but you can't hide. We live in a profoundly interconnected world, after all, and the world is within us. The song may be bad, but its truth remains: we *are* the world.

Across the road from where I grew up, there was a pond. It was in the middle of a fenced cow pasture, so there were always cows dipping in the water or moseying around next to it. The farm was owned by our neighbor Jack and his wife, Nelly, so we called it simply "Jack's pond." Jack's pond was a fixture in my family's life. We saw it every day when we left for work and drove past it when we came home. My dad liked to take pictures of sunsets over the pond and the surrounding fields and cows. He milked cows for many years, so he has a soft spot for the beasts. The sunsets were indeed often quite beautiful, and those pictures of the sun setting over the landscape represent the things we loved about rural life: simplicity, peace, beauty, spaciousness, solitude, nearness to nature.

But the pond had a human history as well. One day my parents told me about a farmer who owned the land before Jack and Nelly. I never knew him, but I knew his wife. She was a local farmer who attended my church, taught Sunday school, and was known for bringing food to grieving families. Maybe she had a special concern for those experiencing loss because she had experienced it so deeply herself. You see, one day, during the farm crisis of the 1980s, her husband succumbed to the economic, mental, and spiritual burdens he carried. He walked out to the pond, stepped into the deepest part, and went under the water. He kept himself underwater until the pain stopped. When he came back up, he was dead. I don't know all the demons he wrestled with, but the tragic truth is that the suicide rate among farmers is stunningly high.

Jack's pond is a symbol of what I call "the paradox of rural life." On one hand, rural life is a lifestyle of serenity, simplicity, and beauty. We move to rural places, or remain in them, because we cherish this way of life. And yet, paradoxically, rural life can be a lifestyle of pain, futility, and hopelessness.

We run to rural regions and cling to small towns to escape from the world's sins and struggles. But they chase after us just as hard. Jesus and the disciples experienced this as they tried to escape from the crowds. They, and we, are being chased by people with great needs—addiction, poverty, domestic abuse, unemployment, and so on. And like the ringing phone that interrupted my serenity at the isolated monastery, the world's problems call upon us to engage them, sometimes even jerking us awake from our peaceful simplicity. When we hear the call, we have choices to make.

As ordinary leaders, we want to get involved, make a difference, and be sources of healing and renewal where we live. But it's easy to feel flooded, overwhelmed, and disoriented. What work is ours to do, and what is not ours to do?

Our decision-making process calls us to a practice commended by our spiritual traditions as the practice of discernment. According to its Latin roots, to "discern" means to "slice," "separate," and "distinguish." Sometimes this means to distinguish between good and bad choices or good and evil forces, but often it means choosing between multiple good options. It involves determining what response is best for a particular person in a particular moment.

CARRYING YOUR CROSS

Sitting on the bed of my monastery room, I hung up the phone with Ashlyn and knew I had some discerning to do—and not much time to do it. I really wanted to make the right decision, but the answer wasn't clear. Just as I could feel panic setting in, I decided I should offer up the matter in prayer, being in a monastery and all. I felt a rising reminder that I could entrust the process to the One who doesn't withhold wisdom but "gives generously to all without finding fault" (Jas 1:5). I went to afternoon prayers, ate a satisfying dinner in silence, then went to an evening talk given by the guest house chaplain.

Father Carlos, a middle-aged Filipino monk with a round belly and generous grin, was the guest house chaplain, and he gave a talk each of the first two evenings as a kind of orientation for retreatants. I assumed that these orientation talks would cover subjects like how to make the most of a retreat, how to embrace solitude and silence, or the spirituality of Thomas Merton. But no, Father Carlos decided to give two half-hour talks on the topics of suffering and evil. Nothing like covering the deepest mysteries of the cosmos in two half-hour segments.

I believed that Father Carolos was being overly ambitious, but nevertheless, I wanted to hear what he had to say. He gave a nice talk, peppered with personal anecdotes and references to Catholic teaching. I found it interesting, but he said nothing particularly striking or applicable to the questions I was asking. That is, until the end of the talk. Father Carlos started talking about his friend who was a mother learning how to live with a wayward child fighting a drug addiction. He related her painful experience to the Christian symbol of the cross: "Problems are meant to be solved; crosses are meant to be carried." A simple truth, though not an easy one. So often our suffering is something that can only be carried and lived, not something that can be fixed or solved. But then Father Carlos said something else that became like an "alive and active Word" (Heb 4:12) that spoke to my condition.

Father Carlos said that while crosses are meant to be carried, we can only carry our own cross. We cannot carry someone else's cross. As if inspired to stop and say it again, he repeated, "We cannot carry someone else's cross." In some mysterious way, the teaching for the group became a Word spoken directly to me: "Andy, *you* cannot carry someone else's cross." The words sunk into my spirit, and I knew what I needed to do. I could not carry this cross for my fiancée, as much as it hurt me to see her carry it. I could not save her or fix her family. Especially if I was carrying my own cross—or baggage and unmet needs. In this moment of discernment, it became clear that the best service I could offer to Ashlyn and the other loved ones in my life was to rest my body and recover my soul and strength.

Discernment is a subtle art, more scalpel than hatchet. And it is a journey that typically requires a good guide. I needed Father Carlos at that particular moment. He kept me from carrying a cross that wasn't mine to carry. In another moment, I may have needed a guide who challenged me to face the cost of discipleship and do some hard things for love. The Word at that point may have been to take up my cross and follow the Spirit of Christ.

Too often, though, human guides place crosses on us that aren't ours to carry. Minister and healer Flora Slosson Wuellner makes an important distinction between harmful manipulation and our "true cross." Flora believes, "Our true crosses, though painful, renew our strength and faith; they never destroy our spirit."[1] Expanding on this principle, she reminds us of a central truth for discerning authentic guidance: "Being guided by God does not guarantee we will have perfect families, perfect jobs, perfect health, with no problems or challenges." Wuellner writes, "But genuine guidance does mean we will experience basic fulfillment and renewal. Abundance will be present at our center."[2] The One who promised abundant life will not always lead us on easy paths, but I agree with Wuellner that Christ's true leading will bring with it a sense of abundance at the center of our being. After all, Jesus was clear that he doesn't "steal, kill, and destroy." No, he came so we can experience abundant life (John 10:10).

INTERRUPTION AND INVITATION

There were many times in Jesus's life and ministry when he refused to carry other people's crosses or be dominated by their demands. As meek and mild as Jesus was, he did not make it a pattern to let crowds dictate his direction. He was what we might call a "self-differentiated person"; he made decisions based on his own values and divine direction, not on the demands of crowds. Over time, Jesus's fame (Greek, *pheme*) spread across the rural countryside, and people sought him out for healing and guidance. Everywhere he went, it seemed, were people desperate to touch him or talk to him.

Most rural and small-town folks aren't much impressed with celebrity, but ordinary leaders can easily become a kind of local hero. Their *pheme* gets around, and the committee hounds start coming after them. There are only so many people in small towns, so anytime "fresh meat" enters the scene, there are lots of hungry and weary people ready to pounce. We need volunteers, committee members, donors, directors, board members, and on and on into world without end. It's like when someone finds out you have a truck and suddenly everyone's moving and needs your truck to haul their precious possessions. It becomes tempting to hide your light under a bushel—or maybe hide your truck under some bushes.

Ordinary leaders in small towns understand why Jesus had to protect his time and energy. He had to protect his solitude and stay in touch with the holy whisper despite the noisiness and neediness of the crowds, doing what he was truly called to do, nothing more and nothing less. Consider the story in Luke 4:

> At daybreak, Jesus went out to a solitary place. The people were looking for him and when they came to where he was, they tried to keep him from leaving them. But he said, "I must proclaim the good news of the kingdom of God to the other towns also, because that is why I was sent." (vv. 42–43)

Jesus wasn't a slave to the crowd's demands. In fact, he often blatantly contradicted or confronted the crowd. To borrow from Gandhi, the only tyrant Jesus accepted was the still, small voice within. In that same chapter of Luke, Jesus said a clear no to Satan's wily schemes in the wilderness then went on to say a clear no to his hometown folks who thought he was straying from the role established by his family name. They got so mad, in fact, that they tried to force him off a cliff. (If you're having trouble as a leader in your hometown, Jesus understands. Be glad they haven't tried to shove you off a cliff . . . yet). Jesus's response? "But he walked right through the crowd and went on his way" (v. 30). There are always people who say to us, "I love you and have wonderful plans for your life." But we have to walk through the crowd and be like Jesus, who "went on *his* way."

I tend to be a peacemaker and people pleaser, so Jesus's example has been critical in my own growth. Jesus taught me that it's okay to have limits, to rest, to preserve boundaries, to say no. So, when I read the story in Mark 6 where Jesus gets out of the boat and goes toward the crowd, I am puzzled by his response. I expect him to say to the mass of needy people trying to hijack his retreat, "Sorry, but we are out of the office right now. We are going on retreat for the weekend, so we will have to talk later. Please leave a message after the beep." But that's not what happened!

Some people may look at Jesus moving into the crowd as a sweet, wonderful moment or imagine Jesus strutting toward the crowd like some kind of Marvel character, ready to show off his powers to feed the crowd. But it seems to me that Jesus caved. Jesus saves, to be sure, but it seems like Jesus also caves. It seems to me that Jesus felt the pressure of the people and felt pity for their sad state, so he gave in and helped them out. I've done it many, many times, but I expect more from Jesus the Christ.

My reading of Jesus's actions has evolved and possibly matured over time. Maybe it wasn't that Jesus caved; maybe he exercised his developed discernment skills in the moment and saw an opportunity that God was inviting him into. Henri Nouwen commented that he used to get frustrated at all the interruptions to his work until he realized that the interruptions *were* his work.[3] Perhaps Jesus knew that, in this case, the interruption was his work. Maybe Jesus saw the hurting people in front of him as a divine invitation, as the Good Samaritan saw the hurting person in front of him as a divine invitation, only on a much larger scale.

Another possibility is that Jesus saw something alive and ready among the people, something the gospel authors call "faith." In the gospels, faith makes amazing things possible. And Jesus loved seeing it in people. A sick woman reaching out to grab Jesus's clothes, a crippled man crying out for Jesus's attention even when the disciples shushed him, friends breaking through a roof so their friend could be healed, children running joyfully to his arms. Jesus seemed to be able to see when that thing called "faith" was present in an individual or group, and it guided him as he discerned what was possible for the exchange. He seemed to be able to tell when folks were "on the verge of a miracle," as Rich Mullins sang,[4] or whether they were only interested in control, self-advancement, or sabotage.

It's also possible that Jesus saw a teaching opportunity. Knowing his disciples needed hands-on, in-person training, perhaps he saw an opportunity to show them the makings of a miracle. Maybe he wanted them to see the surprising possibilities of rural people and places and gain some muscle memory of the possibilities by participating in the making of the miracle. Maybe he saw a chance to help make his disciples into rural leaders. It's possible that this was on Jesus's agenda for the retreat all along. In that case, the problem is with my own narrow definition of retreat. His leadership retreats tended to be both unconventional and unforgettable.

MOVED WITH COMPASSION

We obviously don't know for sure what all went into Jesus's discernment process, but the passage does give us a pretty big clue as to what moved him into action. The pivot point, we learn, was when Jesus was moved with *compassion*: "When Jesus landed and saw a large crowd, he had compassion on them, because they were like sheep without a shepherd" (Mark 6:34). They lacked leadership. They lacked the kind of advocates and companions who could lead them to the abundant life they sought. So Jesus was moved into action; he was moved *with* compassion and *by* compassion.

The word "compassion" has a lot of connotations, but it tends to evoke a feeling of sympathy or pity. In Scripture, however, compassion has more force to it. The Greek word for what happened within Jesus is *splagxnízomai*, and it indicates a deep feeling of empathy and emotion, feeling with and suffering with another from a deep place, literally "from the guts." But compassion is not only an emotion; it is an energy. It is an energy arising from deep within that moves a person to act for the well-being of another.

Biblical scholar Marcus Borg argues that Jesus's core message was one of compassion. "Compassion is the central virtue of a life centered in God as known in Jesus," Borg proposes. To help us see the bigger biblical picture, Borg offers context for compassion:

> In Hebrew and Aramaic, [compassion] is related to the word for "womb." God is "womb-like," giving birth to us, nourishing us, and feeling for us (and the whole of creation) as a mother feels for the children of her womb: willing our well-being, and sometimes becoming fierce when our well-being (and the well-being

of creation) is threatened. We are to be compassionate as God is compassionate. Importantly, compassion is not only a feeling but a doing. The imperative is not simply to feel compassion but to "be compassionate"—to act in accord with the feeling.[5]

Compassion is the bridge between contemplation and action. It was this deep sense of compassion—like the tender nurture and fierce protection of a mother—that moved Jesus out of contemplation into action. It moved him into the crowd, in a posture of engagement and care, rather than away from the crowd.

CONTEMPLATION AND ACTION

The practice of discernment challenges us to learn the relationship between contemplation and action. Compassion is the bridge between them, and we should walk that bridge both directions. The Franciscan spiritual author Richard Rohr started a retreat center called the Center for Action and Contemplation. He says that the most important word in the title is not "action" or "contemplation" but the word "and."[6] Most of us have a leaning and preference toward one or the other. But in discernment, we remember the importance of both and consider what kind of mix the present opportunity calls for. Both my choice to stay on retreat and Jesus's choice to redirect the retreat were expressions of faithful discernment and illustrations of the sacred word "and."

Paradoxically, it is often the process of moving away from the crowds that leads us deeper into their midst. It is in those spaces of retreat and reflection that we can more clearly see what we really need and what is really needed by those we seek to serve. Retreats are revelatory. They tend to reveal at least two things: our true worth and our true work. This revelatory capacity is why contemplative retreats are important for discernment.

"When Jesus and his disciples seek contemplation, they ironically evoke more action," observes Parker Palmer. He notes the dynamic relationship between these two pulls in the story of Jesus feeding the multitude:

> The story tells us that contemplation and action cannot be separated the way that we separate work and vacation. Action will always set up the need for contemplation. But true contemplation is never a mere retreat. Instead, it draws us deeper into right action by getting us more deeply in touch with the gifts that we have to give, with our need to give them, with the people and problems that need us.[7]

Contemplation and action form a circle of faithfulness in which we enter the rhythms of grace that Jesus modeled. Entering those rhythms of withdrawal and engagement, contemplation and action, makes discernment a more organic and dynamic practice. When we learn that rhythm, we are able to discern where we are in the cycle and what may be most needed for the moment. We need to cultivate a contemplative space in which we can discern how compassion is drawing us to particular people and places. We also need an active life of engagement so that our contemplative practice doesn't devolve into escapism and narcissism or get stuck in the "paralysis of analysis."

If compassion is a word with too much baggage or vagueness for you, try another one. My own Quaker tradition has a related concept called "concern." A concern is more than a vague expression of caution or an excuse to gossip. ("I'm *concerned* about Janet and her marriage. I will give you the details of her problems so you will know how to pray.") No, it has to do with discerning our personal work in the world—and discerning God's personal work in the world.

In Quaker spirituality, no one can heal the whole world alone, so God divides the world's suffering among humankind, and we each get a bundle of concerns that are ours to carry. We know a concern is ours when it rises for us in a personal and persistent way. Discerning our concerns and noticing the movements of compassion helps us know when to move away from the crowd and when to move into it.

Quaker author Thomas Kelly writes about our struggle to limit and focus our work, since people of faith so often try to love the whole world: "But in our love of people are we to be excitedly hurried, sweeping all people and tasks into our loving concern? No, that is God's function. But he, working within us, portions out his vast concern into bundles, and lays on each of us our portion. These become our tasks."[8] How liberating to know that we are only responsible for our "portion," and how compelling a vision to see people around the world carrying their own unique joys and concerns. God is both kind and capable enough to distribute these concerns so that no one is unduly burdened.

When we discern and carry our concerns with God, we do not have to be driven by fear and anxiety, which ultimately lead to what Thomas Merton called "a violent form of activism."[9] No, Thomas Kelly offers an alternative vision: "I find [God] never guides us into an intolerable scramble of panting feverishness. The Cosmic Patience becomes, in part, our patience, for after all God is at work in the world. It is not we alone who are at work in the world, frantically finishing a work to be offered to God."[10]

It may be helpful to think of concerns like eggs in a nest. The size of the nest is determined by our capacities, commitments, and callings. Each of us has a uniquely sized and shaped nest, but it is limited. Too many eggs, and one of them is likely to be neglected or pushed over the edge to its literal downfall. We have room for a few core concerns that are ours to nurture, care for, and attend to. God is wise and knows how much each of us can handle. Our small towns are under the care of an infinitely resourceful and eternally faithful God, who, it's important to remember, has lots of friends and followers of all shapes and sizes. As Kelly said, we are not alone in this Great Work.

DISCERNMENT AND TEMPTATION

The gospels teach us the creative tension between contemplation and action by providing two stories about bread and miracles in kind of point-counterpoint fashion. We have the story about Jesus feeding the multitude, of course, but we have another story earlier in the gospels. Long before Jesus's *wilderness feeding* was Jesus's *wilderness temptation* (Mark 1; Luke 4; Matt 4).

In the wilderness temptations, Jesus is faced with variant visions of authority and ministry as he wrestles discerningly with his identity and vocation. He is fasting and, no doubt, acutely aware of his hunger, so the tempter comes to him with stones, instructing him to prove his worth: "If you are the son of God, tell these stones to become bread." In this case, however, Jesus refuses to work a miracle with bread, responding that "human beings do not live on bread alone but on every word that comes from the mouth of God" (Matt 4:4).

Henri Nouwen offers a meaningful reading of this temptation when he proposes that Jesus was resisting the "temptation to be relevant." He describes this as the temptation "to do something that is needed and can be appreciated by people—to make productivity the basis of our ministry."[11] As ordinary leaders, it is easy to base our identity on our productivity. It's natural to evaluate our personal worth based on what people around us say is most needed and important. We want to be "relevant" to our community and our culture by doing what the dominant voices say is most urgent instead of discerning the deeper needs and possibilities before us.

While it is noble to create something worthwhile and contribute to our community, the relevance temptation plays into the harmful, shame-based patterns that prevail in our society. It demands that we earn our value and worth by producing, whereas the God of Jesus invites us to root our identity in the voice that calls us beloved children of our Creator. Nouwen writes that we should hear and heed this voice above all the other tempting voices: "Many voices ask for our attention. . . . But underneath all these often very noisy voices is a still, small voice that says, 'You are my beloved, my favor rests on you.' This is the voice we most need to hear."[12]

This process of sorting through the voices that call us is a critical skill for ordinary leaders. When we know who and whose we are, we are free to take risks and step out in faith as rural leaders because we don't have to prove ourselves. Decision-making may still be daunting, but we can engage the process with a sense of anticipation and adventure because we are not trying to prove our worth but improve the world with God—the God who loves us as we are and lures us into the future.

This temptation can also be tricky for us because it's often veiled in the language of religion, social justice, or civic patriotism. We get stuck in discernment because we are being told this or that opportunity is the call of duty from God, country, or community rather than an offer to which we can freely say yes or no. No wonder Jesus taught us to avoid dramatic vows and simply say yes and no: "anything beyond this is from the evil one" (Matt 5:37). Of course, service, activism, and civic engagement are all important. But discernment teaches us to tune our ears to tell the difference between the Spirit's voice of love and invitation and the twists and tricks of temptation. Nouwen summarizes well: "The temptation to be relevant is difficult to shake since it is usually not considered a temptation, but a call."[13]

This temptation can be especially prevalent in small towns and rural communities. We have many needs and not many people to meet them. We have a void of leadership and not many people stepping up. When we see the local shop shutting down and the young people heading to the cities, a sense of scarcity sets in. When we volunteer for something in a small town, it's not long before others come knocking on our door. After moving back, I learned about this temptation the hard way.

A couple years after I moved back to Morrow County, I took a second job at a local community center. The current director was ready to retire and wanted to hire someone who could potentially take on the managerial responsibilities. I told her that I would get settled into the current job, then after I got more familiar with how the place worked, try out some additional tasks. But before I knew it, I was the heir apparent. People began talking as if I would be at the helm in the next month. Still hoping to slow the process down and make it clear that I couldn't accept something I had not been offered, I asked for a job description and a pay scale. I eventually received this additional information, but people were still talking like I was the definite successor. Half-jokingly, I told a friend that I was "anointed" the leader. Next thing I knew, there was a story about me in the local paper.

The whole thing was strange, and I wasn't sure what to do. My indirect attempts to slow it down or create a clearer process were unsuccessful. I ignored the inner nudges of caution reminding me that this way of doing things had not turned out well for me in the past. But I rationalized my responses because I would be meeting a great need in my community. I could actually make a difference. I could actually make connections with community leaders. I could gain visibility and influence in the county. And besides, people said I would do great. Someone even said that they prayed about it and I was an answer to prayer. It was flattering. I ignored the inner warning signs, but all seemed to be coming together. After all, I just wanted to be relevant! Maybe I could be the one who would turn the stones into bread and feed my people. If not me, then who?

In less than two weeks, the reason for those inward warning signs became clear. It was more than I could handle with my other commitments, made long before this opportunity was handed to me. It was more than I could handle in terms of my mental health; a vicious wave from my old friends Depression and Anxiety made their presence known.

Finally, I listened to those quiet whispers. They told me that I didn't have to perform to prove my worth. They told me that I was deeply loved and accepted. And they reminded me that I have other ways of loving my neighbors and serving my community—ways that are more consistent with how I was made and who I am. With great humility—humiliation, really—I wrote a letter of resignation and contacted the (former and soon to be reinstated) director.

The following week was full of awkward conversations and explanations. One night, I came home discouraged and wondered if I had just chickened out. Then I came across a quote from Parker Palmer that spoke directly to my condition:

> If I try to be or do something noble that has nothing to do with who I am, I may look good to others and to myself for a while. But the fact that I am exceeding my limits will eventually have consequences. I will distort myself, the other, and our relationship—and may end up doing more damage than if I had never set out to do this particular "good."[14]

Palmer's words confirmed my decision and invited me to lean into the hard truth I was facing. I cannot be all things to all people. In fact, I could practically hear the words of the poet Rumi announced in my soul, "If you are here unfaithfully with us, you're causing terrible damage."[15] My decision was the right one. It was best for me, and it would be best for the organization.

DISCERNMENT AND DESIRE

My own foolishness combined with the wisdom of Jesus and Parker Palmer point to an important truth about discernment. The authentic voice of calling is the one that "calls us by name" as Jesus said of the truly Good Shepherd (John 10:3). It speaks to us in a particular way and calls us to particular tasks that are consistent with our nature. The practice of discernment challenges us as ordinary leaders to see beyond the "any warm body" mentality that often prevails in struggling rural communities.

Jewish philosopher Martin Buber illustrates this aspect of discernment in his story called "The Particular Way." The story goes that Rabbi Baer of Radoshitz once approached his teacher, known as the Seer of Lublin, with a question. Seeking wisdom for how he could teach others the spiritual path, he asked the sage, "Show me one general way to the service of God."

To his surprise, the sage replied, "It is impossible to tell all people what way they should take. For one way to serve God is through learning, another through prayer, another through fasting, and still another through eating. Everyone should carefully observe what their heart draws them to, and then choose this way with all their strength."[16]

There are many ways to serve God and our neighbors. Discernment invites us to discover our unique design and explore how that design can be lived in a way that nurtures the well-being of our community. The sage of Buber's tale communicates this call clearly: "Everyone should carefully observe what their heart draws them to, and then choose this way with all their strength." Getting in touch with the drawing of our heart and giving ourselves fully to it is often a difficult task. But it's central to the practice of discernment.

Discernment calls upon us to discover our design by honoring our desires. Noticing the drawings of the heart and honoring of our desires are tasks often met with resistance in religious circles. Some religious traditions encourage us to be suspicious of our desires, assuming that they are reflections of our sinful nature. Desire is often equated with lust, whether for sexual satisfaction, power, or wealth. In my own evangelical Christian tradition, folks are fond of quoting the prophet Jeremiah, who said, "The heart is deceitful above all things"—or "desperately wicked," as the King James translation says. Certainly doesn't sound like something to be trusted when you are seeking direction for your life. Definitely not something we should pursue with all our strength, as Buber's story suggests.

There are indeed expressions of desire in human nature that lead us to harmful and destructive places. But when we move past shallow or distorted desires to our deeper desires, we find a wellspring of passion and purpose that is vital for leadership and spiritual growth. In fact, deep, holy desire is the only sustainable source for spiritual growth. Shame wears off. Guilt gives in. Duty grows old. Piety gets tiring. But the desire for wholeness, meaning, and the Divine Presence will keep us continually seeking the Source and Fulfillment of our desires. Jesus knew this truth and used it for his ministry, which is why he asked the seemingly obvious but actually profound, transformative question to those seeking his help: "What do you *want* me to do for you?" (Matt 20:32; Mark 10:51).

So, how do we discern the desires that we should follow from the ones that lead us astray? The Ignatian tradition is a uniquely useful resource. In the sixteenth century, Saint Ignatius of Loyola created a series of spiritual exercises that guide the discerner through the process of the "discernment of spirits" so they can discover God's will for their particular situation. This discernment process is an invitation to become more attentive to the movements of our inner life, including our desires. We gain a greater awareness of the divine leading through our "felt-knowledge" (*sentir* in Spanish) discovered through the practice.[17]

Jesuit scholar Paul Robb explains that Ignatius "came to recognize that human experiences of joy and desolation, of enthusiasm and depression, of light and darkness, are not just human emotions which vary like the wind in a storm, but are the means by which we recognize the movements within our spirit stirred by the Spirit of Jesus."[18] Indeed, the practice of Ignatian discernment is simply the recognition of what most Christians (and many non-Christians) assume and affirm—that the spirit of God is present and active within the spirit of every human being—but in our distrust of desire and suspicion about emotions, we fail to notice. This is why the central question from a spiritual director in the Ignatian exercises is, "How were you *moved* in prayer?" Remember how Jesus was *moved* with compassion?

Parker Palmer tells the story about a man who attended one of his Circles of Trust retreats. The gentleman was anxiously struggling with a policy decision he had to make. He had been working for a decade in the Department of Agriculture, preceded by twenty-five

years of farming in Iowa. Reflecting with the group about the conun-
drum, he named the tension he was feeling, saying, "My farmer's
heart knows what I need to do, but doing it will get me in trouble
with my superior."

As the retreat came to an end, he told the group that he knew
that he needed to honor his farmer's heart in this decision. Someone asked, "How will you respond to your boss?" He replied with
the resolve and insight he needed to take the next steps: "It won't be
easy. But during my time in this circle, I've understood something
important. I don't report to my boss. I report to the land."[19]

Sometimes discernment doesn't have to involve emotional spe-
lunking down the caverns of our souls or complex tests with proof
texts and quotes from church fathers. Interior exploration and
listening to the witnesses of Scripture and tradition are valuable,
but sometimes the wisdom we need is already there, available and
accessible with a simple nod of recognition. We need only to trust
the "farmer's heart" or "pastor's heart" or "parent's heart" or "social
worker's heart." A passage in Deuteronomy reminds us: "The word
is very near you; it is in your mouth and in your heart so you may
obey it" (30:14).

One of the enduring and trusted practices of discernment that
arose from Ignatian spirituality is the Prayer of Examen. It is a daily
exercise that helps us gain access to divine guidance arising in our
heart. A simple way to practice the Prayer of Examen is to take
about ten minutes at the end of the day to review your day, either
by yourself or with a partner. You look back across your day, recalling the people, places, and experiences and bringing them into the
Light. As you do this, you note what are called consolations and
desolations.[20]

Consolation is a life-giving sense of joy, peace, energy, and movement toward God's active presence. Desolation is a life-draining
sense of anxiety, heaviness, narrowness, and a movement away
from God's active presence. Each day we experience a mix of these
moments and movements. Ending each day with this practice of

examination allows us to notice patterns and trends. When we consistently experience joy and life when engaging a certain task, we sense God drawing us to prioritize that task as part of our work in the world. When we consistently feel desolation around a particular relationship, we discern that this relationship needs to either change or come to an end.

While it's nice when we experience discernment in one dramatic epiphany, it usually requires attention to these daily, weekly, monthly, and yearly patterns of consolation and desolation. "God's grace resounds in our lives like a staccato," wrote Abraham Heschel. "Only by retaining the seemingly disconnected notes do we acquire the ability to grasp the theme."[21] It seems that over time we can learn the patterns and indicators in our lives so that we begin to hear the song with greater ease and speed. Like Jesus, we are better able to discern in the moment whether we are being *moved to care* for the crowd or whether we should *move on* for time away from them.

DISCERNMENT AND HUNGER

Neither our desire nor the world's need alone can tell us what work is ours to do. Discernment happens at the intersection of the two. Frederick Buechner famously advised, "The place God calls you to is the place where your deep gladness and the world's deep hunger meet."[22] So, discernment requires not only the "discernment of spirits" within us but the "discernment of hungers" around us.

It's tragically ironic that our rural communities, many of which are rooted in agriculture, are full of hunger. How strange that people surrounded by acres and acres of corn or wheat or cattle would face food insecurity. According to Feeding America, an organization that supplies and supports food pantries and feeding programs across the country, 2.4 million rural householders face hunger. Three-quarters of the counties with the highest rates of food insecurity are in rural areas, as are 86 percent of the counties with the highest rates of child hunger. Many rural communities are hungry communities. Many rural regions also contain "food deserts," where they lack access to healthy, affordable foods.[23] So they subsist on cheap, highly processed food.

But we are hungry for other things as well. We hunger for social dignity, economic security, and spiritual renewal. We hunger for wholeness in our families and unity in our divided communities. We hunger for vision and purpose that can energize us for a positive future. In our rural feeding story, Jesus discerns multiple hungers at work in the crowd. He discerns their hunger for

- leadership, so he steps up and steps in;
- wisdom and direction, so he teaches them;
- wholeness, so he offers them healing ministry;
- community, so he gathers them into smaller groups;
- belonging, so he hosts them;
- rest, so he instructs them to sit down;
- agency, so he invites them into the miracle;
- purpose, so he reveals the kingdom; and
- good food, so he prepares a meal.

Jesus declared that those who are hungry, whether for food, justice, or healing, are "blessed" because their hunger creates a space in which God can move and reveal God's kingdom. "They will be filled," Jesus promised (Matt 5:6). He seemed to love it when people would "come hungry" when they met him.

Perhaps the present Christ is prepared to fill the hungers within us when we are ready to notice and name them. He asks: What are you hungry for? And perhaps the present Christ is also prepared to show us how to discern and respond to the deep hungers driving the people in our small towns and rural communities. When we are, like Jesus, moved with compassion and attentive to the Spirit's personal movements in our lives, we get to forge a partnership with God. Together we discern the hungers around us and respond by cocreating an abundant community in which everyone gets to experience a life without lack.

CHAPTER THREE

THE PRACTICE
OF STABILITY

They do not need to go away. You give them something to eat.

Matthew 14:16

I'M NOT AN ANGRY MAN. I'd like to think that I'm a pretty congenial fellow. It takes a lot to get me truly upset, and I rarely lose my temper. But like everyone, I have a few triggers. I don't like when people negatively stereotype entire cultures. I don't like when people use abusive language. I don't like when people are willfully ignorant or narrowly ideological. But there is another trigger that may be a bit more surprising. You see, it has to do with corn.

I get very annoyed when someone refers to a place as "just a bunch of cornfields."

I call it the "corn comment."

For most of my life, hearing the corn comment didn't bother me; truth be told, I have used it a few times—about my homeland and other wide-open places in the heartland. But in the past few years, I've become a tad more sensitive about it.

This cornfield-related conflict happens often enough that I've created a compelling speech—a righteous rant of sorts—that, if utilized, would silence any critic's mockery once and for all. It's a nuclear option, which I will only use in self-defense. But it's ready. At just the right time, I can pull out my speech and use it to win the hearts and minds of all those in the room who dare to scorn the corn. Most importantly, the speech is potent enough to humble (humiliate) cynics until they're ready to husk some corn, lobby for ethanol subsidies, and move to Iowa.

My introduction exposes the poverty of the perspective: When I see corn farmers and cornfields, I don't see them as signposts of isolation and irrelevance. I don't see backward farmers and simple yeomen. I see hardworking caretakers of our common home. I see smart, strategic businesspeople witnessing the seeds of investment transform into the fruit of their labor. They know the soil; they know the land; they're responsible for it. And they are feeding the world.

Then, I weave in the personal and cinematic: those fields also carry memory and mystery. They hold the memories of laughing children running through the corn maze at a local fall festival. I remember the fun I had playing with the neighbor kid in the cornfields behind my house; we created some amazing paths meandering through the cornfield. It was awesome until his dad found out and informed us that the green wilderness we were taming happened to be his livelihood. Also, what would *Signs* or *Field of Dreams*, not to mention *Children of the Corn*, be like without cornfields?

I bring the speech home by connecting our kitchens to a long heritage of culture and agriculture: Finally, when I look at these fields, I see food. Indigenous peoples have cultivated corn on this continent going back about seven thousand years. Several American Indian tribes considered corn to be a special gift from the Creator, one of the "three sisters" (corn, squash, and beans) that enabled them to survive and thrive for centuries. It sustained them with hope, nutrition, and trade value.

Not to mention, there is nothing quite like corn on the cob slathered with butter and a touch of salt. It is the taste of summer, of family dinners and picnics on the green grass. And that Mountain Dew in your hand? Check the ingredients. It's mostly high fructose corn syrup. Might not be the most healthful beverage, but it pairs nicely with your corn chips. Until you stop doing the Dew and eating popcorn at the movies, maybe show a little respect.

Okay, maybe I'm just a little too sensitive about corn. And when I stop to reflect on it, I see that it is not really about corn. It's really about how we talk about our place, our home, or someone else's homeplace:

Is it worthless or valuable?

Is it ugly or beautiful?

Is it worth care and commitment, or should it be left behind?

Lots of people see rural America as "flyover country," somewhere we have to drive *through* or fly *over*. There's not much going on there and nothing worth seeing. I always loved the sign that a tiny town called Gas, Kansas, put up beside the road. The sign pleads with passersby: "Don't pass Gas. Stop and visit." Unless we are desperate for fuel or a bathroom break, we do pass Gas, and thousands of small towns like it, without a thought.

But not only outsiders and city folk keep moving, looking for someplace more interesting. The truth is that many rural people themselves grow weary of rural life and want to leave. Many do leave.

In fact, if a young person doesn't hit the road for college or adventure or opportunity, they may get some sideways looks. I left, then came back. And even when I returned, I often felt like I needed to explain why I returned. Even though people seemed happy to have me back, they also seemed to wonder what failure brought me back: Couldn't make it in the big city? Had a mental breakdown? Got a degree in Polish Folk Music Gender Theory and couldn't find a job?

Returning, for me, was not a failure. It was not a concession or surrender. It was a free and intentional choice. I examined my life and how I wanted to live. I decided that I wanted to live and possibly raise a family in a small town, in the Ohio Valley, close to my family. I wanted my future to have a connection to my past—to my childhood and ancestors.

SALVATION BY RELOCATION

People in rural places stay, leave, and return for many reasons. Two sociologists, Patrick Carr and Maria Kefalas, studied the decision-making processes of young adults in the American heartland who were debating whether to stay in or leave their rural hometowns. In their book, *Hollowing Out the Middle: Rural Brain Drain and What It Means for America*, they identified four distinct groups in this population: stayers, seekers, returners, and achievers.

Stayers stick around for old friends and extended family, content to work a low-skilled job for a decent wage, saving up to buy a house; they probably won't attend college and will probably marry a local guy or girl at a young age. They seem "destined to stay." *Seekers* cannot wait to get out of town and into a city where they can meet new people and have new experiences. *Returners* go away but come back, either because they couldn't find their way "out there" or they wanted to go "home" to the simplicity of their small town; they may be returning to their roots and starting a family. Finally, *achievers* stand out as uniquely "gifted." Teachers and parents see the child's potential and prepare them for a future outside their small town where they can flourish and succeed; they are "raised to leave."[1]

Whether due to a discernment practice like the one we explored in the previous chapter or a restless longing to see what's "out there," lots of folks end up leaving. Some, like me, come back. Enough leave and don't come back that it has become a major concern for many small towns and rural communities. They fear that their beloved towns are dying, sometimes because they are. These troubling trends mobilize many to seek change and revitalization. But for others, especially those who consider themselves experts, leaving is a logical survival skill, because these struggling small towns are dying—and they deserve to die.

In an article for *National Review*, conservative political commentator Kevin D. Williamson provides a "subscription for impoverished communities" in which he dismisses the complaints of rural (and other struggling) Americans, offering distilled wisdom for their salvation: "The best thing that people trapped in poverty in these undercapitalized and dysfunctional communities could do is—move. Get the hell out of Dodge, or Eastern Kentucky, or the Bronx."[2] The symbol of this salvation for him is the U-Haul. Apparently, that's what rural Americans in struggling communities need more than any social empowerment or financial investment.

Likewise, Paul Krugman, a Nobel Prize–winning economist (from the opposite end of the political spectrum), has no brilliant plan for rural revitalization. He admits that his solution risks a "social cost" but ultimately proposes that we're all better off moving toward the supercities where new technology and large labor pools will bring the abundance we seek. In his final evaluation, small cities and rural communities "have nothing going for them except historical luck, which eventually tends to run out."[3]

Williamson and Krugman aren't alone. These types of opinions make regular appearances in both left- and right-leaning publications. Some write with sympathy, others with contempt, but they all agree that the last best hope for people in struggling rural communities is to leave and move to a city. The city is where the jobs are, where the growth is happening, where culture and creativity can be found. I call this idea "salvation by relocation."

This supposed solution is nothing new. In fact, we encounter it in our gospel story.

When we left off in Mark 6, Jesus had been moved with compassion, so he offered his presence to the people: listening, healing, and "teaching them many things" (v. 34). Before long, however, the disciples noticed that it was getting late; they also noticed that Jesus didn't seem to be aware of this fact. So they worked up the courage to interrupt him for a moment to let him know.

I have an acquaintance who has a wonderful way of telling guests to leave his house. After dinner with friends and some conversation over a nightcap, he feels himself getting sleepy and worn out from the work of hosting. Instead of saying, "I'm tired. It was great seeing you, but we'd better head to bed," he would say to his wife, "Well, the guests are tired. We had better call it a night." Another strategy I like comes from a pastor who would make his exit by asking, "Shall we pray?" The prayer provided a convenient and spiritual method for ending the visit and parting ways.

The disciples approached Jesus to say, in essence, "The guests are tired (and probably hungry). Shall we pray?"

But they didn't stop there. They seemed to have anticipated Jesus's objection. He is going to be concerned about all these people, they probably reasoned, and will want to make sure they get something to eat. And Jesus will likely forget that we are in the middle of nowhere. So we will need to make sure he knows that the people will need to fend for themselves, and that they will have to fend somewhere else.

So, after encouraging Jesus to wrap things up with a closing prayer, they tacked on some advice. "This is a remote place," they said, "and it's already very late. Send the people away so that they can go to the surrounding countryside and villages and buy themselves something to eat" (v. 36).

Jesus's response to the disciples is straightforward and revealing: "You give them something to eat" (v. 37).

Matthew's version emphasizes the contrast between Jesus's solution and the disciples' solution: "*They* do not need to go away. *You* give them something to eat" (Matt 14:6).

Jesus seems to see what they are doing and decides to flip their "solution" on its head. The answer isn't *there* and *them*, it's *here* and *us*. He seems to be saying "Remember when I said, 'The kingdom is not up above or over yonder but within and among you?' I am going to show you what I meant. Actually, we are going to create and experience this kingdom event together. So, what do you think? How are we going to do it?"

At this point, the disciples are preparing a PowerPoint presentation with charts and graphs, mumbling that Jesus may be a world-class spiritual teacher, but he seriously needs a math tutor. "You see this line, Jesus?" asks Peter, pointing his laser at the graph. "This is the cost required to feed this massive crowd, for just one meal." Then Andrew jumps in: "You see this line *way* down here? That is how much money we currently have." Finally, Thomas steps up for the finish: "It's a very nice idea, Jesus. Truly. But we can't deny this basic math and simple accounting. We simply don't have enough. So, back to our original proposal."

THE MIDDLE OF NOWHERE

I don't want to be too hard on the disciples. They were simply using the tools they had to fix the problem as they understood it. Their logic reflects conventional wisdom. But it hides a set of assumptions about the people and the place. And it masks a set of beliefs about God, human beings, and the nature of the world. It is the same mindset that still sneaks into the souls of restless rural people and ruthless commentators today:

> "Send the people away."
> Problems at home? Leave!
> Get the hell out of Dodge.
> Give them a U-Haul.
> We don't have what we need.
> There is not enough. We are not enough.
> The power and resources are somewhere else.
> Salvation is relocation.

Simply put, the disciples were operating from a mindset of scarcity. They looked out at the crowd and saw a lot of need and looked around them and saw very few resources. In their view, there was a lot of demand and very little supply. They were, after all, in the desert.

The isolation of their location is emphasized through the repeated use of the Greek phrase *eremos topos* (vv. 30, 32, and 35), often translated as "wilderness" or "desert place." In the biblical landscape, the desert is not necessarily the desert as we typically imagine it in the United States, with blowing sand and cacti. It is understood more sociologically and spiritually than ecologically. It is a wild place with little human habitation, making it ripe for both divine and demonic activity.

This wilderness landscape features prominently in Mark's gospel.[4] The book begins with John the Baptist embodying the ministry anticipated by the prophet Isaiah: "In the *wilderness* prepare the way for the Lord; make straight in the *desert* a highway for our God" (Isa 40:3). John, likely a relative of Jesus, would initiate Jesus into this desert spirituality. And only after an extended formational time in the desert would Jesus begin his public ministry.

Translating *eremos* in Mark illustrates the mixed connotation of wilderness. It can be translated as "peaceful" and "quiet" or "barren," "lonely," and "deserted" (even in the same passage). God-filled or God-forsaken, depending on whom you ask. These are exactly the interpretative choices we make when we look at rural places. Some of us see just a bunch of cornfields in the middle of nowhere; others see a place of precious memories, surprising gifts, and special people. Some see a God-forsaken landscape to be avoided, while others see "God's country," a place to be explored and enjoyed.

In the documentary *Look and See*, Kentucky farmer and author Wendell Berry said, "The great cultural failure we have made here in the United States is to mistake millions of individual small places, with their own character, their own needs and demands . . . for *nowhere*."[5]

We often look at a place and see only its problems, not its potential. We see its emptiness but not its capacity. And we do the same with people. Too often, only in hindsight do we see beauty and possibility. We wake up and admit, like Jacob of old, "Surely the Lord is in this place, and I was not aware of it!" (Gen 28:16).

In contrast to the disciples and those of us who only see rural places as deserted space, Jesus was the master of seeing the possibility and potential within people and places. He was able to see healing and wholeness when others saw only brokenness and illness. He was able to see dignity and worth when others saw only sinners and strangers. He was able to see peace and justice when others saw only violence and oppression. And Jesus was able to see abundance and community when others saw only scarcity and desperation.

Instead of scarcity, Jesus looked out at the people and the place and saw *hidden abundance*.

Moving from the mindset of scarcity to the mindset of abundance is one of the most important shifts required for rural renewal. It is an essential skill for ordinary leaders. As Parker Palmer notes, this mindset change makes all the difference:

> The quality of our active lives depends heavily on whether we assume a world of scarcity or a world of abundance. Do we inhabit a universe where the basic things that people need—from food and shelter to a sense of competence and of being loved—are ample in nature? Or is this a universe where such goods are in short supply, available only to those who have the power to beat everyone else to the store? The nature of our action will be heavily conditioned by the way we answer those bedrock questions.[6]

Because Jesus sees abundance in the place and the people, his plan of action in our feeding story is markedly different from the one proposed by the disciples in their assumption of scarcity.

Perhaps, learning from Jesus, we need to reframe the phrase "middle of nowhere." If we break the word *nowhere* into two parts, we discover a trite but true word play: "now here." If this is God's world, filled with divine presence, and unfolding in the divine process, then the place we find ourselves is a good place, an important place, a holy place. In fact, when we are shaped by the theological landscapes of Scripture, we realize that it is often in the undervalued and unexpected places where God is discovered and revealed. Those places considered the "middle of nowhere" are often the middle of the "now here" of God's presence and activity—the middle of the "now here" of God's work of repair and renewal. And that is a good place to be.

STABILITY IN THE DESERT

The disciples were clear on the best course of action: get these people out of this God-forsaken place in the middle of nowhere and let them figure it out and fight it out for themselves. Jesus was also clear on the best course of action: stay put and present, take another look at where you are, and recover the abundance hidden within this place and these people. Jesus was reaffirming both the resources and the responsibilities of the disciples. What they needed was there and theirs.

If we are honest, most ordinary leaders in rural places and small towns can identify with the disciples. We see great needs but few resources. We grow weary and discouraged—even resentful—and we are tempted to tell people to move on and move away. Go to the city or suburbs where there are jobs and opportunity and activities. But the wisdom of Jesus comes to today's ordinary leaders as it came to those disciples: "They do not need to go away." The resources will be revealed and miracles made possible, but only if we are willing to *stay put and stay present*. We will be able to discover and recover abundance only if we are willing to root ourselves in the present moment and present place. Spiritual teachers have a name for this commitment: the practice of stability.

The practice of stability is found throughout the Bible and religious history but is most clearly demonstrated by the witness of monastic communities. The desert monastics fled to the deserts of Egypt in the fourth century to seek Christ in solitude and silence because they were disillusioned with the corruption of both the church and state of their time. Living in caves and other simple dwellings, they practiced their faith in the context of a rugged, rural environment. In time, many seekers from the surrounding villages came to visit these hermits, hungry for their wisdom and ministry. Under the ministry of these desert fathers and mothers, spiritual seekers were taught the spirituality of *hesychasm,* through which disciples learned to nurture interior stillness and a life of continual prayer. They were taught that the depth of their spirituality was connected to the strength of their stability.[7]

I first learned about the spirituality of the desert fathers and mothers when I was in college. If ever there was a college "in the middle of nowhere," it was the small Quaker college in rural Kansas I attended. The town in which the school was located lost half its population every year when the students went home for the summer. The community had one store, one restaurant, and two churches. My first weekend there, some students had a campfire and ate a snake cooked over the fire. So, naturally, I was a bit homesick. Life in rural Kansas was boring, and I was lonely.

About halfway through my first semester, the college chaplain, Dave Williams, asked me to join him for a lunch meeting. The school was so small that he was able to meet personally with most of the students during their first year. Over a cafeteria lunch of chicken-fried steak and mashed potatoes, we talked about how things were going with classes and the transition. I confessed that it had been a bit of a struggle. He smiled and nodded knowingly. As he often did, he adjusted his glasses, looked me straight in the eyes, then asked, "Does it feel like a desert experience?" It was a simple question, some would even say a trite one. But something about the way he asked it and the way I was feeling connected, and the desert metaphor spoke to my condition.

He had guided many students through the transition, so he knew the spiritual and psychological landscape well. It so happened that Dave was also from Ohio—Cleveland, no less. So he knew well the experience of feeling far from home in a rugged region. As we finished our lunch and slid aside our trays, Dave told me the story of Saint Anthony. Anthony was about to become a strange new friend.

Dave told me the story of how Anthony had left his city and family inheritance to seek God in the desert, making his home in a cave for several years. During his time in the desert cave, Anthony's friends would come to visit and, from outside the cave, could hear him struggling and arguing within. Anthony himself would describe these experiences as wrestling with the devil and the beasts and seductresses that were sent to him. After years of interior struggle and spiritual formation in the cave, Anthony emerged. Much to the surprise of his concerned friends, he came out glowing. He was a new being. He would spend his next years counseling seekers and directing disciples.

The application wasn't hard to grasp. If I would stay put and stay present through the temptations to flee or avoid questions and conflicts, I would be transformed. I would emerge from my time in rural Kansas as a new being, someone prepared for ministry.

A few months later, I went to a bookstore in Wichita and found an odd, wonderful icon from the Eastern Orthodox tradition. It was called "The Temptation of Saint Anthony." The icon pictured Anthony in his cave, wrestling with all manner of creatures and demons, with the city far in the background. I hung it up by my bed as a reminder and a promise. I would stay put and stay present. I would do the work the desert called upon me to do as God did God's deep work in me. And if I would refuse the temptation to check out or move away, I would emerge as a new creation.

Even within early monastic communities, the temptations of excessive mobility and consumerism were strong. Abba Antony advised, "Whatever place you live, do not easily leave that place."[8] Another desert teacher named Abba Moses similarly counseled, "Go, sit in your cell, and your cell will teach you everything."[9] They were confronting a trend among some seekers to move from one place to another, from one experience to another, without putting down the kind of roots from which a flourishing, fruitful life can grow.

In fact, the eleventh-century Benedictine monk Anselm of Canterbury used the analogy of a tree to describe this troubling trend:

> Just as any young tree, if frequently transplanted or often disturbed by being torn up after having recently been planted in a particular place, will never be able to take root, will rapidly wither and bring no fruit to perfection, similarly an unhappy monk, if he often moves from place to place at his own whim, or remaining in one place, is frequently agitated by his hatred of it, he never achieves stability with roots of love, grows weary and does not grow rich in the fruitfulness of good works.[10]

Anselm's solution to this restless, fruitless mobility was the voluntary and joyful practice of what became known as a "vow of stability." In taking the vow of stability, a monk or nun was committing themselves to a place and its people, usually for their lifetime. Anselm advised his disciples to strive "with total application of his mind to set down roots of love in whatever monastery he made his profession." He went on to remind the reader of a truth that is easily forgotten. Belonging to a community is a gift: "Let him rejoice at having at last found a place where he can stay, not unwillingly but voluntarily, for the rest of his life, and having put away all anxiety about moving from one place to another."[11]

STABILITY AND SPIRITUAL RENEWAL

The wisdom of Anthony and the desert fathers and mothers spoke to my personal situation all those years ago, but it also speaks to contemporary rural leaders. The temptations of life and leadership haven't changed all that much. So, while the mobility of modern life has many advantages, it has psychological and spiritual side effects as well. Among them is the feeling among many that we should always be looking for a better life, often in a better place. Some people are ever restless and never happy. They refuse to stay in one place or with one person because they are always finding some flaw that can't be overlooked or worked through.

That restlessness exists in all of us and has both creative and destructive potential. We walk around with a vague uneasiness and restlessness, haunted by the fear that we should be seeking someone or somewhere else out there. Sometimes we even mask it in spiritual language, telling ourselves and others that we are doing missionary work or going on pilgrimage. While those are legitimate, important practices in a life of faith, they can easily be used to justify a fear of commitment and leave us blown around in a spirit of consumerism, escapism, and what I call "adventure addiction."

Wise teachers across the ages remind us that these energies need to be named and channeled. When we commit to staying put and staying present, we get to "put away all anxiety about moving one place to another." We are free to "set down roots of love" and "grow rich in fruitfulness." Our roots have the time and space they need to grow down deep because we are not being constantly uprooted and transplanted. The roots are able to soak up all the nourishment and energy of the land, and the branches reach wide. Our lives, families, congregations, and businesses can be fruitful because we are secure, rooted, and stable.

The desert saints had a word for the urges of restlessness that keep us moving and uprooting: *acedia*. The struggle with *acedia* was considered akin to the sin of slothfulness, but it wasn't about laziness, exactly. It was more about the sense of despair or craving for escape that comes with living in the desert (literally or spiritually).[12]

With remarkable psychological insight, the abbas and ammas described the temptations of this particular demon, sometimes called the "noonday devil." This demon, they noted, often comes to the monk in the middle of the day. He makes it seem like the sun is barely moving at all. Before long, the monk grows so bored and frustrated that he develops a hatred for the place, sometimes even for life itself. The demon then brings up every offense from every brother, causing the monk to hate the people as well as the place.

Evagrius of Pontus, a fourth-century monk, describes the final, fatal temptation: "He leads him on to the desire for other places where he can easily find the wherewithal to meet his needs and pursue a trade that is easier and more productive; he adds that pleasing the Lord is not a question of being in a particular place, . . . and he deploys every device in order to have the monk leave his cell and flee the stadium."[13] Evagrius exhibits impressive psychological insight in his description of *acedia*. This is a thought process with which most of us are familiar.

The wisdom of these spiritual teachers is that we must withstand these temptations, staying put and present, before we can find the wholeness and fullness of life for which we long. We have to wrestle with the restlessness of *acedia* before we can discover and recover the abundance within and around us. The path that leads to abundance first leads us through *acedia*

STABILITY AND SOCIAL CHANGE

The practice of stability is not only essential for spiritual growth, but it is critical for social change. The temptations of *acedia* and the possibilities of stability are not just about interior freedom and private piety. The principle of stability is key to the process of recovering abundance in our rural communities.

I agree wholeheartedly with the poet Gary Snyder: "One of the key problems in American society now, it seems to me, is people's lack of commitment to any given place. . . . Neighborhoods are allowed to deteriorate, landscapes are allowed to be stripmined, because there is nobody who will live there and take responsibility; they'll just move on."[14] I wonder what projects of repair and renewal were abandoned because folks decided to "just move on" instead of working together to create new solutions. And I wonder what injustices are able to continue because folks aren't rooted and invested enough to risk a stand against them. or, perhaps, they don't have enough social capital and connection to know how to organize against them.

Almost a thousand years after monastic philosopher Anselm used the analogy of the rootless tree, the social scientist Robert Putnam put forth the "re-potting hypothesis." In his landmark book *Bowling Alone*, Putnam attributed the decline in social capital and civic engagement in part to the rise in mobility. Like a plant that is repeatedly repotted, mobility disrupts the root systems of our communities and makes it harder to connect with one another and accomplish projects together.[15] Mobility has advantages, to be sure, and plenty of people who are rooted are also isolated and antagonistic. But I think Anselm and Putnam are both pointing to a critical principle. Like other living things, human beings and our communities thrive best when we have solid, established roots.

Community renewal happens when ordinary leaders take personal responsibility for their place and trust that resources will be provided to fulfill those responsibilities. They dare to believe Jesus when he says, "They do not need to go somewhere else (and neither do you)."

When extractive industries move in and wound the mountains, pollute the water, and clearcut the forests, there are rooted people who will stand in the way. They are energized to protect the land and the community not because they are activists but because it's their home and they expect it to be respected. It is where their grandfather farmed, where their children play, where they hunt, fish, or hike. It's more than mere real estate.

Consider Widow Combs. On Thanksgiving 1965, a recently widowed Kentucky farmer named Ollie "Widow" Combs spent the holiday in jail. Why? Because she had lain down in front of a bulldozer to stop the coal company from strip mining her farm. She didn't set out to be an activist, but she loved her land and her home and she wasn't about to let it get destroyed. Combs later stated, "It's where I raised my family and it's the only home I ever really owned." Her efforts led to strip-mining legislation in the Kentucky general assembly in 1967. Ten years later, she was a guest at the White House for the signing of the Surface Mining Control and Reclamation Act.[16]

Consider Maria Gunnoe. Maria and her family live in West Virginia on a piece of land her family has owned for generations. Her Cherokee family taught her that nature is sacred and should be treated with respect. During times of poverty, they had to rely on resources from the mountains for food and medicine. In the early 2000s, a coal company started blasting off the top of a mountain near her home. The runoff and flooding from the practice of "valley fill" poisoned her water, spread toxic chemicals across her land, and nearly washed away her home. So she took a stand and set out to protect her home, then moved on to stopping mountaintop removal. Gunnoe began organizing, educating, and training neighborhood groups to report illegal behavior from coal companies. She won numerous awards for her work as an environmental activist. But she hadn't considered herself an activist until her beloved home, land, and family were threatened.[17]

It would have been easier for Maria and Ollie to just give up and leave. No one would blame them. They were just two people in the face of powerful corporations. But they stayed put, stayed present, and fought for the people and places that they loved. That's the power of stability.

BRAIN GAIN

The practice of stability requires commitment, but it doesn't have to be a cold and bitter stability, where we stay put out of sheer stubbornness or self-righteousness. Some people are trapped in small towns or can't find a way out of their rural region. But with all the emphasis on rural decline and brain drain, it's easy to miss the rest of the rural story. While brain drain is a real phenomenon, sociologists like Ben Winchester are telling a more complex story about the data. Winchester reports a countertrend of individuals and families moving *into* small towns and rural communities, especially in the thirty-to-fifty age range.

According to Winchester's research, these folks are moving into our communities for three main reasons. They are looking for a slower pace of life, safety and security (especially for families with children), and lower-cost housing. These migrants believe small towns and rural regions have something valuable to offer. And when they move into our communities, they bring their experience and education with them. Brain gain is just as real as brain drain.[18]

Alongside these migrants are a rising number of young folks who are choosing to stay, or return, not because they are trapped but because they love their home, and they want to have a role in its revitalization. The exciting part is that they aren't just talking about doing something; they are working together in projects of renewal, bringing new life to their hometowns.

In the Pacific Northwest, Madeline Moore was having cocktails with two friends when she confessed a dream she had been carrying: "Wouldn't it be cool if we got a room full of millennials together and just get them talking about how to change the future of rural?!"[19] Her two friends joyfully joined the dream, and together the three women started Rethinking Rural. The organization brings together rural millennials to learn about projects, network, and share best practices. This network includes artists, farmers, entrepreneurs, health-care workers, and many others who celebrate rural together in all its expressions and dedicate themselves to "creating resiliently vibrant communities."[20]

In the South, a group of rural youth started talking about the challenges they faced, seeking to find ways they could get involved in social movements in their region. They wanted to gain new skills and access to opportunities that would enable them to build a more "economically and environmentally sustainable Central Appalachia where young people have the power to build and participate in diverse, inclusive, and healthy communities." So they started the STAY Project (Stay Together Appalachian Youth). A number of like-minded nonprofit organizations from Kentucky, West Virginia, and Tennessee offered support and sponsorship. Since 2008, the STAY Project has been helping rural youth reverse the exodus from Central Appalachia and make their hometowns places where they can stay—and want to stay.[21]

Demographer Richard Florida defines three categories of Americans he studied in his research on place and mobility: the mobile,
the stuck, and the rooted. The mobile are those with the means and
connections to move toward opportunities. The stuck are those who
are unable to leave their current geographical location because they
don't have those means. Those are familiar categories to most of
us, but Florida also talks about a third category: the "rooted," those
who have the means and opportunities to leave but choose to stay
where they live.[22]

I believe "rooted" folks are central to rural renewal. Unlike the
mobile, they are not using their energy to chase new jobs and opportunities in other parts of the country. Unlike the stuck, they don't
have to use their energy to escape their current situation. Instead,
they can use their energy to live, love, and lead in their hometown
because they are there by choice. They are ordinary leaders.

STABILITY IS TESTIMONY

In the 1940s, a Georgia couple named Clarence and Florence Jordan started an intentional community called Koinonia Farm in
rural Georgia. This community was to be a "demonstration plot
for the kingdom of God" in which white and black folks would live,
work, and worship together as an alternative to the prevalent racism and poverty across the American South. When the interracial
nature of the community became more obvious, citizens from the
surrounding towns grew outraged. The local chamber of commerce
demanded that businesses not buy their products, and a seventy-car
motorcade of the Ku Klux Klan (KKK) drove out to the property to
terrorize and intimidate the group into leaving the state. When the
boycott didn't destroy the community, some opponents turned to
bombs and bullets.

Though nobody in Koinonia Farm wanted to let violence and
prejudice win the day, many members were concerned for their
safety and believed that the integrity of their life together was more

important than taking a courageous stand at that particular location. About half of the community left. Clarence Jordan saw the impact the threats and violence were having on his community and contemplated whether his choice to stay put and stand strong was really the right one. After all, due to the intimidation, the agricultural classes, vacation Bible schools, and summer camps had been canceled for the foreseeable future. Nevertheless, after intense prayer and personal wrestling, Jordan decided to take a vow of stability and maintain the farm's local witness. He describes his decision in a sermon given in 1958:

> Fifteen years ago we went there and bought that old run down eroded piece of land. It was sick. There were gashes in it. It was sore and bleeding. I don't know whether you've ever walked over a piece of ground that could almost cry out to you and say "Heal me, heal me." I don't know if you feel the closeness to the soil that I do. But when you fill in those old gullies and terrace the fields and you begin to feel the springiness of the sod beneath your feet and you begin to feel that old land come to life and when you walk through a little old pine forest that you set out in little seedlings and now you see them reaching for the sky and you hear the wind through them ... and you go on over a hill where your children and all the many visitors have held picnics and you walk across a creek that you've bathed [in] the heat of the summer, and men say to you "Why don't you sell it and move away?" they might as well ask, "Why don't you sell your mother." Somehow God has made us out of this old soil and we go back to it and we never lose its claim on us. It isn't a simple matter to leave it.[23]

When we make a commitment to stay put and stay present, to learn and love our place, "it isn't a simple matter to leave it." And it isn't a simple matter to use and abuse it or let others do so. It is our home. It is the center of our responsibility and source of our resources.

As ordinary leaders, stability is our testimony. Our commitment to staying put and present testifies to our value as people and places created by God. It reflects our insistence that our places are worth knowing, loving, and preserving. The practice of stability also testifies to the possibilities of God's renewing work. When we are rooted, we become strong enough to rise and join God's work in way that makes our communities, like Clarence Jordan made his, a "demonstration plot for the kingdom of God."

By the way, after the Jordans committed to staying in Georgia and continuing the community's witness, new opportunities arose. They were able to start a successful mail-order business for the farm. Koinonia Farm became a place of renewal and hospitality for burned-out activists and leaders. And in the 1960s, a housing ministry was born from their work called Habitat for Humanity.

Abundant life is possible for everyone in every place. The kingdom is within us and at work among us. But abundant communities require ordinary leaders who are willing to stay put and stay present, taking the time and building the trust upon which a flourishing future can be built. It's a privilege to participate in this Great Project, but it's also work. We will wrestle with the demon of *acedia*. We will come face to face with the shadow side of our communities, witnessing a spirit of violence and prejudice from folks we previously respected. But if we will linger in our love and leadership, we will develop rich relationships that surprise us and discover resources we didn't know existed.

CHAPTER FOUR

THE PRACTICE
OF INVENTORY

How many loaves do you have? Go and see.

Mark 6:38

THERE IS A HASIDIC TALE about a poor Jewish man who lived in the city of Prague. One night he had a dream in which he traveled to Vienna and found a treasure chest buried underneath the bridge to the king's palace. The prospect of finding treasure and escaping poverty sounded wonderful, but he dared not believe it. It was only a dream, after all.

Night after night, the dream kept returning, until he finally gave in. He left his home, village, and family behind to seek the treasure. After a long journey, he arrived at the bridge near the king's palace but found that it was heavily guarded by the king's soldiers. Day after day, he paced across and around the bridge, waiting for the moment when he could get under the bridge and dig out the treasure.

After almost two weeks of this, however, the guards grew suspicious. One day, the captain decided that he'd had enough, so he walked over to him, picked him up by the collar of his shirt, and demanded, "What are you plotting, Jew? Why do you keep coming here day after day?"

Startled and afraid, the man decided to come clean with the honest truth. He told the captain about his dream, the bridge, and the treasure. Upon hearing the man's story, the captain broke out in loud, uncontrollable laughter. The poor dreamer looked at the soldier in astonishment, letting out a few nervous chuckles.

When the captain finally caught his breath and his laughter subsided, he explained, "You came all this way because of a foolish dream? Well, if I was guided by dreams, I'd be halfway to the city of Prague by now! Just last night I had a dream that some poor Jew in that city had a treasure buried in his cellar, waiting to be discovered and claimed."

Secretly elated to hear the captain's dream, the man quietly but quickly returned home, the soldiers all laughing as he left. Daring to believe there was something to all these dreams, he went into his cellar and started digging. Much to his surprise and excitement, he found the buried treasure. He was amazed to realize that the wealth he dreamed of was always in his possession, hidden in his own house.

When it comes to renewing our rural communities, it's tempting to think that all the resources we need are somewhere else. As we discussed in the last chapter, it's easy to start thinking that our salvation will come from relocation. It's also common for rural communities to fall prey to the "white knight" myth, putting our hopes in the prospect of attracting a large corporation to move into our town and save us. Whether we bring in the jobs from somewhere else or send our people away, the relationships and resources we need are "not from around here."

The Hasidic story, however, reminds us that the wisdom and wealth we need is often closer than we think, maybe even hidden within our own household and community. We might need to take a transformational journey somewhere else to realize it, which is why we should value our "returners," but the sooner we learn that what we need is nearby, the sooner we can start uncovering and recovering the treasure hidden within us, within our homes, and within our neighbors and neighborhoods.

There is a wonderful story in the Hebrew Bible about a desperate widow and the prophet Elisha (2 Kgs 4). The widow's late husband had been connected to Elisha through the "company of prophets" (v. 1), so she appealed to him for assistance. Now a single mom in a patriarchal society, the widow knew what the future would hold if there were no intervention: "His creditor is coming to take my two boys as his slaves" (v. 1). She was dealing with both the heaviness of death and the bondage of debt. So she hoped that Elisha, being a man of God, could facilitate a miracle.

Upon hearing the widow's needs, we might expect Elisha to turn his attention to heaven. Perhaps he would lift his eyes and hands to God above and ask for a mighty miracle. Perhaps God's power would be displayed if Elisha prayed and coins materialized into the widow's hands, created out of nothing. But that's not what happened. Elisha heard of the widow's situation and asked a critical, creative question: "Tell me, what do you have in your house?" (v. 2).

Elisha believed there was wealth hidden in her house. Like the man in the Hasidic tale discovered, she had hidden treasures waiting closer than she could imagine. So, the prophet encouraged her to take a closer look at what was already present, what she already had.

Elisha's question was apparently confusing, possibly frustrating, to the woman. If she had what she needed, she wouldn't be there pleading with the prophet for help. "Your servant has nothing there at all," she informed him, "except a small jar of olive oil" (v. 2).

It wasn't much. Who could blame the widow for feeling like it wasn't enough, barely even worth mentioning? But there is a bit of humorous irony in her response. She said there was *nothing* there at all, then sheepishly mentioned, *except* the jar of oil. I imagine Elisha responding, "Aha! Something we can work with!" Then I imagine Elisha engaging the situation with prophetic improvisation, seeing the problem and possibilities and moving forward in a spirit of partnership. God, Elisha, and the widow were figuring out the solution to her problem together, trusting that the makings of a miracle were present, waiting to be discovered.

Then Elisha moved from the household to the neighbor-hood. There were community resources that could be shared. He instructed the widow, "Go around and ask all your neighbors for empty jars." He added, "Don't ask for just a few" (v. 3). The Torah taught the people of Israel that the peace and prosperity of shalom was possible if neighbors shared wealth within the community, especially caring for widows and orphans. Perhaps Elisha went with the widow into the neighbor's houses to remind them of their cove-nant responsibility to secure the common good, especially on behalf of the most vulnerable among them.

Elisha told her to take all the jars and containers she has col-lected and start pouring oil in them, inviting her kids to join in as well. Only when all the jars were full did the oil stop flowing. After this incredible display of abundance, Elisha provided a final instruc-tion: "Go, sell the oil and pay your debts. You and your sons can live on what is left" (v. 7).

What is interesting and instructive about this story is that the miracle is not performed ex nihilo, out of nothing and out of nowhere. It happens by reclaiming household resources, sharing neighborhood gifts, and exercising entrepreneurial creativity. The miracle is not above and beyond but within and between. It hap-pens as a partnership of humans creating and collaborating, with God's power flowing through the process to bring abundance into being.

INVENTORY AND INQUIRY

Several hundred years later, in the spirit of Elijah and Elisha, Jesus stands amid a hungry crowd and doubting disciples and sets out to solve a problem with a similar prophetic inquiry, not "What do you have in your house?" but "How many loaves do you have?" The ques-tion isn't rhetorical. It comes with an imperative: "Go and see." It's nice that Jesus doesn't just insist—"think this way"—but invites—"try this." Jesus invites the disciples into the practice of inventory.

He asks them to leave the huddle and figure out what they have to work with, to count and declare their loaves and fishes. This practice shifts the focus from what is absent to what is present, from the problem to the possibilities.

In both stories, the inventory inquiry is where the story turns. Before then, the focus is on the need, the problem, the scarcity of resources. Naming the issue is understandable and necessary. But these stories teach us that a good leader turns the attention toward what is present and what is possible. If we want to begin the process of *recovering* abundance, we must start by *discovering* the abundance that is already present.

Interestingly, this same shift is happening today among people and organizations doing the work of community development and social change. The conventional wisdom used to be that change and growth began by interviewing the community and finding out what needs and problems they were facing. Then the experts would respond with a list of recommended solutions and systems. Over time, however, people began to see how this approach could be disempowering and instead pivoted to asset-based community development (conveniently abbreviated ABCD). After all, as ABCD pioneers John McKnight and Peter Block said, "You don't know what you need until you know what you have."[1]

In the conventional approach, the interviewing process itself centers on problems, often reinforcing a community's sense of despair and dependence. We may think of questions as neutral, but they are actually powerful directors of energy and attention. In some sense, all questions are leading questions. Ordinary leaders, then, have the responsibility of stewarding questions and conversations in ways that call forth the gifts and possibilities of their communities.

In his book *Community: The Structure of Belonging*, organizational consultant Peter Block writes, "Restoration is created by the kinds of conversations we initiate with each other. These conversations are a leverage point for an alternative future. The core question that underlies each conversation is 'what can we create together?'"[2] Moving toward this creative, collaborative orientation will require that we watch our language. Block suggests that we shift our language in the following ways:

- from retribution to restoration
- from problems to possibilities
- from fear and fault to gifts, generosity, and abundance
- from law and oversight to social fabric and chosen accountability
- from corporations and systems to associational life
- from consumerism to citizenship[3]

When we change our language, we change our questions. When we change our questions, we change our conversations. When we change our conversations, we change our cultures. When we change our cultures, we change our futures.

This process of using positive questions to re-create communities is sometimes called Appreciative Inquiry (AI). Developed by Case Western Reserve professors David Cooperrider and Diana Whitney, the AI process invites ordinary leaders to craft questions that will help identify the "life-giving forces" (not unlike the Examen practice we explored earlier) already present within the community. The inquirer follows those forces and listens to the responses so they can discover metaphors and stories that will draw the community forward. The group also works together to create "provocative proposals" about how that positive future can be enacted through prototypes, programs, and other innovations.[4]

The shifts Block and AI suggest may be subtle in some ways, but they have the power to redirect a community in significant ways. But those shifts make all the difference for the direction and vitality of communities. Likewise, shifting from the question and direction of the disciples to the question and direction of Jesus is game-changing. How different would the outcome have been had the disciples been in charge? How would the energy and momentum of the moment have changed if the disciples' questions instead of Jesus's had been prioritized?

WORD WORK

In the small town of Eastport, Maine, a group of local women began to notice a troubling trend in the media's stories about their town, as well as the way locals were talking about the town. They seemed to be stuck using what the women called "DE-Words": depressed, dependent, decline, and despair. Even positive stories somehow always came back around to those DE-Words in describing schools and services and their economy. So these women, who call themselves the Women of the Commons, started a campaign to replace the DE-Words with RE-Words: rebound, rediscover, redesign, reverse, renew, reenergize, and reemerge. The campaign encouraged community members, especially public figures, to "watch their language" when they talked about the town.

As they worked and watched, they began to see the shift in language result in a shift in culture around town. As the culture shifted, the people became more open and supportive of new ventures. So the women restored a historic building on Eastport's waterfront and began making their shared dream for the community into reality. The Commons Eastport became a shop space for over one hundred local artists and artisans to share their craft and sell their products. The second floor was renovated and made into seaside vacation suites. And they aren't done. An article in *The Atlantic* says, "They have built this place, and three among them are planning a second more ambitious project. The women have been at this a long time, about a dozen years now, building with conservative patience and care, and yet the enthusiasm of a startup."[5]

Renewal requires that ordinary leaders take risks with that combination of "conservative patience and care" and "the enthusiasm of a startup." But it's important to remember that making change and creating new opportunities first require the kind of "language planning" utilized by the Women of the Commons. When we shift our language, we shift our focus to the resources and possibilities already present.

GOLD IN THEM HILLS

My beloved Morrow County doesn't make it into international publications very often. Unfortunately, we did a couple of years ago when a state representative was caught having sex with another man in his statehouse office. I should mention that he was married to a woman and an outspoken opponent of same-sex marriage. It was also revealed that he had a history of "homosexual activity" (often in the name of "mentoring" young conservatives in their late teens), all the while standing strong for family values and "traditional marriage." The media crowed, the public gawked, and locals hung their heads.

It wasn't our proudest moment. But about fifty-three years earlier, Morrow County had made the news for something very different: oil. No, not like the widow's oil. Oil as in "black gold, Texas tea," per the *Beverly Hillbillies* theme song. In February 1964, an article in *TIME* magazine reported how the small, sleepy county in central Ohio was completely transformed by an oil boom.[6]

"Boom" was exactly the right word. It came suddenly and exploded. And it was the last unregulated oil boom in the United States. Wells were drilled in backyards and parks and cemeteries; one was drilled on a local school's baseball field (where home plate used to be). Almost fourteen hundred wells were completed in Morrow County in 1964 alone. Visitors could send home a postcard of the orange glow of gas flares lighting up the night sky over Cardington.

I know some people were concerned about the economic and ecological chaos. Surely folks shared those concerns. But it's hard for small towns to criticize anything that's bringing in a lot of money. And the oil boom was definitely bringing in a *lot* of money. Hotels popped up as the county scrambled to find housing for the laborers; restaurants and grocery stores were packed. Struggling farmers were suddenly wealthy. My grandfather on my mom's side of the family was one of them. Suddenly he became dramatically more "financially secure." He was able to purchase a vacation home in Florida and pay for his in-laws who lived in a Kentucky holler to get indoor plumbing. He made investments in his own farm and helped some of his children buy homes.

As the cycle goes, the bust followed soon after the boom. There are still oil wells around the county; some provide supplemental income for a farmer or landowner here and there. A couple entrepreneurs put their oil money to work and started businesses or invested in real estate in the county. But mostly, the wells ran dry. The laborers and executives went home or moved on. Hotels and restaurants closed. Our county's small towns took a hit after the storm quieted, and we had to find our bearings again as a quiet, rural county largely dependent on agriculture with a side of manufacturing.

We recovered fairly well. The people who remained were resilient. They rebuilt and reorganized; they tended their households and cared for their neighbors. In the past ten years, we have developed our interstate exit areas and taken advantage of the ever-growing Columbus metropolitan area. We have a new sports bar, winery, Mexican restaurant, pizza shop, four fast-food restaurants, a succulent greenhouse, and a community center. We have two new doctors' offices, a new daycare facility, a new pharmacy, and a much-needed public transportation initiative. We have our struggles, to be sure. We face persistent poverty, substance use, food insecurity, stagnant wages, domestic abuse, and more. But growth is taking place; good things are happening. Good people are taking ownership of their community and working to invest its assets for a positive future.

Not every Ohio community recovered so smoothly from the boom and bust of extractive industries. Appalachian Ohio—a region of forty-two counties across the southern and southeastern parts of the state—has been particularly devastated by these cycles. Like much of Appalachia, this region developed around natural resource extraction, mainly iron, coal, and timber. Again and again, there would be a frenzy of economic activity that left as quickly as it came, without any substantive development in infrastructure, economic diversification, or social capacity. The irresponsible practices of these industries left the land eroded, unusable for agriculture, and the waters severely polluted. In the first half of the twentieth century, almost half the population left. In fact, Route 23, which leads from Appalachia to Detroit, was nicknamed Hillbilly Highway because it was used by so many to move out of the hills and hollows to midwestern factory towns further north.

While natural gas discoveries have injected some money into families and towns here and there, Appalachian Ohio is the most depressed part of the state by any economic or social measure. People in my part of the state may enjoy hiking and outdoor recreation here but mostly see their home area as even more backward and backwoods than the "normal" rural folks up north do. Some derisively refer to the region as "northern Kentucky."

Some people, however, view the region differently. Appalachian Ohio is their home, by choice. They want to see it survive and thrive. And because of this commitment and affection, they are able to see the possibilities of abundance in the region. This has required a critical shift in focus, however. The people here have had to stop looking for big business or big government to solve their problems. While government programs and large business attraction can be important to a region's renewal, they're rarely the salvation people often want them to be. Ultimately, these communities have had to look in their own households, to their neighbors, and across their own landscape to find the assets and gifts already present.

COMMUNITY CAPITAL

This asset-based approach, developed by sociologists Cornelia and Jan Flora, is called the Community Capital Framework (CCF). In this framework, entrepreneurs and community developers discover and invest seven kinds of capital in the community that can be used to support growth and renewal:

1. *Natural capital*—a community's water sources, forests, wildlife, soil, parks, and places of natural beauty that make up a healthy environment in which to live, play, and work. These resources can also be developed for tourism and recreation.

2. *Cultural capital*—values, assumptions, perspectives, symbols, and the like that cultivate a sense of shared meaning and identity in the community. These sources of cultural capital can range from ethnic diversity to a strong work ethic.

3. *Human capital*—education, skills, health, self-esteem, and other attributes of individuals and groups that shape their character and capacities. This includes the quality and availability of local leaders who can bridge differences and bring people together to create a positive future.

4. *Social capital*—the bonds, connections, and networks between people and organizations that hold the community together. *Bonding social capital* creates cohesion and close connections; *bridging social capital* creates ties among different people and organizations, allowing for new relationships and enterprises.

5. *Political capital*—ability of a community to translate its vision and values into law and ensure that those standards, rules, and regulations are enforced. This reflects access to local and regional power brokers and decision-makers.

6. *Financial capital*—savings, income generation, loans and credit, charity and philanthropy, and tax policies that can be mobilized to improve economic conditions.

7. *Built capital*—human-constructed infrastructure in various forms, such as roads, bridges, factories, broadband wireless, daycare centers, wind farms, and technologies.[7]

How are these sources of capital being used to recover abundance in Appalachian Ohio?

- Cultural and built capital was developed in the town of Muskingum when a group of people set about restoring their old opera house into a theater for old movies and new plays.
- The natural and human capital of the region was highlighted when the town of Athens revitalized its farmers market, incubated new farm enterprises, and created the 30 Mile Meal project.
- A group of citizens and naturalists, aware of their region's natural capital, came together to start the Arc of Appalachia preserve system, protecting an ecological niche that is one of the most biodiverse temperate forests in the world. It also utilizes the cultural capital of the region by preserving the burial mounds of the Native American tribes who first inhabited the region.
- The founders of ACENET (Appalachian Center for Economic Networks) came together because they saw the human capital in Appalachian Ohio among people who knew how to work in the farm, food, wood, and manufacturing sectors but had been left behind by large companies that fled the region. The organization enabled them to utilize their skills and creative capacities to start businesses, microenterprises, and worker-owned cooperatives that created wealth, jobs, and hope in the region.
- A local entrepreneur in MacArthur, Ohio, saw the fields and farms around Vinton County and the potential for a local grocery store. He started Campbell's Market in the middle of a region considered a "food desert." There are now new jobs, fresh food, and affordable groceries in a county that didn't have a single grocery store and where 21 percent of the people live in poverty.
- A woman in Nelsonville noticed the loneliness and desperation of her community, especially in the local kids, so she opened a hang-out space called The Hive in a downtown storefront. It's a clean, bright, safe place for kids to come after

school or on a snow day; there's a shower, washer and dryer, and Wi-Fi (some families have had their utilities shut off and many have no internet). They have fresh food for snacks and community meals, do crafts and art projects, and go on field trips to parks, the pool, and other fun places.

- The Presbyterian church in Nelsonville used its spiritual, natural, and built capital to renovate the Presbyterian Farm it owns, creating a place for camping, retreats, recreation, and outdoor education. The church partnered with Rural Action, the Hive, and a local Boy Scout troop to clean it up and make it a place for the whole community to enjoy.

- Folks from across Appalachian Ohio with a passion for social justice and economic revitalization in their region joined forces to found Rural Action. Rural Action is a member-based organization that collaborates with a long list of local, regional, and national partners (both public and private) to renew the region through zero waste initiatives, watershed restoration, social enterprise coaching, sustainable forestry and agriculture, and environmental education. They envision and empower a just transition from the old extraction economy to the new emerging economy by developing the region's natural resources, rich history, resilient people, and ecological diversity.

These initiatives, businesses, and organizations began when people came together to solve their own problems and create their own futures using the gifts and resources already present within their communities. And these ordinary leaders are rooted in their region, familiar with their neighbors, and hopeful about what they can do in their place, with their people.

LOCUS OF POWER

This recovering abundance process can be greatly helped or harmed depending on where local leaders and community members locate the *locus of control*. Psychologists use "locus of control" as a way of

determining whether a client sees themselves as the victim of powers outside themselves and beyond their control (an external locus
of control) or as the agent of self-determination and self-control
(internal locus of control). Neither is technically "correct" or "incor-
rect," but these beliefs about power have a great impact on how we
live, love, and lead.

Rural folks tend to have a paradoxical mix of internal and external loci of control. On one hand, we tend to value self-reliance and
independence, working hard to provide for ourselves and our families. On the other hand, we can devolve into a kind of politics of
resentment, complaining about how the powers that be don't care
about people like us or care more about this or that other group than
us. This is understandable when you consider how global economic
forces and multinational companies have negatively impacted
many rural communities, leaving them with a devastating loss of
jobs, income, pride, and opportunity. Combine these economic
forces with disinvestment from the federal government and a prevailing preoccupation with identity politics, and it's not hard to see
why rural folks begin to feel like their lives are being determined by
centers of power far away. It's also easy to see why we might begin to
see these outside centers of power as our sources of salvation. If we
elect the right president or attract the right big-box stores, we can
be made great again.

Understandable though it may be, this mindset of waiting for
outside powers to save us is stifling. When we are constantly watching the horizon (or the stock market or cable news or signs of an
impending rapture), we are diverted from looking around us for
the loaves and fishes. There are indeed resources to be sought and
claimed from government grants, foundation funds, and corporate
donations. Public policy and economic incentives matter, and we
ought to rightly use them. Ultimately, however, they are secondary.
The resources *out there* will flow into places where resources are
being invested *right here*. The paradoxical principle has been proven
true repeatedly: "For whoever has will be given more, and they will

have an abundance. Whoever does not have, even what they have will be taken from them" (Matt 25:29).

POWER AND DISPOSSESSION

This practice of self-empowerment and reclaiming resources is exceedingly challenging for some groups of rural folks who have to overcome a history of oppression and dispossession. They are fighting against stories and systems designed to keep them from claiming their power. One of the most devastating examples of this disempowerment is the Pine Ridge Indian Reservation in southwestern South Dakota. The community of over thirty thousand people reflects the effects of colonization and despair. About 80 percent of residents are unemployed, and almost 98 percent live below the federal poverty level. The infant mortality rate is five times the national average, and the teen suicide rate is four times the national average.[8] It is a tragic story of increasing isolation and continuous decline.

But that's only part of the story. There are also groups there like the Thunder Valley Community Development Corporation (TVCDC). The TVCDC was initiated and incubated by a small group of youth and young families who started talking about the future of their people, reflecting on their eroding cultural and spiritual identity. They carried their ideas about the future into their spiritual ceremonies and spent hundreds of hours consulting with the community.

What the group developed was a comprehensive vision for renewal that was place-based and in alignment with their local assets and tribal history. Instead of trying to copy and paste revitalization techniques from other cultures and outside groups, they decided to inventory and invest their own gifts. Their Indigenous and Lakota-inspired vision combines the wisdom of their ancestors with the best of contemporary theory and praxis of change. *After* they had gathered and developed their own ideas, dreams, and assets, they were *then* able to find outside sources of support and funding. They brought together coalitions within the reservation and applied for grants and additional financing sources, even receiving assistance from the White House through President Obama's Promise Zone Initiative.[9]

The corporation started by purchasing thirty-four acres of empty land on the reservation to make their vision of a "regenerative community" a reality. Currently, they have completed several components of the vision, and there is more to come. The plan is community driven and comprehensive:

- Build homes to buy or rent with little to no utility cost (homeowners can build equity instead of paying high utility bills).
- Ensure quality food options, such as community gardens, a grocery store, and an aquaponics greenhouse.
- Establish retail space for local entrepreneurs.
- Develop Lakota-language educational resources.
- Erect a cultural center and powwow grounds.
- Launch a workforce development training center.
- Form an employee-owned construction company.
- Construct youth spaces, playgrounds, and basketball courts.
- Create a youth shelter.
- Design an outdoor amphitheater.
- Form an artists and farmers market.
- Designate walking paths and community gathering spaces.
- Establish a daycare and fitness center.

As if this plan wasn't ambitious enough, they envision their resilient, regenerative community being an example ("a show-me place"), particularly for other tribes and reservations, of what is possible through community collaboration and development based in place and cultural assets.[10] They hope they can inspire and empower others to develop their own regional equity and shared prosperity. In a rural region most consider too remote and rundown to develop, these ordinary leaders are reclaiming their cultural, spiritual, and economic capital to create opportunity and hope. This new life seems almost miraculous, rising out of nothing and nowhere, but it's the fruit of inventory, investment, partnership, spiritual renewal, vision-casting, and grassroots ownership—and, as with all stories of renewal, a lot of faith, hope, and love from ordinary leaders.

By the way, a critical part of their renewal is, like the Women of the Commons, the use of "language planning." Except, in this case, it's not just about word choice; it's about reclaiming their native language and teaching it to the next generation through common use at home and in school curricula.

MAKING A MIRACLE

The dynamics of our community work relate closely to our theology. They reveal an embedded belief system about the locus of *divine* power. Is the locus of divine power up in heaven, with God reaching down to save from time to time? Or is it here and now, within and between us, always working to bring about abundant life for every person and place?

In the gospel story, Jesus did not magically pull loaves and fishes from his cloak, like a rabbit from a hat. No, Jesus drew out the resources already present among the people and the place. He invited the disciples to take inventory of the gifts they had between them, then sent them out into the crowd to discover the resources from among the people. Perhaps Jesus wasn't just displaying divine power. Perhaps he was also channeling and stewarding the divine power that was already active all around. Perhaps Jesus was showing the disciples and the gathered community how to respond to the Creative Spirit moving among them, attending to what Quakers call the "Presence in the midst." Jesus was able to make himself available to that Presence in a spirit of trust in the One "who is able to do immeasurably more than all we ask or imagine, according to [the divine] power that is at work *within* us" (Eph 3:20).

This understanding of divine and human power does not mean we are all on our own. It does not mean that God is simply an absent abstraction. Instead, it means that God uses power to *em*power, not *over*power. God's power is not about dominating intervention but gracious interaction and interrelationship. It is a power that calls forth and draws out our gifts, revealing an abundance we had no conception of before our Christ encounter. It is an infinitely persistent and persuasive power that lures us forward through the possibilities of abundant life in God's kingdom.

This paradoxical and partnership understanding of divine power revealed in Jesus invites us to revisit our understanding of miracles. They are something we receive and experience, to be sure, but miracles are also something we co-create and participate in. In doctrinal language, they happen *by* grace and *through* faith. In the words of Archbishop Desmond Tutu, paraphrasing St. Augustine, "We, without God, cannot. God, without us, will not."[11] Whether the miracle is recovery from addiction, a reconciled family, a revitalized downtown, a restored river, an abundant harvest, or the transformation of unjust structures, we all have a part to play in the making of the miracle.

Barbara Brown Taylor said it beautifully, discussing the miracle of loaves and fishes: "Miracles let us off the hook. They appeal to the part of us that is all too happy to let God feed the crowd, save the world, do it all. But in this story God tells us, out of God's own deep pain and sadness for the world, 'Stop waiting for food to fall from the sky and share what you have. Stop waiting for a miracle and participate in one instead.'"[12]

Taylor's quote highlights a surprising aspect of miracle making in our communities. Miracles not only require that we trust in God; they also require that we embrace God's trust in us. God would not call us, through Christ, to "give them something to eat" (Mark 6:37) if God did not believe we were capable of doing so (in partnership with God). In fact, it seems to delight God, like a parent observing a child, when we adopt new skills, create new things, and meet new people as we learn to be ordinary leaders in the kingdom of God. "What God does first and best and most," writes Walter Brueggemann, "is to trust his people with their moment in history. He trusts them to do what must be done for the sake of his whole community."[13]

Miracle making is risky business. Miracles can be messy. But Jesus helps us bring them into being through the practice of inventory, discovering our gifts and assets and inquiring into the life-giving forces at work in our midst. We shift our language and initiate new conversations. And we start claiming a new locus of power that generates a new set of affirmations. We start repeating after Jesus, saying things like "The kingdom of heaven is within you" and "The kingdom of God is at hand."

For the last few years, I've been working with an affirmation I learned from Wendell Berry in his poem "Wild Geese":

And we pray, not for new
Earth or heaven, but to be quiet
In heart, and in eye clear.
What we need is here.[14]

"What we need is here." That's a powerful statement. And a statement of faith. If we take it too literally, it breaks down pretty quickly. Of course we still need knowledge, support, and resources from other places. But I believe something powerful and beautiful happens when we look inward and around first. When we think local first. When we start asking new questions and making new connections. When we get into the same room and invite diverse people to the table. When we turn the focus to what's present and positive. And, as Berry reminds us, we also need to quiet our hearts and clarify our vision, taking on both a contemplative and collaborative posture. Who knows what will rise? Who knows what we will find? It just might be the beginning of a new possibility, partnership, or project that transforms the trajectory of our small town or rural region.

Sometimes ordinary leadership isn't about a daring venture or exciting new program. Sometimes it's about stepping up to ask a new set of questions, uncover hidden resources, and make fresh connections. It's about engaging local people and processes and asking, "What if what we need is here?"

CHAPTER FIVE

THE PRACTICE OF IMAGINATION

Bring them here to me.

Matthew 14:18

I SPENT MOST OF MY childhood years in Morrow County, Ohio, but my story actually began two counties to the east. According to my birth certificate and the baby book my mother kept, I was born Andrew Floyd Henry in October 1987 in Millersburg, Ohio, the county seat of Holmes County. The name of that county may not mean anything to you. If you are familiar with Holmes County, though, you probably heard about it in relation to the Amish community. It is the home of what is arguably the largest Amish population in the world (the Amish community in Lancaster, Pennsylvania, is similarly large). Nearly half of the county's population is Amish; some project it could surpass the "English" (non-Amish) population in the county within the next decade. Locals throughout the state refer to the region as "Amish country."

Amish country was the homeland of my birth; I'm told that I was the only non-Amish baby in the hospital at the time. The little Henry boy was brought into the world surrounded by a great cloud of Amish witnesses with names like Yoder, Stoltzfus, Hershberger, and Miller. A little Quaker baby among the Amish. How could I not be a peacemaker?

We lived in Holmes County because my dad worked there with the Farm Service Agency (FSA). FSA is a county government agency under the USDA (United States Department of Agriculture) that resulted from the consolidation of several New Deal era agencies. Today, it essentially implements conservation, regulation, and aid programs, as outlined in the federal farm bill that's passed roughly every five years. My dad worked for FSA for almost thirty years before retiring. He enjoyed working with farmers, getting to know all the farms and farm families in the county, and connecting them with the assistance they needed. After a few years in Holmes County, my dad got a job with Delaware County FSA, where he eventually became the executive director. This gave him the opportunity to travel to Washington, DC, every year and to work at the national office, which he loved. It also gave him the opportunity to move back to Morrow County, where most of his family and closest friends lived. My mom's family mostly resided in the county as well, so it worked out nicely, but Holmes County still has a special place in their hearts.

When my family returns to visit Holmes County today, after having lived elsewhere for about thirty years, they find an "Amish country" very different from the one they knew when I was born. Sure, the buggies and beards and horse manure on the streets are still the same. Some of the same cheese factories and restaurants remain. But the region has experienced significant growth, leveraging its Amish heritage and culture to start antique stores, museums, restaurants, inns, agritourism, food stores, craft furniture shops, delis, bookstores, bicycle shops, quilt barns, lumberyards, backyard barn sales, and even a hotel-theater-restaurant entertainment center for Amish-inspired plays and clean comedy shows. This industry injects millions of dollars into the regional economy. It's not your parents' Amish country anymore. At least, it's not my parents' Amish country. What happened?

Every year, tens of millions of people swarm to Amish country, whether in Ohio, Pennsylvania, Indiana, or elsewhere. They shop the stores, eat the food, and drive the countryside because they are seeking, it seems, a sense of wholesomeness, peace, and simplicity that they don't experience in their everyday lives. The Amish lifestyle points to an alternative way of life that many desire but see as out of reach. Visitors may not want to shun all modern conveniences and take on the Amish lifestyle entirely, but they want to touch and taste it from time to time, to remember that it's possible, and perhaps to carry its spirit into their lives in small ways (at least in the form of a few bags of Amish-made goods).

In her book *Selling the Amish*, researcher Susan Trollinger suggests that the tourist industry of Amish country is ultimately selling *nostalgia*, comfort in the reminder of how things used to be or hope in seeing how things could be again. "It seems to me," she concludes, "that as long as we have eyes to see the Amish as strange, they will ask us whether we have the courage or the creativity or the vision or the faith to embrace a future that we have not yet seen and in which we become . . . truly strange ourselves."[1] We are drawn to Amish country because we see the Amish as what the King James Bible calls a "peculiar people," and we receive from them an invitation to become peculiar ourselves. Sometimes we accept the invitation, and sometimes we take our peanut butter pie, hop in our comfy cars, and return to our smartphones and ESPN.

Whether we change our lifestyles or enjoy a quiet getaway, I agree that something about Amish country and the Amish way draws us. Whether out of our desire for a simpler life or the necessity of scaling back and becoming more reliant on local land and labor, the witness of Amish communities feels necessary, somehow. Occasionally, when I'm passing around a buggy or driving beside Amish farmsteads with drying clothes flapping in the wind across the clothesline, I ponder a possibility. If we were ever hit by the apocalyptic future some claim is coming—whether they be zombie enthusiasts, global warming prophets, or end-times preachers—would we end up knocking on the doors of Amish houses, begging for help?

One day at the library, I discovered a local author and farmer named Gene Logsdon who had a similar idea. In *At Nature's Pace: Farming and the American Dream*, a book largely about "Amish economics," Logsdon states, "Sustainable farms are to today's headlong rush toward global destruction what the monasteries were to the Dark Ages: places to preserve human skills and crafts until some semblance of common sense and common purpose returns to the public mind."[2] Maybe it is these Amish farms and rural families who are holding the world together while the rest of us are throwing off the old ways as we head down our own pathways to destruction.

Thank goodness some things in this world never change. When everything else is rising and falling, coming and going, heading to hell in a handbasket, at least there will always be this remnant of faithful, stable saints nestled in the hills. The only problem is, it's not true. It's partly true, perhaps. But it's far from the full story. The truth is, the Amish have had to adapt and innovate and negotiate the changing world.

In their book *Amish Enterprise: From Plows to Profits*, sociologists Donald B. Kraybill and Steven M. Nolt tell a fascinating story about how Amish communities, particularly in Lancaster County, Pennsylvania, navigated a significant transition away from exclusive reliance on small family farms. Since their separation from other Anabaptist congregations and exile into rural regions in the late seventeenth century, Amish faith and practice were rooted in the family farm. Farming was central to Amish spirituality; it linked people to creation and enabled Amish families to remain tight-knit and separated from the harmful influences of the world. Their conviction about the importance of farming to their faith and practice was so central that nonfarmers were barred from ordination and church leadership.[3]

Some Amish districts began permitting men to leave the farm to work in factories if they absolutely had to. This proved to be troublesome, as they were kept from quality time with their families and had difficulty getting time off for Amish holidays. Some got involved in betting pools with other factory workers, and their benefit packages disconnected them from the communal system of mutual aid and shared labor. Church leaders feared that this factory work was drawing people away from the core relationships of farm, family, and faith. One even commented, "The lunch pail is the biggest threat to our way of life."[4]

Since factory work did not allow the Amish to get ahead financially without leaving behind their core values, they had to consider other options. Kraybill notes that the viable options before them were limited to seven primary paths: (1) migration, (2) subdivision of farms, (3) purchase of additional farmland, (4) use of artificial birth control, (5) non-Amish employment, (6) higher education, (7) microenterprises.[5] The first six solutions were tried and found wanting. Though any of them may be used in pockets of Amish populations, they did not provide the kind of satisfactory outcome needed to maintain both ethical integrity and economic sustainability.

It was the seventh option, starting and expanding microenterprises, that won the day. In the 1980s, when the farm crisis reached its peak (impacting Amish farms negatively, though sometimes without the depth of devastation that others faced), Amish businesses grew exponentially. Small shops and cottage industries sprang up, and Amish business owners found ways to maintain kinship ties, moral values, and community solidarity while using entrepreneurial tools to grow their businesses. Sociologically, the Amish were dealing with the tension between *cultural restraints* and *cultural resources* so they could reach an acceptable *cultural revision* that allowed them to move forward in a positive way.[6]

The prosperity of today's Holmes County, Ohio, is an anomaly to most outsiders. It exists as a kind of alternative economy. Job growth, population, and median household income have been on a path of upward growth when other rural counties in Ohio continue to bleed. How? The county has no major highway or rail system and is almost two hours from a large city or major university. No huge company moved in.

Amish prosperity grew from within, and the English folks around them benefited as well. The Old World values of solidarity, community, and mutual aid are central to this microeconomy's success, as is the spirit of entrepreneurship. The combination of strong social ethics and entrepreneurial energy seems to be the secret to their surprising success. In the end, it has been a creative combination of tradition and innovation that has allowed the Amish to survive and thrive.

Maybe Amish folks aren't so different from other rural folks. Generally speaking, we rural folks are resistant to change. There are many reasons for this. We see trends come and go, so we don't get too worked up about new ideas. We see people come and go, so we don't get too excited about new people with big dreams or a fancy degree. We've seen tornados and other severe weather level our towns and blow away our buildings, so we don't get too worked up about a newfangled store or business center. We've seen the boom and bust cycle, so we just give up trying anything different. Rural folks can be skeptical because we've been used and abused, and sometimes we are just plain stubborn and stuck in our ways.

Sometimes, the only change we really desire is the kind that takes us *back*, back to the way things were. We want something "again." Take us back to the way things were in the good ol' days. It is the temptation of nostalgia. We want change for the same reasons we want to visit Amish country. We want to get back to simpler times. Back when rules and roles were clear. When folks took care of each other. When families stayed together, and the factory stayed in town.

However, if we wish to recover a spirit of abundance for our own communities, we must learn from the true example of our Amish neighbors. We don't need to imitate their particular practices, but we all need to learn from their willingness to imagine something new being born out of the old. If rural communities are to survive and thrive, we need to adopt practices that help us negotiate transitions and tradeoffs in a way that honors our values and heritage while utilizing our communal capital. We need a practice of imagination that will help us stay open to the Creator's renewing and surprising work in our midst.

RELEASING OUR RESOURCES

The disciples had inquired, gathered, and inventoried the loaves and fishes from within the group. What would be their next step? Matthew's gospel tells us Jesus's next instruction: "Bring them here to me." Jesus instructed the disciples to gather all the gifts and bring them to him. This instruction wasn't just a matter of bringing the food to one location so that it could be efficiently or perhaps equitably distributed. Just distribution is an important concern we will address in a later chapter, but Jesus's invitation in that moment was about something more.

The loaves and fishes Jesus received were not the same ones he shared. Whatever the mechanics of the miracle, something changed when the gifts were handed over to Christ. When the people released their resources to Christ, they were releasing them to God and the community. In doing so, they were surrendering their ideas about what was present over to One who works (and plays) with an infinite range of possibilities. "What we will be has not yet been made known," says the first letter of John. Indeed, and what our communities can be has not yet been made known either.

When Jesus instructed, "Bring them here to me," he was asking the disciples and the people to believe that things could be otherwise. When we make our lives and resources available to the Eternal One, we are opening ourselves to a much larger story with a much wider range of possibilities. We are also enacting a willingness to negotiate the transitions and trade-offs of a new future.

For ordinary leaders to dream and scheme with God about something new in a small town is a risky thing. It's not for the faint of heart. We may fail; it's hard to recover from failure in a small town. We may face opposition; it's not hard to make enemies in a small town. And there's not only a risk but a guarantee that our ideas, solutions, and resources will be incomplete. That's why we must release them and offer them over to God and our community.

Biblical scholar N. T. Wright reminds us that the disciples were not the heroes of our gospel story. They didn't have all the answers; in fact, the text portrays them as pretty slow learners. But Jesus asked them to offer the ideas and insights they did have, to lay aside both ego and timidity. He knew what to do with their incomplete offerings, and he had a way of animating and multiplying those offerings into something larger than the sum of their parts. Wright says:

> Jesus takes ideas, loaves and fishes, money, a sense of humor, time, energy, talents, love, artistic gifts, skill with words, quickness of eyes or fingers, whatever we have to offer. He holds them before his father with prayer and blessing. Then, breaking them so they are ready for use, he gives them back to us to give to those who need them. And now they are both ours and not ours. They are both what we had in mind and not what we had in mind. It is part of genuine Christian service, at whatever level, that we look on in amazement to see what God has done with the bits and pieces we dug out of our meagre resources to offer to him.[7]

When we practice imagination, the innovations and enterprises that emerge are not ours alone. As Wright says, they are "both ours and not ours." We are co-creators with God and our neighbors in bringing about the new creation.

FAITH FOR FOOD

If you travel a couple hours south of the Amish Country in Holmes County, you will find a region of the state that has a much higher poverty rate: Appalachian Ohio. There are Amish folks there, as well, and they are similarly partnering for prosperity in this region.

Multiple times a week you can attend a produce auction, packed with volunteers and shoppers and auctioneers who come in pickup trucks, Priuses, and horse-drawn buggies. Some are farmers (both English and Amish) who have come to sell their produce; others are restaurant owners, grocers, and food-conscious consumers who come to find quality food (often in large quantities) at a good price. If you've never been to a produce auction, you should find one and go. It's a fascinating experience that inspires a sense of connection to land, food, neighbors, and local economy. How did something like this come to be in such an out-of-the-way place?

The story of the Chesterhill Produce Auction began with a couple named Jean and Marvin Conkle. Jean and Marvin retired to the village of Chesterhill in 2003. As they settled into their retirement and into the region, they noticed the prevalent poverty and lack of both fresh food and economic opportunity in Morgan County. They were troubled by what they saw and believed things should be different, insisting, "People want and deserve good quality food; just because they live in a remote area doesn't mean they can't have good, fresh produce."[8]

They not only believed that things *should* be different, however. They also believed things *could* be different. The Conkles had a vision, one informed by the experience they had in their previous home of Bainbridge, Ohio, where something called a "produce auction" had made locally grown fresh fruits and vegetables available to local residents, increased economic activity, and opened up markets for local farmers (most of whom happened to be Mennonite).

The Conkles envisioned a produce market opening in Chesterhill that could have the same positive outcomes for their new neighbors. So they began talking with other folks in the community, gauging interest and gathering ideas. They didn't know exactly how it would work, but they kept the vision, shared their ideas, and offered them to the community. It was an act of imagination, and an act of faith. After all, as Eugene Peterson argued, "The imagination is almost, not quite, the same thing as faith. It's that which connects what we see and what we don't see and pulls us through what we see into what we don't see. Now when that imagination involves trust and participation in the unseen, it's faith."[9]

The Conkles' was certainly not a case of faith without works. Though retired, they worked tenaciously to turn their vision into a reality. They talked with neighbors, held meetings, and attended conferences. It wasn't long, however, before they realized they couldn't do it alone. So they joined forces with a locally based development group called Rural Action, which had the experience and connections necessary to help them create this new social enterprise. Rural Action helped expand their network, extend their marketing, and form new relationships with nearby colleges, organizations, and foundations.

After a few years and more than a few changes, the auction became profitable and was purchased by Rural Action. As it grew in scope and influence, Rural Action was able to expand its reach by partnering with local organizations to offer grower education, food donations, and targeted distribution to food insecure places through the "Country Fresh Stop" program, which places fresh food stands at gas stations and corner stores. They also expanded their outreach to local schools through "School Day at the CPA"—an annual field trip to educate youth about composting, nutrition, food systems, produce, and auctions.[10]

Through the produce auction and the market and community it helped create, Chesterhill has been transformed from a food desert to a food hub. Morgan County still has its share of struggles, but the Chesterhill Produce Auction stands as a testament of hope for other towns and families in Appalachian Ohio and beyond. It reminds us what is possible when ordinary leaders embrace an imaginative vision, offer incomplete ideas to the community, collaborate with neighbors, and own an innovative future that builds on local assets and heritage.

GRIEF AND PROPHETIC IMAGINATION

I once heard a sermon on an Easter Sunday that spoke to me in a surprising way. The pastor remarked at the beginning of her message, "Easter almost always begins with grief." This comment caught me by surprise, because I tend to think of Easter as a time of celebration and joy. In my mind, the cross of Good Friday is the time of loss, pain, and sorrow. Then Easter Sunday comes, and we are immediately greeted with news of great hope. O death, where is thy sting?

But when we read the Easter narrative more closely, we see people responding to resurrection in various ways. Some respond with joy and faith while others responded with skepticism and confusion. And some, like Mary Magdalene, responded with grief: "Now Mary stood outside the tomb crying" (John 20:11). As she grieved, she wept and searched inside the tomb. Even after an angel and the risen Christ had appeared to her, she still didn't recognize the moment, or her teacher and friend in his new manifestation.

In one form or another, we have all been in Mary's position. We find ourselves grieving over the loss of the old and the disorientation that comes with the new. The old manifestations were safe and familiar, even if not satisfying or life-giving. The new manifestation may sound great, but it requires a lot of adjustment, even transformation. We weep at the loss of the former and cannot see the new that is present around us. The thing is, if we want God to make all things new, we first have to let God deal with all things old: "the old order of things has passed away" (Rev 21:4).

We need ordinary leaders who are able to guide communities through times of grief over the old order. We need folks who can be patient with people who struggle to release their nostalgia without letting the emotional anxiety create gridlock. This requires a mix of emotional, social, and spiritual skills that we might call "prophetic imagination."

The concept of prophetic imagination comes from the biblical scholar Walter Brueggemann and his work on the Hebrew prophets. He argued that one of the critical roles of the prophets was to nurture and evoke an "alternative consciousness" to help the people imagine a future that is different from the way things are now. Societies need these prophets because it is easy for us to become entrenched in the current system, either out of discouragement and fear or out of self-interest. "It is the vocation of the prophet to keep alive the ministry of imagination," wrote Brueggemann, "to keep on conjuring and proposing future alternatives to the single one the king wants to urge as the only thinkable one."[11]

The trouble is that some people like things the way they are. Maybe because they're familiar and stable. People in positions of power fight against change because they benefit from things remaining the way they are. And, they typically have the most resources to ensure that the current system does not change. This is why prophets have to be willing to confront the powers that be. It's also why so many prophets were (and are) killed.

Prophetic ministry is driven by a dual purpose. It must simultaneously offer an inspiring, compelling vision of the future *and* challenge communities to take an honest look at their reality, to discern why things cannot remain the way they are. Brueggemann describes these two roles as *energizing* and *criticizing*. The prophet energizes with a positive picture of a possible future for the people. But they also criticize the current order and how it is leading to decline and destruction.[12]

Many times, leaders lean toward one role or the other. Either they like to inspire and energize with vision and possibility thinking, or they like to critique and confront with passionate protest and moral clarity. But prophetic ministry requires both, and they must be held in creative tension. The prophetic leader must ensure that criticism does not end up in despair and energizing does not end up in denial.

In order to ensure that neither despair nor denial become overwhelming forces, the prophetic leader must offer rituals, symbols, and language for grief. We cannot simply shame people into the future. And we may not be able to pull them out of the past with a positive vision. They need ways to grieve the old, to celebrate its gifts and lament its pain, before folks can take brave steps into the disruptive but liberating future.

A couple years ago, my wife and I attended a church service at a small, local mainline congregation. Afterward, as we attempted to sneak out, a woman came up to us with a huge smile. As she shook our hands, she told us how glad she was that we were there (something we were used to hearing when we were the only young couple in a very old congregation). And after expressing her gladness at our presence, she went on to share her gratitude about something else.

"I just wanted to thank you two for sitting on this side of the sanctuary," she exclaimed. We nodded our heads and smiled, saying something about how we just gravitated toward those pews when we arrived. There was no planning involved; we snuck in late and sat toward the back in the section closest to the entrance. I did notice that most of the people sat in the back rows. It's a common pattern in churches. The congregants believe their strategic seating arrangement keeps the preacher from getting too close and noticing the fellow nodding off or hearing the lady scramble through her purse to retrieve a mint with the world's loudest wrapper. As someone who has done a fair bit of preaching, I can tell you that we still notice these things. The other part of this seating design has a social shaming purpose. It ensures that the latecomers have the least convenient places for seating; they have to take the walk of shame to the front, where their sinful arrival time is observed and judged by all. As someone who has done a fair bit of late arriving to church services, I can tell you that this is noticed as well.

As we took a step toward the door, ready to wish her a blessed day and decide our lunch menu, the nice lady decided to explain further: "It used to be that people spread out and sat in each section. But for some reason, nobody will sit over here, so we get lonely." Then came the punch line: "We have been sitting in that same pew for sixty-six years, and I just can't sit anywhere else." Trying not to look stunned or amused, we smiled politely, and I said, "Well, must be a good place to sit. Glad we could join you."

As I thought about that short conversation later that day, I chuckled but also wondered what was behind her words. Why was the devotion to her pew so important to her that she made a point of stopping and thanking the new couple for sharing her loyalty, before even learning our names, where we live, or what brought us to her faith community? Maybe she was just one of the quirky people every congregation has, but I couldn't help but wonder if her comment represented an entrenchment of beliefs and practices shared by many in that same church.

The congregation was searching for a new minister, so I began to ponder what a new pastor might face if they came with the intention of bringing in new faces and families or wanted to implement some of their own ideas. It might be tempting for a newly minted minister to come in and immediately start changing things. Upon hire, the congregation may say that they are excited to find a talented, faithful young person and look forward to their new ideas and the new people they will bring in. Naively, the new pastor would believe them.

After the new pastor changes the order of service, so the prayers of the people are before announcements instead of after the sermon, they will be met with a campaign of emails and passive-aggressive comments after the service. When they put the American and Christian flags in the back room to create a simpler, less-nationalistic aesthetic, they are visited by several upset members who inform their unpatriotic pastor that those were donated by a local group of World War II veterans who fought the Nazis so we could have American and Christian flags in our sanctuaries.

Imagine what would happen if this new pastor decided it was more seeker-friendly to have chairs instead of pews. How do you think the couple with sixty-six years of loyalty to a particular pew would respond to this? I have a feeling the pastoral search committee would need to start meeting again.

Of course, I am poking a bit of fun at the tendency of some congregations to get stuck in their ways and develop a resistance to change. But I am also pointing out the way pastors often overlook the symbolic and spiritual meanings of things they seek to change. It

doesn't mean things shouldn't change. A number of changes probably need to be made if the church is going to survive and thrive. But
the prophets remind us that change requires both energizing for the
new and grieving the loss of the old. It's as if the eyes of imagination
must be washed clean with tears of grief before they can see clearly
an alternative future before them.

Perhaps our hypothetical new pastor would have more success
shepherding the congregation into a new season if they provided
language and rituals for the transition. For example, while changing
to chairs might be worthwhile, the pastor would need to recognize
that the pews may have great meaning for some folks. They may
have sat in that pew when they saw their daughter get married in
that sanctuary, or their son baptized there, or laid a relative to rest
after weeping through a funeral service there. The pews are more
than some lumber nailed together; they have been the stable, sacred
holding structures for many life transitions and holy experiences.
Before the chairs are moved in, it may be helpful for the pastor to
acknowledge the grief that comes with the change and facilitate a
worshipful time for people to share memories of how they encountered God and beloved community while sitting in those pews.
Maybe some of them could be offered as gifts or sold for a donation,
so that they could find a second life in a congregant's home.

However trivial a change may seem, the old order must be
grieved before the new can come in its fullness. The best leaders are
able to guide the transitions by tenderly hearing and recognizing
the grief of leaving the old behind while still insisting that an alternative, positive future is possible.

STEWARDING SACRED SPACES

As important as recalling and grieving the old is to the process of
renewal, I don't want to give the impression that it's all about weeping and wailing as we reluctantly step into something new. No,
the practice of imagination invites us into a playful, prayerful, and

prophetic posture in which we get to participate in the co-creative work of God. We state the facts and squarely face our realities. Then we explore possibilities, argue over ideas, discern the spirits, dream dreams, and see visions. And eventually a way opens that we didn't see before.

Appropriately, the words *inventory* and *invention* share the same root. Citing neuroscience research, Casey Tygrett wrote about the connection between memory and creativity: "Invention was the product of inventorying. . . . In order to invent, one first needed to make a proper inventory, a bank of existing ideas to draw from."[13] We practice inventory to get a fuller view of reality—what we actually have to work with. We practice imagination to get a fuller view of possibility—what we can create with those resources. Holding reality and possibility in a creative tension, we find the "third way."

It is critical that this process be engaged with a spirit of prayerful playfulness and not an anxious search for saving solutions. Yes, we are searching for solutions, but the practice of imagination is about building community as we co-create a positive future. As pastor Steve Willis notes in his book *Imagining the Small Church*, "What is lost in our rush to find the solution to our decline is the exercise of a lively faith imagination."[14] When we approach our declining congregation or restaurant or village as a desperate system in need of salvation, we will inevitably fall victim to a failure of imagination, narrowing our vision to a dualistic win/lose, die/survive, now/never framework.

What does this "lively faith imagination" look like for leaders and helpers who are stewarding groups and institutions in transition? Let me put forth some examples.

Driving across rural regions in my home state, I'm always fascinated and heartbroken at the (not uncommon) sight of two sacred structures breaking down and falling apart: barns and churches. I wonder what story of neglect, abandonment, or loss they have to tell, or what they looked like during better times.

When it comes to barns, I'm glad to report that a number of organizations are working diligently to preserve and restore historic barns. Grants and tax incentives and charitable donations are available for folks who have a barn on their property that is historically, culturally, or architecturally valuable. What about the other barns? Well, thankfully, many barns are still being used by our nation's farmers. But beyond agriculture use and restoration, many barns are getting "barn again." These old barns are getting new life as wedding venues, restaurants, event spaces, stores, and even as houses. Other barns that pose a safety risk and are not suited for either restoration or renovation are skillfully torn down and the lumber reclaimed. They are "barn again" as furniture, flooring, support beams, shelves, or any number of other projects. My parents had a contractor friend use reclaimed wood from a nearby barn to build a long picnic table where the growing family can all fit for our get-togethers.

You may be familiar with the ways old barns can be restored, renovated, and reclaimed but not heard about church buildings getting new life. An organization called Partners for Sacred Places does fascinating and holy work with these kinds of spaces. Their mission involves the work of "building the capacity of congregations of historic sacred places to better serve their communities as anchor institutions, nurturing transformation, and shaping vibrant, creative communities."[15] The partnership brings together professionals who are able to come alongside congregations to assess needs, name assets, and imagine the best possible ways to use their space.

Many churches face declining attendance and giving. And while it may be less true for some rural congregations, the Christian church does not garner the respect it once did as a central civic institution. These consultants help congregations and their stewards utilize the practices of inventory and imagination to see how, with the support of new funding sources, they can preserve and revitalize their existing space while exploring new ways to benefit the community. Churches and synagogues have reimagined underutilized spaces in their building for community arts projects, farmers markets, afterschool programs, health and wellness centers, event spaces, and much more.

A surprising alliance called Nuns and Nones brings together two divergent groups in order to imagine and discover what is emerging—spiritually, socially, and economically. Like many mainline churches, monasteries and convents are declining in perceived relevance within Western society. They too are facing hard choices about how to live their faith and how to steward their land. So the group brings together Nones (those who checked "none of the above" as a religion on the US Census, largely millennials) and Nuns (women with a monastic religious vocation in the Roman Catholic Church). Through dialogue, spiritual practices, activism, service, and even a residency program, these two groups form an "unlikely alliance across communities of spirit."[16]

These two groups are also coming together to engage difficult questions of land stewardship. As they face heartbreaking choices about closing convents or selling off a retreat center to a developer, the nuns use their catalytic conversations with Nones to consider how they can address fiscal challenges, navigate emotional transitions, and find alternative futures for their spaces that don't involve a wrecking ball. They come together across their differences to use the practice of imagination to discern possibilities for their future. Some of the visions that have emerged through their dialogues and research include:

- Creating co-living spaces for seekers and sisters in covenantal communities
- Building affordable housing
- Selling easements to conservation land trusts
- Converting to ecological spiritual centers and farms
- Developing transition to Catholic worker houses or special care facilities
- Returning land in restitution and reconciliation to black and indigenous communities
- Establishing tiny house villages
- Anchoring partnerships with other community organizations.

These stories of barns, convents, and churches demonstrate the practice of imagination. They remind us that the choice isn't between saving a building as is or tearing it down. When we practice imagination, we see a wonderfully wide range of possibilities for the future. Barns can be "barn again." Churches can be "born again." Convents can be repurposed. And our organizations, institutions, and traditions can be renovated, restored, and reclaimed.

Of course, we still see churches and barns in rural landscapes slowly surrendering to gravity. Some convents are torn down to make room for luxury apartments. Likewise, not every organization, business, or congregation will survive. The hard truth is that sometimes rural towns themselves die. Sometimes they are killed. The hopeful truth is that some can be resurrected.

The willingness or unwillingness to negotiate the new order that resurrection brings will be a significant factor in whether a positive future is possible. Congregations and communities may need to receive assistance from organizations and governments that goes against their independent spirit. They may have to do some consolidating and collaborating. They may have to let some cherished institutions go to make room for new ideas and ventures. They may have to re-story community culture, retool community leaders, and remove some of the power brokers who stand in the way of the reborn, resilient community that's possible.

As the many Amish communities discovered, a renewed future requires, in the language of Kraybill and Nolt, a negotiation of cultural resources and cultural restraints. But for many communities and organizations, a positive future—one in which heritage and values are maintained—is possible, albeit within new forms and functions. This future is possible if ordinary leaders are willing to offer their resources to God and their community so they can create a future together.

HERITAGE HOUSE

Two rural leaders I admire greatly are my friends Kate and Jeff Stuttler. I went to school with both of them, and Jeff was one of my closest friends through high school. We felt like we were destined to be buddies, since we were born on the same day of the same year. As close as we were, though, we had a lot of differences. We had very different views on theology and politics, and our personalities were quite different. Jeff was Pentecostal, musical, and extroverted, while I was an introverted contemplative Quaker. But we shared a deep desire to live fully and faithfully.

After high school graduation, we went separate ways, catching up occasionally on summer or Christmas break. But when I moved back to Ohio, we were able to reconnect quickly. We were both returners; we left the state for a while but came back and wanted to be a positive presence in our community. I was excited to learn more about what Jeff was up to, because he is someone who has an idea and just goes out and does it. He's a dreamer and an entrepreneur. His wife, Kate, is amazing as well. She is sharp, grounded, and creative. They make an excellent team.

One of the big things Jeff and Kate had been up to while I was gone was starting their own bed-and-breakfast called Heritage House. The story of Heritage House started way back in the 1850s with a home that was built by Kate's family. It had been kept in the family ever since, but as it came time to pass it on to the next generation, there didn't seem to be anyone with energy or interest to move into it or do anything with it. Jeff and Kate had the idea to turn the house into a bed-and-breakfast. They pitched the idea to the family, and after receiving their blessing, they began planning and renovating. After a little over a year of renovating and restoring the house, they opened their doors to guests.

One of the great things about this bed-and-breakfast is that it literally builds upon the history of the house. The new additions and renovations were built on the solid bones of the house. The new enterprise was built on the stories and memories of the family. Jeff and Kate couldn't have done it all; thankfully, others in the family dedicated countless hours to making the dream into a reality. Each of the suites in the house bears a family name from their heritage.

Jeff and Kate have continued to expand the enterprise and find new ways to serve the community through their business. They restored the barn on the property to create Heritage Barn, a rustic but elegant event venue. People use the barn for graduations, showers, weddings, and other parties. I officiated my sister's wedding inside Heritage Barn. It's inspiring to see how an entrepreneurial dream became a reality through hard work, faith, family support, a strong network, and a long list of DIY YouTube videos. It was all done in a way that honored the history and values of the family while creating something new for a new generation.

Every thriving rural community is a heritage house. It honors the best of its history, maintains its values, and utilizes its community capital, all while working to create something new and intergenerational. Neither nostalgia nor neglect of history will move a community forward. We must build our house on the solid bones of our heritage and come together across generations to build a restored and renovated home. Beautiful things are possible when ordinary leaders practice imagination by offering their ideas to God and their neighbors and discovering ways to bring new life to old structures.

CHAPTER SIX

THE PRACTICE OF
ORGANIZING

Jesus directed them to have all the people sit down in groups.

Mark 6:39

MEET OLIVER HUDSON KELLEY. KELLEY was a Minnesota farmer in the 1800s. Though he grew up in New England and started his adult life as a writer, the vocation of farming called to him so continuously that he decided to purchase a plot of land in Minnesota and put his hand to the plow. Oliver loved farming, but he also loved innovation and entrepreneurship, so he was constantly experimenting with new seeds, equipment, and techniques. People took note of his innovative leadership, and he began to rise through the ranks of national institutions. In the 1860s he took a job with the Department of Agriculture in Washington, DC.[1]

In 1866, Kelley received a commission from President Andrew Johnson to travel the South on a tour of farms to assess the state of their agriculture and communities. What he saw disturbed him. Poverty was widespread. Many towns were decimated from the war, and the social and economic systems dependent on slavery had collapsed. The cultural landscape was full of despair and resentment; the economic landscape was devastated. On top of all that, many southern farmers lacked the tools and techniques that could help them carve a living from their land.

Kelley was ready and eager to assist these fellow farmers. After all, he had both the expertise in farming practices and the connections to people in power to improve their political fortunes. But because he was a Yankee from the North, many southern farmers were guarded and resistant, even hostile, to his visits. That is, except for one group. One group of people were warm to his presence and open to his ideas: his fellow Masons.[2]

Despite the geographical and cultural differences, Kelley's fellow Freemason farmers welcomed him because of their shared identity and connections. Their bond as Masons transcended regional and political differences. This connection was not lost on Kelley, and he returned to Washington with this insight at the forefront of his mind. In fact, he ruminated on an idea until it began to form into a vision. He could use the structure and power of the fraternal organization to overcome barriers of isolation, powerlessness, and outdated farming practices. These groups would have exclusive meetings and secret rituals that bonded them together. And they would be organized in levels, whereupon members could climb the membership ladder, learning something different about agriculture and morality on each rung.

Upon his return, Oliver started forming his team and working out the details to make his vision a reality.[3] In 1867, Oliver and his leadership team founded The National Grange of the Order of Patrons of Husbandry, better known as simply the Grange. It would be a national organization, but farmers and farm families would form and gather in local Grange groups, hosting social and educational events, sharing ideas and best practices, and organizing for their own interests. The Grange would be a powerful force in overcoming isolation among farmers, promoting progressive farming, strengthening rural communities, and advocating for the well-being of farmers.

Grange organizers spread the word about this new organization and began gathering farmers into groups. The movement exploded, particularly in the Midwest and West, but also in the southern states, where these local groups (supported by a national network) advanced the work of healing and rebuilding their communities. By the early 1870s, the Grange had expanded to over 1.5 million members.[4]

Local chapters thrived and built new Grange Halls across the country. People joined together to form cooperatives, collectively purchasing machinery and seeds, and built their own grain elevators. Many even started their own stores. They welcomed women into membership and created a program for children that became the precursor to Future Farmers of America. Grangers seemed to be on top of the world, and Kelley's vision was transforming the face of agriculture across the American landscape.

Farmers were hit hard, however, by the Panic of 1873, when commodity prices plummeted, railroads extorted them for high rates, and creditors began seizing land and equipment. The bonds and networks formed by the Grange movement became more important than ever. Oliver Kelley saw this pain and plunder and put his organizational mind to work.

In the next year, the Grange transformed itself from a fraternal association for fellowship and mutual edification into a powerful political force. By 1874, Granger Parties controlled the legislatures of Illinois, Wisconsin, Iowa, and Minnesota. Leveraging their political influence, they advocated for a series of "Granger Laws" that regulated the dominating powers of corporations, banks, and railroads. These legal restraints and regulations kept big businesses from exploiting farmers and manipulating the market. Grange legislators also encouraged innovative programs, such as Cooperative Extension Services and the Farm Credit System, to strengthen rural communities. These laws set in motion a legislative trajectory that led to clusters of legislative reform in the Progressive Era and the eras of the New Deal and the Great Society. This movement was born out of grassroots community building and organizing.[5]

Not quite a hundred years later, a farmworker and organizer named Cesar Chavez was crisscrossing California on his own commissioned farm tour. Unlike Oliver Kelley, Chavez wasn't commissioned by the president of the United States. He wasn't even commissioned by the Community Service Organization with whom he had been working for the previous several years. He had proposed an organizing tour to his organization but was denied support. So he left. And he did it anyway. The commission in this case was his own sense of calling and conscience.

Chavez was a devout Catholic, greatly influenced by the social justice teachings of Jesus and the church, as well as the examples of St. Francis and Mahatma Gandhi. He was also shaped by his own life story. When he was a young child, his family had a small farm and country store in Arizona before they lost it all in the Great Depression. The family was forced to move, so they relocated to California. Chavez lived his childhood as a farmworker; his family moved from farm to farm, harvest to harvest, and often had to sleep on the side of the road.

But now he was old enough to change things. So he traveled and toured the farms across California, listening to the farmworkers' struggles and ideas and then recruiting them to join his new organization, the National Farmworkers Association. This network provided a sense of empowerment and dignity to overcome the prevailing spirit of isolation and despair. The members felt like they were part of something larger than themselves and that they might finally have the power to create safer and more just work environments.

Chavez combined the ideals of his Catholic faith, which was shared by many of the workers, with the strategic practice of nonviolent action he learned from other social reformers. Chavez fasted and prayed and led pickets and protests. In 1965, the National Farmworkers Association appealed to the public to stop buying Delano grapes. It was the only way this group of impoverished farmworkers could gain the attention of the big businesses and landowners that worked to suppress them. At its height, they were able to get over 13 million Americans to support the cause by boycotting grapes, and in 1969, a history-shaping contract was signed with the growers that improved conditions for over ten thousand workers. By the end of the campaign, Cesar Chavez and the alliance of Filipino, Mexican, and other allied members had joined together to create the United Farm Workers (UFW).

The UFW was a game changer for farmworkers and for the American political landscape. They became a political force to be reckoned with, especially in California, leading the fight for overtime pay, state standards, and immigration reform, and against the use of disease-causing pesticides.[6]

Chavez's organizing was ultimately about empowerment, calling forth the dignity and collective strength that manifests when people come together for a just cause. This is illustrated perfectly by the motto of the UFW: *¡Sí, se puede!* (Yes, we can!) That's right, the phrase didn't originate with Barack Obama. It originated in 1972, during Cesar Chavez's twenty-five-day fast, when he and UFW cofounder Dolores Huerta came up with the slogan.[7] It demonstrates the sense of possibility and empowerment that comes with joining together to work for positive change.

Organizing is a powerful practice. There's only so much we can do by ourselves. And when we act alone, it is easy to grow discouraged and disillusioned. Remaining isolated and divided also benefits what Walter Wink called the "Domination System."[8] But something powerful happens when we come together across differences for a common cause. When we reclaim our power and dignity, a spirit of "Yes, we can!" develops among us, and we learn how to "be the change" we want to see in the world.

In some ways, Oliver Kelley and Cesar Chavez (as well as the Grange and the UFW) couldn't be more different. They were leaders in different eras and areas. One was fighting for farm owners, and one was fighting for farm workers. One was based in the Midwest, while the other was based in California and the Southwest. One was a white New Englander, the other was Latino.

But their work had much in common. Both were rural leaders who cared about rural people and those who worked the land. Both were inspired by listening and learning tours where they engaged the stories of actual people doing the work of agriculture. Both focused their efforts on empowering people to shape their own destiny through social capital and political advocacy. Both built enduring networks and institutions that would sustain their ongoing objectives. Most importantly, both brought together people who had been desperate and divided and enabled them to reclaim their dignity and agency. In other words, they were organizers.

JESUS THE ORGANIZER

Jesus of Nazareth was a community organizer. You may not have thought of him that way before, but organizing was an important part of his kingdom work. When we read the gospels as if they were collections of isolated incidents and punctuated pious stories about personal salvation and morality, we miss something important about the bigger picture of Jesus's ministry. He didn't just wander around the ancient Near East, angering Pharisees and sharing pithy sayings with peasants. No, Jesus moved with intention, because he intended to start a movement.

The context in which Jesus's ministry grew was one in which the majority of people inhabiting the Galilean countryside were feeling increasingly oppressed by a spirit of decline, devastation, and disinheritance. They were heavily taxed and increasingly dispossessed of their work and their wealth. Their lives were dominated by decisions and decrees made by far-off elites, Roman political authorities, and Jewish religious leaders who used each other to maintain power and privilege. Instead of representing the interests of their people and the ethics of their tradition, the Jewish leaders in Jerusalem added temple tithes to the heavy Roman taxation, financing lavish lifestyles and massive building projects. It became nearly impossible for people dependent on farming and fishing to get ahead. This led to a rise in debt and exploitative lending, further forcing agrarian villagers to become sharecroppers, then day laborers, and sometimes even slaves.[9]

Many lost their homes, farms, and ancestral lands as property and power were consolidated into a more centralized agribusiness system that drove many to low-wage work or forced them to migrate to the cities. This economic, social, and spiritual environment was one in which the powerful elites coerced the peasant class into a pattern John Dominic Crossan described as "Romanization by urbanization for commercialization."[10]

The problems weren't just "out there" in Rome or Jerusalem, however. The pain and pressure put on these rural villages inspired disturbing trends in which traditional bonds of family, village, and land were breaking down. Rural villagers were charging excessive interest on loans to their already vulnerable neighbors. They were taking out their stress on each other through quarreling, abusive language, and cutthroat competition for scarce resources. For many individuals, families, and villages, the sense of covenant community was breaking down, and their bonds were eroding. Biblical scholar Richard Horsley explains, "Unfortunately, under the press of debt and taxation, Roman legal standards, not the Torah, began to take precedence."[11] Villagers who used to provide mutual aid during times of distress looked only to their own. Local feuds were no longer resolved quickly but instead spiraled into violence. Spouses were divorcing, leaving wives and children vulnerable. "The simple fact was that the people of Israel were badly divided. Villagers who could have cooperated in each other's liberation were at each other's throats."[12]

Jesus's ministry of organizing provided healing encounters and liberating teachings that turned the people back to God and one another, where right relationships were restored and new energies released. Jesus moved with mission from village to village, organizing folks to renew their covenant commitments to one another and forming what some scholars call "renewal-resistance movements." The people were gathered together and sent out, while typically remaining rooted in their local village. Horsley writes that Jesus called upon the community to "recommit themselves collectively to the covenantal principles and commandments of mutual cooperation and support in the village community."[13] The kingdom of God was coming into being through these networks of covenant communities where God's ways were put into practice and God's redemptive actions were experienced.

In this new and renewing movement, God was acting in a decisive way, but God was acting *through* villagers, most notably through Jesus of Nazareth. Yet Jesus famously said that those who followed him would do "even greater things" than he did (John 14:12). "In the gospel story," Horsley comments, "Jesus not only mediates divine power to the people but also generates power among the people, power of renewal in family and villages and power in opposition to the rulers who had been draining away their strength."[14]

Jesus, in the spirit of a community organizer, overcomes the isolation and division of the community by turning its members toward one another. In this turning, "repentance" in biblical terms, the people renew their spirits, repair their relationships, and revitalize their villages. This experience of renewal comes as Jesus not only "mediates" but also "generates" power among the people, as Horsley notes.

POWER HUNGRY

We explored the dynamics of power in an earlier chapter, exploring the "locus of power" and how divine power is at work between, within, and among us. But another complex issue has to do with seeking and claiming power. The reality is that many of the people Jesus ministered to longed for power.

We tend to view "power hungry" people with suspicion. And rightly so. We have seen Lord Acton proven right too many times: "Power tends to corrupt and absolute power corrupts absolutely." However, powerlessness is not a virtue either. Congregation-based community organizer Dennis Jacobsen reminds us: "Powerlessness also corrupts. Powerlessness is also a tool of evil."[15] He goes on to list the fruits of powerlessness, such as loss of dignity, addictions, broken families, crimes of desperation, and so forth. Oppressed communities have often had to "build power" through community organizing and political action.

The American civil rights movement is a prime example of a repressed and oppressed community rising up and reclaiming its power. It's worth noting, by the way, that there were various "fronts" of the movement. Some were marching, preaching, and boycotting. Others, such as the hundreds of farmer cooperatives started by Black leaders like Ralph Paige, were starting new food and credit systems.

One of the movement's most prominent leaders, Dr. Martin Luther King Jr., guided by philosopher Paul Tillich, traced the connections between power, love, and justice. King stated clearly and compellingly, "Power without love is reckless and abusive, and love without power is sentimental and anemic. Power at its best is love implementing the demands of justice, and justice at its best is power correcting everything that stands against love."[16] It is neither just nor loving to expect that people accept their own powerlessness as if it were an inescapable fact of history, or worse, a fact of God's will.

The journalist J. D. Vance, in his best-selling memoir *Hillbilly Elegy*, critiques a common attitude he encountered during his Appalachian childhood. This attitude, "learned helplessness," limits people because of their beliefs about how the world works. They believe that the powers that be are conspiring against them, so they can never get ahead:

> We'll get fired for tardiness, or for stealing merchandise and selling it on eBay, or for having a customer complain about the smell of alcohol on our breath, or for taking five thirty-minute restroom breaks per shift. We talk about the value of hard work but tell ourselves that the reason we're not working is some perceived unfairness: Obama shut down the coal mines, or all the jobs went to the Chinese. These are the lies we tell ourselves to solve the cognitive dissonance—the broken connection between the world we see and the values we preach.[17]

Vance observed the impact this perspective had on his friends and family members, trapping them in poverty and addiction. They then passed on this helplessness and hopelessness to the next generation. It becomes a kind of self-fulfilling prophecy.

For Vance, the solution is largely about taking personal responsibility. He concludes, "I don't know what the answer is, precisely, but I know it starts when we stop blaming Obama or Bush or faceless companies and ask ourselves what we can do to make things better."[18] He argues that good public policy helps, education is important, and "mediating institutions" such as churches are vital. But ultimately, he argues, if rural folks are going to be lifted and liberated, we have to reclaim our agency and responsibility.

As numerous critics of *Hillbilly Elegy* have argued, Vance's picture of Appalachia is severely lacking. He leaves out the innumerable stories of organizing, activism, and innovation among Appalachian folks. I agree with these critiques, and I agree that Vance's partial story has done damage to the narrative about rural communities in our national imagination. That being said, what if he has a point about the way we give up our power? This is a real temptation among rural folks. We focus so much on the state capital and the nation's capital or the elites and liberals and neocons as the sources of our problems. What if we have more power than we think? And even if those centers of power are indeed responsible for our problems, how are we going to organize to create change and recover abundance?

Sometimes our power is stolen, and sometimes we give it away. Yet the powerful and empowering God of love and justice awaits the partnership of ordinary leaders and waits for us to seek the promise: "You shall receive power when the Holy Spirit comes upon you" (Acts 1:8). After all, Scripture reminds us, "God has not given us a spirit of fear, but of power and of love and of a sound mind" (2 Tim 1:7). In both passages the Greek word for power is *dunamis*, which has to do with energy, force, ability, and capacity that drives something or someone to its fullest potential, possibility, and purpose. This power is not self-serving power but a divine empowerment that energizes us to experience abundant life and extend it to others.

Maybe being "power hungry" in its truest sense isn't a bad thing at all. Maybe it's like the "hungering after righteousness" that Jesus talked about. Maybe it's part of the Spirit's lure to greater love and justice in the world. Maybe it's an indicator of a hunger that God is ready to fill and ready for us to claim. And, for some of us, maybe seeing that hunger in our neighbors means it's time for us to claim and share some of our power, so we can recover abundance in our communities together.

CROWD CONTROL AND COMMUNITY CULTIVATION

In our gospel story, Jesus faced a power-hungry crowd. Many felt left out and left behind. Many were waiting for a strongman messianic leader to rescue them or hoping for a singular act of divine judgment to deliver them. Though Jesus would redirect their power hunger, he didn't chastise them for it. He knew their deeper hunger was for the empowerment and fulfillment experienced when you "taste and see" the kingdom of God. So he prepared them for a taste. Actually, he prepared them for a feast.

First, however, he had to deal with the matter of the crowd. Jesus didn't really trust crowds. He saw throughout his ministry that crowds were fickle and shallow, even violent at times. Later on in his life, crowds would chant both "Hosanna!" and "Crucify him!" Crowds may channel a collective longing for salvation, but they are too easily possessed by anxiety, violence, and "extraordinarily popular delusions."[19] No, a crowd would not do. He could have deputized the disciples for crowd control. But crowd control was the way of the empire, not God's kingdom. And Jesus knew the kingdom of God doesn't advance by crowd control but by community creation and cultivation.

So, Jesus begins to organize the crowd. In a strategy of "divide and empower," he tells the disciples to reorganize the people and gather them into smaller groups. This action imitates the work of the Creator in Genesis when God separates, orders, and organizes the elements of nature to create a cosmic community that works together in harmony and generates abundance.

Jesus is creating an ecosystem where harmony and abundance can emerge. And he is acting to order the chaos, transforming a crowd into a community—or rather, a collection of communities. Through Jesus's organizing initiative, the crowd dissolves into an array of diverse communities: unique individuals, couples, families, covenants, associations, partners, neighbors, strangers, new friends, renewed connections, villagers, members—all about to be knit together through the saving, salvaging, surprising works of Jesus.

Parker Palmer, himself a community organizer, makes note of Jesus's wise actions in the story: "His miracle begins with the simple act of gathering the faceless crowd of five thousand into smaller, face-to-face communities. This is the stock-in-trade of every good community organizer, this clustering of people into more intimate settings where everyday miracles have a chance to happen."[20] What a powerful transformation. From a faceless crowd to face-to-face communities. That's where the good stuff happens.

Both our humanity and our divinity shine through in small groups. When we turn toward one another and nurture face-to-face relationships, we begin to truly see one another. We see both our beauty and our brokenness. In the words of Martin Buber, we make that shift from an I–It to an I–Thou relationship. We encounter each other as whole and holy people, though we are yet flawed and wounded. We see both our profound commonalities and our real differences. And we sense that *dunamis* at work between and among us as we share, listen, and practice.

Palmer notes another dynamic of crowds and communities. Crowds carry a spirit of scarcity, while community awakens abundance. "In the faceless crowd we experience scarcity—a scarcity of contact, of concern, of affirmation, of love. But as the crowd is replaced by community, an invisible sense of abundance arises

long before the community produces any visible goods or services."
Where does this abundance come from? "True abundance resides
in the simple experience of people being present to one another and
for one another."[21]

No wonder community organizers exert so much energy connecting and networking folks, building social capital and strong
bonds. Without those central and strong webs of connection, nothing else is possible. Until the crowd becomes a community, no miracle can take place. But with that community in place, surprising and
amazing things emerge. Abundance is recovered. Indeed, as Palmer
proclaims, "The experience of community is itself abundance."[22]

Quaker Rufus Jones said, "I pin my hopes to quiet processes
and small circles where vital and transforming events take place."[23]
I agree. And apparently Jesus did too. Indeed, "vital and transforming events" were about to take place within and between these new
small groups.

THE KINGDOM IS BOTANICAL

The Greek text for this story provides two helpful images for Jesus's
organizing actions. Jesus instructed the disciples to organize
the crowd into groups, but the Greek wording for these groups is
the repetition *prasia prasia*. It means, essentially, "garden plots." The
groups were ordered like garden plots, planted in particular clusters
and cultivated in rows. Some scholars suggest the word picture also
calls to mind the colors of the diverse garments worn by the people
in the crowd.

I worked in landscaping for several years, and I've been an ama-
teur gardener for about a decade now. Folks who have never tried
landscaping or gardening might think it's rather simple. You toss a
seed or plant in the ground, and nature does the rest. Voila! Beauty
and fruitfulness.

Anybody who has actually done landscaping and gardening,
on the other hand, knows it's not nearly that simple. It requires

knowledge of what soil and amount of sunlight work best for the plant and what kind of cultivation is required for fullest fruitfulness. It requires work and attention to proper watering, weeding, and pruning. And it requires vigilance: all kinds of critters, diseases, and insects seek to "steal, kill, and destroy."

When I moved to Kansas for college, I got a work-study job on campus. When the maintenance team heard that I worked in landscaping, they were eager to toss me into the various landscaping projects going on. They actually put me in charge of a few. Eager to show off my skills, I planned and designed several lovely beds around a couple of the main buildings. I picked out my favorite plants, plopped them into the ground, and gave them a good soaking. Then I made another pivotal change. I switched out the ugly pinkish red bark they were using for mulch and replaced it with the rich, dark black mulch we used in Ohio. It would provide a picturesque contrast to the surrounding grass and emphasize the color in my plants.

Initially, everything seemed to go well. But things didn't go—or grow—as I had hoped over the first month after installation. After about two months I realized that it was a colossal failure. You see, the plants were scorched to death. That's what happens when nonnative plants are submerged in heat-attracting mulch in a dry climate where summers see temperatures in the triple digits. I wasn't in Ohio anymore. I had to admit defeat, and the college had to swallow the loss of several hundred dollars.

When we know the nature of our place and people and we work in concert with their nature, however, it's much easier to organize in a way that promotes flourishing and fruitfulness. When we try to force activism and revitalization projects that don't fit the community, we fail. And it's tempting to simply blame it on the apathetic and fearful people. But community requires cultivation, and abundance is the result of the right mix of organization, nourishment, and pruning.

Ordinary leaders are organizing leaders. When we are at our best, we organize our people, according to the nature of our place, in such a way that they can thrive and flourish together. We encourage their roots, cultivate relationships, provide nourishing resources, and invite new connections. We learn from Jesus, the wise gardener of relationships, about how to order and organize our community in a way that promotes abundant life for all. As a friend once reminded me, the kingdom of God is botanical, not mechanical. It is a dynamic, organic, (agri)cultural process of growth. It doesn't work like a machine. Jesus's parables almost always use natural and agricultural analogies to describe the kingdom.

IT'S ALSO A BATTLE

Implicit in the passage, however, is another metaphor for organizing. The report that the crowd includes five thousand men and that they were formed into groups or "companies" of hundreds and fifties may have military implications. Biblical commentator David Garland explains, "Dividing the assembly into orderly rows suggests the grouping of an army and recalls Israel's encampment. Five thousand was also the typical number in a Roman legion and the number of Galilean troops Josephus said that he assembled for the battle against the Romans in A.D. 67. Rebel movements were known for gathering in the desert during this era."[24] John's version of the story may also indicate this military connection, stating that the crowd wanted to coerce Jesus into becoming their "king" (John 6:15), a role that had both military and political dimensions.

Here again we see the people's hunger for power. They were marginalized and oppressed and longed to regain their former dignity and glory. Garland observes, however, that Jesus is feeding a spiritual army, not a military company. He doesn't shame the people for their desire but redirects the energy. They will reclaim their power and renew their strength but not for a military victory or political power grabs. They will build power to live faithfully and abundantly as a covenant community and become a force that advances peace and justice in the world.

As a Quaker, I tend to be uncomfortable with military language used in religious settings. Quakers are committed to a testimony of peace and following the nonviolent teachings of Jesus. Yet it's hard to deny that life and leadership can feel like a battle. And it's hard to deny that Jesus himself acknowledges the forces that oppose his kingdom of peace and justice. Indeed, passivity and niceness are not enough to advance God's commonwealth. In one striking passage, Jesus is reported to have said, "From the days of John the Baptist until now the kingdom of heaven has suffered violence, and the violent take it by force" (Matt 11:12). The Greek word for "violence" here has to do with taking or seizing something by force.

In the weeks following the murder of George Floyd in 2020, my wife, Ashlyn, and I were inspired by the protests and anti-racism work happening in small towns across the country. There was something sacred taking place, and we were feeling called to participate in some way. We weren't sure how, exactly. And we preferred to let a person of color take the lead. However, in our small town, no such person emerged. So we felt clear to meet with a small group of people to discern our role in that moment and begin planning a local event.

What arose was the idea of holding a vigil. It would begin with a walk around town, holding signs calling for racial justice and healing. Then we would meet in the downtown square, where we would offer prayers and reflections, read the names of black citizens killed by police violence, light candles, and hang up the signs we were carrying.

We planned the vigil collaboratively with local folks, and we decided not to affiliate with any national organizations. We emphasized that it wasn't a riot or protest; it was a time for grieving, praying, and reflecting on our role in the work of racial justice and community healing. Our little town is called Mount Gilead, so in my address to the group, I drew from the prophet Jeremiah and his words about the "balm of Gilead" and the need to grieve and repent instead of "treating the wounds of [God's] people lightly" (Jer 6).

The gathering was truly beautiful. We brought together about twenty-five neighbors from many different backgrounds and belief systems who walked and stood together in a sacred space, one where people could bring their grief and anger and questions. Ashlyn and I were grateful for the opportunity to lead the gathering, and the event felt right for our community and in alignment with our vocations.

But it wasn't all kumbaya. In fact, it almost didn't happen. The day before, we received word that a man was planning to bring an armed posse to our gathering. We were familiar with him; he had made threats to our lives on social media. He was known locally as someone who was unstable due to untreated posttraumatic stress disorder (PTSD) from his service in the military. I wanted to believe these threats were just the rantings of an angry, insecure, and tragically wounded man. But I knew better. He was heavily armed, and he was dangerous.

Rumors about the vigil were spread. Despite our efforts to emphasize that the gathering was locally led and for folks in our county, claims were made that paid activists were being bused in from Cleveland and Columbus and Cincinnati and that all kinds of destruction to our little peaceful town was inevitable. We organizers got the sense that some folks couldn't conceive that people in their own town would lead an anti-racist event or that such a gathering would not be filled with rioting and looting.

These rumors concerned us in part because we had seen what happened in Bethel, Ohio, a small town near Cincinnati. A local substitute history teacher planned a small demonstration in solidarity with Black Lives Matter. About fifty people showed up. When they did, they were met with counterprotesters . . . hundreds of them. And the counterprotesters meant business. They brought rifles and handguns and a bag full of bats. The counterprotesters began screaming threats and using the N-word and telling the protestors that they had "come to the wrong f***ing town."

"People were screaming at us to go back where we came from," recalled local Anwen Darcy, who came with her mom and sister. "But I was looking around, and I saw Mrs. Dennis, who'd been a teacher for thirty years. I saw my mom, who'd been on the PTA for years and served as the drama director. I saw the woman who ran all the prom fundraisers and a city councilman. The people yelling at us weren't from here, because if they were, they would've known we were home."[25]

We didn't want another Bethel. We wanted a peaceful gathering to support healing and justice in our region. After hearing about the threats and dangers, Ashlyn and I had to do some soul searching. A lot of emotion and energy had gone into planning this vigil, and we believed it was something we were called to do. We felt clear in our own hearts that we were willing to take the risk for our convictions. But should we put other peoples' safety at risk for those convictions? Ultimately, we decided to let people decide for themselves. We also hired a private security guard and asked others to help us cover the event in prayer.

During the actual event, we weren't accosted by an armed posse. Thanks be to God, there was not a "Bethel situation." The man who made the threats did show up and did bring a gun, but he sat across the street on a bench. A few people drove by and screamed hateful and obscene words. But I was focused on these compassionate and courageous neighbors who came together to stand for justice and pray for healing.

Local residents offered mixed reviews about the event, but we did what we were called to do. And we communicated something that needed to be said: this is *our* town and belongs to *all* of us. It doesn't just belong to angry armed men "defending their town." It also belongs to the folks who gathered at the vigil, people who want to build a more just and inclusive community. And if more Black and Brown folks decide to make our town their home, then it will belong to them as well.

The symbolism of standing together on the town square struck me. We were reclaiming our territory. Our membership. Our belonging. Our agency. Our community. "From the days of John the Baptist until now the kingdom of heaven has suffered violence, and the violent take it by force." Can I paraphrase Jesus's words? "From the days of John the Baptist until now, the kingdom has received threats of violence. But we seize it back with soul force."

About three years before our vigil, a woman named Lacy Hale, who grew up in the mountains and coalfields of eastern Kentucky, was concerned about her hometown, Pikeville. The KKK was planning a rally there. What should she do? Well, she's an artist. She had studied art at the Pratt Institute of New York City before returning home as an artist and art teacher. So she used her art. In a workshop, a phrase came to her: "No hate in my holler." She made a print of it and shared it. Lacy had no idea, however, how far and wide this motto would spread. It was printed on T-shirts and bags and painted on buildings and shared all over Facebook, Twitter, and Instagram. She was surprised but glad—and proud of the people in Appalachia who came together around this simple but powerful affirmation. She said, "We get a bad rap here. I've talked to people of color who don't want to come because of the stereotypes about the area, but to hear so many people attach to that phrase and use it was super-encouraging."[26] Organizing, whether by creating art, founding organizations, or planning events, creates opportunities to say together "No hate in my holler," "Hate has no place here," "We are stronger together," "Black Lives Matter," and maybe even "The kingdom of God is here."

As ordinary leaders, we are called to make sure our small town or rural region truly belongs to everyone. If folks are being left out, left behind, or excluded, we use our power to bring them in. Better yet, we use our power to empower them. We cultivate the kinds of spaces where they can grow and thrive. If our power has been lost or taken away, we take it back. We need everyone to recover abundance and claim the kingdom.

Let's organize our community in a way that creates beauty, builds power, makes new connections, and cultivates fruitfulness. And when a soul-level struggle is called for, let's fight the good fight. This land is our land. This kingdom is our kingdom. And we are called to dwell in our place with justice, faithfulness, and love.

CHAPTER SEVEN

THE PRACTICE OF HOSPITALITY

Taking the five loaves and two fish . . .

Mark 6:41

I WAS A BRAND-NEW PASTOR, excited to step into my new role as pastor of leadership support and development. There were so many ideas I wanted to implement as I transitioned from a rookie intern to a member of the pastoral team. I was eager to discuss the opportunities and responsibilities that came with my position. So I sat down with the lead pastor to discuss my new job description. I would oversee and support existing small groups. Great; they needed some nurturing, and I would love to learn more about how to support them. I would also assist with worship planning and participate in the preaching rotation. Excellent—right in my sweet spot. And I would oversee the Wednesday night programming we called Wednesday with Friends (in reference to both our Quaker heritage and our close-knit fellowship). Right on; teaching classes and organizing learning and worship options was right up my alley.

Wednesday with Friends, though, wasn't just a gathering for classes and small groups. It was also a meal. A big meal. The programs and the church had been growing, so we were getting up to eighty and ninety people for these dinners. For some seasoned folks on the fellowship committee, this was no problem. These ladies were expert organizers of potlucks and community meals and meal trains. But that core group had done so much for so long that they were burned out. It would be my job to provide fresh leadership for the kitchen and to recruit new volunteers.

I was terrified. I could barely plan and prepare meals for myself. The lead pastor knew this wasn't exactly my "area of giftedness," but she was pretty insistent that this was part of my job. It needed to be done, and it could be a valuable learning experience for a young pastor like me.

As much as I fought the feeling, part of me felt like this assignment was a waste of my talents. The passage from the book of Acts kept coming to mind when the apostles were made aware that the widows were being neglected in the food distribution. They delegated the task to some newly chosen deacons because "it would not be right for us to neglect the ministry of the word of God in order to wait on tables" (Acts 6:2). While perhaps not an apostle, I was a teacher and preacher. "It would not be right" for me to use my time and energy on something as mundane as training volunteers, making meal plans, shopping for food, setting up tables and chairs, and washing dishes—"waiting on tables."

Right or not, however, there was no escaping the church kitchen. It would become my home away from home, and some fine folks stepped up to join me in making our weekly meal together possible. One evening, I looked out at the people sitting around the round gray tables we had set up before they'd arrived, eating the food we had made together. Some folks were laughing and having a good time catching up. Others were talking about a struggle happening at home or at work. I overheard folks at one table discussing a theological topic they had been pondering. And suddenly I realized that I wasn't just doing a job; my crew and I weren't just providing calories so they could be fueled up to learn about God afterward (the important part). No, we were setting the table for a sacrament. That meal was just as important as the classes and worship experiences. We prepared a space where folks could come together to have an authentic encounter with God and neighbor in the way Jesus promised—at the dinner table.

What I learned from that experience was that *ministry is hospitality*. It is about preparing space for people to encounter God, self, and neighbor. Ordinary leadership is about providing a hospitable presence to folks, whether in an office, home, classroom, or sanctuary. Perhaps no other symbol represents hospitality better than the table.

I was once at a congregational retreat where the speaker asked us to think about our dinner tables growing up. He asked questions like: Did you have a dinner table? What did it look like? Did you have assigned seating? How often did you eat together? What was the shape of the table? How much room was there at the table? How often were there guests at the table? The speaker invited us to reflect on these questions and then make a drawing of our family table. If we didn't eat at a table, we were invited to draw the space where we typically ate our dinner. After a few minutes, we were asked to share our drawings and memories with others in our small group, if we were comfortable doing so. It was a fascinating and revealing exercise.

In my own childhood, while we were on our own for breakfast and typically at school for lunch, my family always had dinner together at our dining room table. Occasionally, on a Friday family night, we might eat pizza in the living room while we watched a movie. But every weekday the whole family sat together and at the same table. And we all ate what was put before us with those whom God had joined together, whether we liked the food (and family) or not.

Sunday dinners were particularly sacrosanct. Most Sunday mornings, my mom put something in the Crock-Pot for us to eat after church, and she made enough so that we could invite friends to join us. My parents wanted us to feel free to bring home guests, believing they were blessed with a nice house so that they could bless others who were in need. On multiple occasions, our finished basement was home for a struggling couple or family finding their way. So when I drew my picture of the table, I drew a long rectangle with spots for Mom, Dad, my sister, my brother, me, and then an empty chair for a guest.

It all seemed normal at the time. But my wife, Ashlyn, tells a much different story about her childhood dinner table. She didn't have one. Her extended family has massive meals around long tables during the holidays; I can attest to this. My belly bears witness. But she confesses that growing up, she thought dinner tables were for "rich people."

What was your table or eating space like as a child? What is it like now?

This exercise is evocative because it brings up all kinds of topics that you wouldn't expect. Eating meals together is about not only cooking and food selection but also family dynamics, feelings of belonging or estrangement, harmony and conflict, vulnerability, and all sorts of implicit theology. Henri Nouwen summarizes it well:

> The table is the place of intimacy. Around the table we discover each other. It's the place where we pray. It's the place where we ask, "How was your day?" It's the place where we eat and drink together and say, "Come on, take some more!" It is the place of old and new stories. It is the place of smiles and tears. The table, too, is the place where distance is most painfully felt. It is the place where the children feel the tension between the parents, where brothers and sisters express their anger and jealousies, where accusations are made, and where plates and cups become instruments of violence. Around the table, we know whether there is friendship and community or hatred and division.[1]

Tables tell us important truths—truths about identity, theology, and the quality of our relationships. You can learn a lot about a person or a family (or yourself) by their table and table practices. Table practices are hospitality practices, and they have a surprising capacity for stirring controversy and for bringing about healing and transformation.

THE MEAL IS THE MESSAGE

Before Jesus was associated with the cross or the empty tomb, he was known for his table practices. When we read the gospels, we see that everybody knew about Jesus's unique approach to table fellowship and had strong opinions about it. Love it or hate it, amazed or angered, the gospel attests that "the Son of Man came eating and drinking" (Luke 7:34). He was criticized for spending too much time at peoples' tables, wining and dining so often that he was called a glutton and a drunkard. He was also criticized for who he was willing to eat with. The Pharisees complained and condemned: "Why do you eat and drink with tax collectors and sinners?" (Luke 5:30).

Like our tables, the tables of Jesus's day told important truths. In a sense, the household table was a microcosm of the larger society. The practices of hosts, guests, and servants communicated truths about proper social roles and power dynamics. They told a story of how society should be ordered and who belonged in what space. Jesus deliberately undermined those rules and taboos. He practiced what John Dominic Crossan calls "open commensality,"[2] where the table is open to "whosoever wills." Even if Jesus was a "guest," he was always opening up the table like a host. Regardless of gender, class, race, or purity status, Jesus welcomed everyone to the table. Jesus's table practices illustrated and demonstrated the inclusive reach of his kingdom message. They enacted and embodied the welcome of God. "Wherever, whenever, however the kingdom manifests itself," wrote Krister Stendahl, "it is welcome."[3] That welcome can be hard to believe, and receive, so it needs to be experienced in our very bodies. Indeed, the meal becomes the message.

This open table was a metaphor for the kingdom of God. But it was also more than a metaphor; it was an actual meal. It was an enactment of that kingdom, experienced in an intimate and embodied way. Biblical scholar Peter Leithart says, "As Jesus announced the feast of the kingdom, he also brought it into reality through his own feasting."[4] Human beings are relational, embodied, hungry creatures. We don't just hear and reason our way into a new way of being; we have to experience a truth with our full self. Jesus knew that people needed to "taste and see" the kingdom. So he taught it through words, yes, but also offered it through food. Jesus made the wideness of God's grace tangible—and edible.

Sometimes stepping outside my own faith and culture helps me to gain a fresh understanding of a truth or practice. For example, something from the Sikh religious tradition enriches my understanding of how Jesus's table fellowship was both controversial and transformational. Sikhs have a beautiful tradition of hosting a communal meal, open to both devotees and strangers, called the *langar*. The *langar* takes place after their worship service, and everyone gathers to sit together on the floor and enjoy a meal from the common pots prepared by volunteers.

When the food is ready, a small portion of each dish is poured into a bowl and placed before the guru. The guru then recites a prayer, dedicating and offering the food to God. Sometimes this prayer also involves the guru touching the food with a ritual dagger, making the food "God-intoxicated." The food is then returned to its respective pot so that the blessing can be spread to everyone who takes and eats. Servers then distribute the food to the people, who are seated on long rugs.[5]

It's not hard to make connections with the Christian practice of the Eucharist or the agape feasts of early Christian communities. The *langar* involves collection, consecration, and distribution. The meal also becomes the message by enacting Sikh values. It demonstrates hospitality, charity, service, and equality in a tangible and tasty way.

In the context of sixteenth-century India, in which Sikhism emerged, meals were not to be shared with those of another caste or another religion. There were all kinds of rules about how and with whom food and drink could be consumed. From the time of its founding by Guru Nanak, Sikh communities have hosted the *langar* as a countercultural practice that emphasizes their belief in the oneness and equality of all people. The meal breaks down the divisions and castes of the community when participants sit on the floor (literally "on the same level"), mixing rich and poor, men and women, Sikhs and guests. They shared a common meal that symbolizes their common humanity and common Creator. In fact, all *langar* meals are vegetarian, not because Sikhism requires vegetarianism, but because it allows the broadest range of guests to partake of the meal.

Jesus was doing something similar with his practice of open commensality. He was breaking down divisions and prejudices by making an alternative meal that would remind his followers of an alternative lifestyle in an alternative kingdom. Eating with Jesus provided a taste, or "foretaste," of the abundance and equality that characterize the loving reign of God. It is characterized by an environment of hospitality where rich and poor, pure and impure, women and men, gay and straight, and so forth are all warmly welcomed and fully fed.

This is all great, you may be thinking, but what does this have to do with the story of Jesus feeding the multitude? I mean, they didn't even have tables! Well, this principle of hospitality has a lot to do with the story, actually. Imagine this massive crowd made up of tens of thousands of people. There was no way to clearly differentiate between Jew and gentile, sinner and holy, rich and poor, and so forth. There was no way to maintain ritual purity and proper table manners with such a huge group in the wilderness. So Jesus set that aside. In fact, I wonder if Jesus saw this intermingling and decided it was the perfect moment for a miracle. Maybe he was setting up a massive demonstration of open commensality, a tangible, tasty, and transformational sign of God's extravagant hospitality and inclusive

kingdom. Perhaps Jesus was preparing a prophetic picnic to provide the disciples and the crowd an unforgettable, undeniable experience of God's dream.

CONFIDENCE

Folks in small towns and rural regions are often known for their hospitality. Hospitality is the friendly farm family in the Midwest who
opens their house to someone whose car broke down on their country road. It's the southern Thanksgiving meal where Granny and the
gang make enough food to feed an army, so if anybody wants to bring
a friend, they are welcome to do so because "the more, the merrier."
Hospitality is also the northwestern neighbor who invites their
friends over to stay warm by the fire because their power went out
and it might be a while before someone gets it working again. I know
so many good and hospitable people in rural regions who open their
hearts and homes to folks in need of resources and relationships.

But sometimes we excel at a form of "exclusive hospitality,"
where we are generous and welcoming to those who are like us but
skeptical of and even prejudiced toward those outside our circle.
This closed-circle hospitality betrays a kind of insecurity and lack of
confidence in the value and vitality of our own household. In their
book *The Abundant Community*, John McKnight and Peter Block
note:

> Hospitality is the signature of not only an abundant com-
> munity, but also a confident one. The extent of hospitality
> becomes the measure of the belief that people have in their
> community. When you do not have confidence and you feel
> threatened or separated, you are unable to be hospitable.
> When you have a life in a connected and confident commu-
> nity, it is welcoming; hospitality is generated because people
> feel so good about themselves that they want others to share it
> and they want to share the joy of others.[6]

This connection between exclusive hospitality and insecure identity may seem counterintuitive to some, but I see it play out all the time in small towns. My own small town and rural county have been experiencing an influx of opportunity due to their proximity to the growing city of Columbus. Some locals are excited about the new folks coming to visit. They are excited about the economic revitalization that's possible as local shops and new restaurants benefit from these new customers. These folks are happy to host out-of-town guests in their parks, businesses, houses of worship, and so forth. Think of my friends I mentioned in the "Imagination" chapter who host both locals and visitors at their wedding venue and bed-and-breakfast.

But other folks in my town and county are less excited or optimistic about these visitors and in-movers. They worry that this influx of outsiders will undermine the local, rural flavor of our county. The newcomers will want specialty coffees and chic decor and will probably vote Democratic. They will bring trouble to our town, "trouble with a capital T" (to borrow from *The Music Man*). Or even worse, they will bring change.

I'm being a bit playful, of course, but this is a real tension within my county, and we have real debates about how our region will stagnate or grow. And there is some truth in each of these perspectives. Our region has a valuable and unique character that should be honored and preserved; it would be tragic if we lost our best qualities in order to become a "little Columbus." "Progress" and "development" don't always mean saying yes to every economic opportunity, corporate bid, or cultural trend that comes our way. But stagnation is not inherently virtuous, either. Neither the memories of our ancestors nor the futures of our children are honored by allowing our town to die a slow, stubborn, and painful death as people increasingly find unattractive and impractical the prospect of making a home and a living in our county.

The third way, which leads to abundant community, is the way of confident hospitality. We are secure in our identity and value; we are "at home" in our home. We embrace our uniqueness as a town and own our assets. And because of this secure confidence, we are open to guests. We are open to new ideas and ventures and friends. We aren't afraid that new people with new ideas are going to steal the heritage of Morrow County. In fact, it is our affectionate and effective marketing of our small-town charm that draws them in.

Exclusive hospitality is death dealing for small towns and rural regions. As the Hebrew and Christian Scriptures remind us, the arrival of the "stranger" often comes with unexpected gifts and restorative blessings. The advice of the author of Hebrews is worth following today as well: "Do not forget to show hospitality to strangers, for by so doing some people have shown hospitality to angels without knowing it" (Heb 13:2).

Confident hospitality involves expanding our relational reach to include both neighbor and stranger, those like us and those different from us. The newness, risk, and surprise that come with the presence of a stranger are the very qualities required for renewal. So we treat strangers with kindness (perhaps even reverence), both because they are image-bearers of God worthy of respect and because they are potential messengers of God. "The strangers at our door can be both gift and challenge," observes Sister Ana María Pineda, "human and divine."[7]

Building a community of confident hospitality requires bonds of trust, connection, and networks that sociologists call "social capital." There are two kinds of social capital: bonding and bridging. Bonding social capital describes the connections *within* a group of tight-knit groups like families, close friends, neighbors, and those of a similar social location and economic status. Bridging social capital, by contrast, describes the connections *between* social groups. This kind of social capital bridges across geographic, demographic, and socioeconomic divides and differences.

Both kinds of social capital are important and necessary for cultivating abundant communities. Both require hospitality. Generally speaking, however, folks in small towns and rural regions tend to be more adept at strengthening the connections of bonding social capital. We are often generous, hospitable, and loyal, but in a more exclusive way. This isn't a condemnation; most individuals and people groups function this way. It's necessary to some degree; it takes time and testing to gain the trust and confidence required for common ventures of increased intimacy. The sad fact is that social capital as a whole seems to be decreasing, as Robert Putnam argued in *Bowling Alone*, so I celebrate these bonds wherever I see them. We need them to survive and sustain our communities.

Understandable though it may be, it's also inadequate. For one, bonding social capital alone falls short of the widely welcoming hospitality Jesus modeled at his tables. "If you love those who love you, what credit is that to you?" Jesus asked. "Even sinners love those who love them" (Luke 6:32). To put it bluntly, the KKK excels at bonding social capital but has a long way to go when it comes to bridging social capital.

Second, bonding social capital tends to maintain the status quo. It helps keep us connected and alive for the moment, but it doesn't lead us to renewal. Robert Putnam makes the distinction this way: bonding social capital is good for "getting by," while bridging social capital is good for "getting ahead."[8] If we want to recover abundance in our small towns and rural regions, we are called upon to get ahead by practicing an inclusive, bridging hospitality that welcomes both neighbors and strangers. We need both for renewal, and ordinary leaders can lead the way with confident hospitality.

INTENTIONALITY

Hospitality also requires *intentionality*. Yes, sometimes a neighbor needs help in an emergency or the stranger just shows up in town, but typically hospitality happens by design, not default. Hospitality is about what Henri Nouwen called "the creation of a free space"[9] where we can find the safety and sanctuary to share our true self and have a mutual encounter. But even "free space" requires some preparation.

We can easily miss this detail, but when Jesus told the people to divide into groups and sit down, he was designing a hospitable space for the guests. The word used here for "group" in Greek is *symposia*, indicating a formal dinner party, not unlike the symposia practiced by Greek philosophers and students. New Testament scholar Gerhard Lohfink explains:

> People in antiquity had two ways of eating. Normal, everyday meals they took, as we do, while seated. But whenever they celebrated a festival or invited guests to a special dinner, they reclined at table. They lay on pillows and bolsters, leaning on their left arms and eating with their right hand. . . . [This] meant that an evening meal was about to begin at which people would take time for a banquet at which everyone could eat his or her fill. The bolsters and pillows were lacking, but they were replaced by plenty of green grass, which Mark expressly mentions.[10]

What a beautiful picture this paints of Jesus's hospitality. He discerns the moment, the people, and the place and responds by carefully creating a space where a miracle could emerge. His companions must have been perplexed, but Jesus had an intention for the event. Interestingly, though the "church" in this story is anything but small, he creates the small church experience by organizing the massive crowd into small groups.

Mediator and event facilitator Priya Parker writes about the intentionality of hospitality in her book *The Art of Gathering: How We Meet and Why It Matters*. She draws out the tension between the organic and open qualities of hospitality and the necessity of design. Hosting an event is not a democratic activity, she says bluntly. And she exposes what she calls the "fallacy of chill":

> Behind the ethic of chill hosting lies a simple fallacy: Hosts assume that leaving guests alone means that the guests will be

left alone, when in fact they will be left to one another. Many hosts I work with seem to imagine that by refusing to exert any power in their gathering, they create a power-free gathering. What they fail to realize is that this pulling-back, far from purging a gathering of power, creates a vacuum that others can fill. These others are likely to exercise power in a manner inconsistent with your gathering's purpose, and exercise it over people who signed up to be at your—the hosts'—mercy, but definitely didn't sign up to be at the mercy of your drunk uncle.[11]

Jesus was masterful at managing the tensions of hospitality. He left room for surprise and unfolding revelations, but he also exercised leadership. Every parent knows well that getting everyone to the table when it's time to eat is not easy. People are staring at their phones, working outside, finishing up a chapter in their book. Children are impatiently waiting to eat or complaining about their sibling's portion size. *Setting* the table requires preparation, and *settling* the table requires even more leadership.

Jesus knew that simply being "chill" with the crowd wouldn't get them what they most needed and deeply desired. And if he left that leadership vacuum empty, the "drunk uncles" of his day would take over. Jesus was well aware of the uncouth truth that Parker writes about when she says, "In gatherings, once your guests have chosen to come into your kingdom, they want to be governed—gently, respectfully, and well. When you fail to govern, you may be elevating how you want them to perceive you over how you want the gathering to go for them."[12]

What was at stake for Jesus, however, wasn't just a bad party. These folks were "like sheep without a shepherd," and lots of leaders had designs on their lives. Without Jesus and the "kin-dom" he was inaugurating, they were left to the mercy of those leaders and the exploitative systems they served. Jesus created a kingdom space through intentional hospitality and provided step-by-step guidance for the groups as they stepped and settled into that kingdom space.

We need rural and small-town leaders who know how to practice hospitality with intentionality, who avoid the "fallacy of chill" and take the lead by designing events and gatherings that model the possibilities of abundant community. Thankfully, ordinary leaders across the country are doing creative and courageous work. I think of Minnesotan Anna Claussen, who carried a concern about climate change and wanted to facilitate dialogue with farmers and rural folks who are impacted by those changes. Skilled in group mediation and creating space for empathic conversations, she founded Voices for Rural Resilience and hatched the idea of rural climate dialogues—dialogues that take place by design, not default. They arise within the framework of a three-day convening in which a small group gathers for informative presentations, guided discussions, and idea sharing. This symposia-like experience builds social capital across different demographics and encourages participants to recommend ways to cultivate greater resilience in their rural region. They get people around the table who often feel left out of climate conversations and invite them into a "deep engagement process to inform and improve climate policy and invigorate local action and public will."[13] In other words, the fruit of this hospitality is agency, in addition to the learning and community building.

I also think of my friends Ben Brazil and Kaia Jackson in Richmond, Indiana, who started Warp & Woof. Four times a year, once per season, they bring people together from across Wayne County to share stories around a theme. They are convinced that their region is overflowing with stories and that with the right invitation and the right design, these stories can be woven together to strengthen and enrich that region. They also believe the arts are critical components to community development and that small towns aren't barren of artistic gifts. So they exercise intentional hospitality by collaborating, designing, creating, inviting, and hosting. The stories that emerge are surprising, inspirational, and powerful.

Stepping into the role of host requires courage. Sharing stories takes courage. Asking people to share their sacred stories takes courage. Facilitating dialogues around controversial topics takes courage. Jesus creating a kingdom space where a miracle may or may not have happened definitely took courage. Anytime we risk practicing hospitality, we are called upon to exercise courage. Community organizer Whitney Kimball Coe uses the term "civic courage" to describe these kinds of hospitality initiatives that renew our small towns and rural regions. She states, "Civic courage looks like persistent, dedicated, and determined people showing up and speaking up for themselves and for those in their communities who cannot speak. Courage looks like vulnerable acts, like overcoming anxiety to become connectors and bridge-builders. We all have it within us to be courageous for our communities."[14]

Hospitality means creating safe spaces for guests. But sometimes, it's more demanding than that. Sometimes hospitality means creating brave spaces, spaces where we can have hard conversations, dine with folks who are different from us, and risk sharing a story or idea that may bring new life to our place and people. Sometimes the tables in these places are small and exclusive; the old guard is used to a small table. Sometimes we simply wait our turn. But sometimes we remember the advice of human rights activist Shirley Chisholm: "If they don't give you a seat at the table, bring a folding chair."[15] And in the spirit of Christ, we pull up a chair for one more person at the table. Such is the work of ordinary leadership.

PARTICULARITY

Hospitality also requires particularity. It's much easier to offer hospitality to folks in the abstract. It's harder to practice hospitality with specific people.

I confess that sometimes I love my hometown a lot more than I love particular neighbors in my hometown. They drive loud trucks. They put up signs for political candidates I don't support. They fight against a local tax levy that would support our neighbors with developmental disabilities. They are too busy to spend time with me or too needy and won't leave me alone. "The Bible tells us to love our neighbors, and also to love our enemies," observed G. K. Chesterton, "probably because generally they are the same people."[16]

Hospitality is hard to practice. One reason it's hard is that it's complicated. I only have so much time, so who do I prioritize? Do I focus on maintaining and deepening existing relationships or making new connections? When do I protect boundaries, and when do I make myself available? When do I confront my neighbor about his dog that poops in my yard? When do I buy pies or mums or raffle tickets for the neighbor kid's fundraiser?

To be neighborly in an abstract sense is easier. We care about the "poor" in a general way, at least enough to pay our taxes and give to a charity at Christmastime. But the "trailer trash" around the corner are not worth our time. Peruvian theologian Gustavo Gutiérrez calls us out on this habit with a prophetic inquiry: "You say you care about the poor? Then tell me, what are their names?"[17]

The practice of hospitality asks us to name names. It challenges us to learn the ways of redemptive name calling. Abstract relationships involve generalized hatred or love based on labels. We pity the poor. We stand with the oppressed. We hate Muslims or Trump supporters or liberals. But what are their names?

Speaking of the people he grew up with in Kentucky and Southern Ohio, journalist J. D. Vance wrote, "Americans call them hillbillies, rednecks, or white trash. I call them neighbors, friends, and family."[18] Labels serve a purpose. They help us analyze and discuss big topics and complex issues. But labels should always be starting points to invite discovery, not end points to shut down discussions. "Neighbors, friends, and family" is a great start. Names are better. Hospitality calls us to move toward "Sarah, Carlos, and Ahmed." As a host in God's kingdom, we invite people to the table and learn their names. Ordinary leaders call their neighbors by name.

Learning our guests' names is the bare minimum of hospitality, though. Anybody having guests over for a meal also makes sure to find out if they have any food preferences or allergies. Maybe we learn about their favorite food or beverage, so they feel fully welcomed. We make sure the house is at a warm enough temperature for our elderly aunt and the music is quiet enough so my nephew with hearing loss can participate in the conversation. My parents keep a ramp in the garage so their home is accessible for those who use a wheelchair. My wife, Ashlyn, has a gluten intolerance. It's more than a preference; I've seen the hell unleashed when gluten gets into her body. We try to let folks know this when we join them for a meal. Sometimes people who know us forget about this. Ashlyn is gracious and tries to find something she can eat. But this failure of hospitality can be painful. Whether or not it's intentional (it probably isn't), it still feels like an act of exclusion and marginalization.

If you're wondering how to practice this particularity, wise people tell us to start at home. Mother Teresa, for example, said, "It is easy to love the people far away. It is not always easy to love those close to us. It is easier to give a cup of rice to relieve hunger than to relieve the loneliness and pain of someone unloved in our own home. Bring love into your home, for this is where our love for each other must start."[19] It's all well and good to be concerned about "starving kids in Africa," but we can't neglect the hungers in our own home. If we want to practice a just and generous hospitality for the world, we can start at our own table. We ask questions about our partner's day. We engage fully with our child's horribly delivered knock-knock joke. We tell an embarrassing personal story to our roommates.

Then, we can expand to our literal neighbors. As religious folks, we often talk about loving our neighbors as a moral imperative but make the category of "neighbor" so broad that it sweeps up folks in Haiti but bypasses the folks next door. When we love neighbors as if they are nameless, we risk dehumanizing them with our vagueness, "fixing" them or "helping them" from a disempowering distance. "Without supper, without love, without table companionship, justice can become a program we do to people,"[20] notes Murphy Davis.

I'm an introvert, and sometimes I don't want to engage with my neighbors, to be honest. But I'm learning. I've learned their names and a bit more about their stories. Ashlyn and I shared baked goods with one family at Christmastime, and we took over a pot of soup to another neighbor when her husband died. They reciprocate too. When we go on a trip, they keep an eye on the house and feed our chickens. We've had a couple of cookouts together. Initially, these encounters felt a bit awkward, but I left them feeling more secure, more whole, and more connected to my place and its people. It's these little acts of hospitality that move us closer to one another and open up possibilities for abundant life and community.

As much as these particularities can make us feel annoyed or resentful of our neighbors, they also have the capacity to break down barriers and nurture new respect and affection. I think about the winery in my county. Yes, my rural county has a winery. The business partners who started the winery do a great job offering something new to the community while also maintaining a local flavor. They partner with the local market for a lasagna and wine date night on Fridays and have an indoor space and outdoor patio that people can rent for gatherings. They host "taco Tuesday," when people can come get a free taco and pair it with a glass of local wine. People love it.

As it turns out, however, the two guys who opened the winery are more than business partners. They are committed, loving, romantic partners. This may be a problem for some people in our neck of the woods. There is more of a "gay community" than you would assume for a small town, but we are not known for our extravagant hospitality to LGBTQ folks. It seems, however, that the locals are fairly disinterested in the vintner's sex life. They like these two guys, these particular guys, because they are active members of our community. They are friendly folks who live nearby on a little homestead. They highlight local businesses in their shop and support local initiatives. These two men are more than "the gays"; they are neighbors, colleagues, community leaders, and entrepreneurs. They are ordinary leaders who practice hospitality through their building and their business. And I think people are responsive to that hospitality in a way that undermines any homophobia that may linger in their hearts and minds.

Of course, this hospitality doesn't necessarily mean a community gay pride parade is on the horizon. But it does point to the power of hospitality. In a meaningful experience of hospitality, both guest and host are impacted. Talking about "gay rights" or "homosexuality" as an issue of popular culture or academic debate is entirely different from the experience of talking with gay folks face to face, as folks who are tied to the same place you are, caring for the same community you do, and pouring you a glass of wine.

Such is the power of hospitality. And such is the power of "third places" where we learn the names and stories of our neighbors. In case the concept is new for you, "third place" is a term coined by sociologist Ray Oldenburg to describe those "great good places" that are semiprivate and semipublic, neither home (first place) nor work (second place).[21] Restaurants, coffee shops, pubs, gyms, dog parks, and barber shops are all examples of third places. In rural communities, think of the general store or corner market where farmers meet early in the morning for coffee and gossip. Or the library where parents take their littles for story time and check out a few books and DVDs. Or maybe the VFW hall where locals meet for a fundraising fish fry or spaghetti dinner.

It's hard to overstate how critical these third places are for the flourishing of our small towns and rural regions. They provide space for gatherings that overcome the common ailments of loneliness and isolation. They have a leveling effect because they attract people from different demographics and put them all into the same room. They nurture "place attachment" and solidarity as people share favorite foods, drinks, games, resources, and the like. As the winery example illustrates, third places tend to have an overall humanizing

and connecting influence on customers and patrons. This humanizing is the result of the particularizing that happens in these settings.

Don't forget that churches are third places—places with a lot
of potential for personalized hospitality. Country churches typically have a small number of attendees and members. We are often
embarrassed and frustrated by our small size. But in the spirit of
asset-based inquiry, we can recognize the positive possibilities of
our setting and size.

Brandon J. O'Brien, author of *The Strategically Small Church*, has
learned through his research that many large churches, which are
envied by many small churches, are seeing the limitations that large
numbers bring. Building deep and intimate relationships in a large
church setting is difficult. So are nurturing a felt sense of belonging and inspiring enduring commitments. Oddly enough, these
churches that labored to get large are trying to recreate the small,
family-church experience within their congregations. O'Brien then
makes the point that leaders of small churches should recognize the
strategic value of our size. O'Brien explains:

> A strategically small church is one that has become comfort-
> able being small, because it has learned to recognize the unique
> advantages of its size. A strategically small church realizes it can
> accomplish things that larger churches cannot. This does not
> make it better or godlier. But it means it can proceed in ministries
> not from a sense of its deficiencies, but from confidence in its
> strengths. Strategically small churches are strategic for the king-
> dom of God, because when they embrace their identity, they can
> make an enormous impact.[22]

"Small is beautiful," taught E. F. Schumacher. Small is also powerful,
O'Brien insists. This matches the liberating reminder from Mother
Teresa that we're not all called to do great things but we can all do
"small things with great love." And, I would add, we can be "small
churches with great love." This belief in the spiritual and strategic

value of smallness also matches the message of Jesus when he compared his message and our movements to the smallness of a seed that grows, disrupts, and produces abundance. Among the greatest strengths of our small size is the unique capacity to nurture a sense of intimate and personalized belonging.

In *Imagining the Small Church*, pastor Steve Willis points to the feeling of belonging that comes when a church practices hospitality. So many of us are searching for a place and sense of belonging, especially in our unsettled and radically mobile culture. Willis argues that if small congregations can overcome the temptation to be exclusive and inward, they have a unique potential to offer that welcoming community to other folks. In a small church, it is possible to know and be known by every member of the congregation. "Over time this intimacy creates strong attachments and deep commitments that make the small church strong and tenacious," writes Willis. "In a time when the mainline church is losing many of the old cultural props, feelings of belonging and gifts of hospitality may be the small church's greatest gifts."[23] Once again, we are invited to flip the disadvantage on its head and see it as a possible advantage in the kingdom of God and the building of beloved community.

I'm inspired by the folks at the Church of the Mountain in Delaware Gap, Pennsylvania. This little Presbyterian church has become a much-beloved sanctuary for hikers on the Appalachian Trail (AT). It was the first hiker center on the AT; in 1976, the church opened up its basement (built in 1853) as a space for rest and rejuvenation. Hikers can recover or connect in the common room, sleep in the bunk room, or enjoy the precious bathrooms and showers. Church members provide rides into town, hold potlucks with home-cooked meals, and bring in local bands.[24]

I love the way this little church embraces its small size, rural location, and placement along the AT. Members used the assets they already had, like a simple and many-storied church building in rural Pennsylvania and good folks seeking to live Christ's message, and created something important and interesting. They get to help these hikers in a practical way with food, shelter, showers, and rides. But these guests give back; they tell their stories of struggle, accomplishment, major life events, and the stirrings that put them on the trail in the first place. It just so happens that the embrace of this mission may well have saved the church. They were down to fifteen people when they started the hostel. Today, there are one hundred fifty members, and they have added several ministry initiatives, locally and internationally.[25] Indeed, stories of hospitality like these remind us of the ancient wisdom: "Whoever refreshes others will be refreshed" (Prov 11:25). May our small and rural congregations all find ways to welcome and host the weary, wounded, and wonderful pilgrims traveling through life. May we all find room within our hearts and buildings for spaces of missional hospitality, even if it seems small and simple.

CHAPTER EIGHT

THE PRACTICE OF GROUNDING

There was plenty of grass in that place, and they sat down.

John 6:10

I'LL NEVER FORGET THE TIME I got lost in the woods as a kid. I was ten or twelve years old at the time and pretty familiar with the woods that stretched across several acres behind our house. In fact, I had forged my very own trail in those woods—the Henry Trail— which wound through my favorite spots, sometimes following streams or deer trails and occasionally intersecting with the well-worn four-wheeler paths. It led me past special landmarks, such as the teepee I built with the neighbor kid, the old shack where a scary squatter supposedly lived, and the only spot on the property where ferns grow. The Henry Trail was my preferred path, and it was reliable enough to take me out into the mysterious woodlands, then circle me back home.

But this time was different. I had just watched a John Wayne movie, so I was feeling rugged and adventurous. My imagination was running wild, and my spirit was soaring. I needed to set forth beyond the trustworthy paths I had pioneered and conquer a new territory. So I threw on my flannel shirt, grabbed my hat, and packed a canteen of water and a package of crackers for rations.

The journey was perfect for the first hour or so. I took the Henry Trail past the usual sites, stopping occasionally to check for deer near the field or beavers by the pond. But mostly I was pressing on, heading past these usual spots for new, untamed regions. I got to the place where the four-wheeler paths circled back, then I paused and stepped confidently off the beaten path into a brave new world. It was exhilarating. What new plants or animals would I encounter? What old glass bottles or discarded farm equipment or unused tree stands might be awaiting discovery? Might this be the beginning of a new and expanded Henry Trail?

My enthusiasm waned, however, when I realized that I was hiking outside the bounds of my friendly neighbor's woods. When I looked around, absolutely nothing looked familiar. I couldn't even tell where I had come from or which direction would take me back to the familiar paths. In the distance I saw some light peeking through the trees and realized there must be a field nearby. So I jogged over and did indeed find a field. But not a familiar one. After a couple more of these frantic and failed attempts to get back to a familiar place, or at least to regain my orientation, I began to panic. I froze as the terrifying truth sunk in: I was lost.

That moment of recognition when we realize we are lost is truly terrifying. Thankfully, after a couple hours of wandering, I found the road and followed it back home.

I would learn later that some smart folks have distilled the wisdom of hikers across the ages and come up with an acronym for just such an occasion: STOP. STOP stands for:

Stop. Sit down, stay put, and don't panic.
Think. Review the things you do know about your location
    and situation. Recall the advice of the United States
    Forest Service: "Do not move at all until you have a
    specific reason to take a step."

Observe. Look around and see if you can gather any more
information. Any signs or markings? Any distinctive
features that provide clues?

Plan. What are your options and potential course of action?
Choose one and proceed. Remember that this could
mean either pushing through or staying put, even
overnight if circumstances require.[1]

We all get lost at some point or another. We step off the well-
worn path and lose our way in the new country. Or we feel like the
old paths just loop round and round, taking us through the same
patterns when we need something new. Crossroads. Fork in the
road. Road less traveled. You know all the travel metaphors. And
you've probably lived them.

Small towns and rural communities get lost too. We lose our
way. Scarcity thinking and fear-based reactions take over. Even if a
previous path led us to abundance and renewal, we can't find our
way back to it. Before we recover our abundance, we have to reorient our thinking. Reorientation, it seems, precedes restoration.

How do we regain, or perhaps reset, our orientation? The STOP
acronym offers unexpected wisdom, even if you're not a small child
seeking adventure in rural Ohio. When we lose our way, the natural
reaction is to panic and start pushing one direction or another, hoping to find a place that's familiar and safe. But the voice of wisdom
tells us to stop, be still, and pay attention to what's around us.

SAVING STILLNESS

It turns out this STOP concept is not a new or novel idea. The Hebrew
Bible implores the people of Israel at several points to cease their
desperate and destructive behaviors and sit still. Standing between
a sea and an army of Egyptian oppressors, Moses told the people,
"The Lord will fight for you; you need only to be still" (Exod 14:14).
"Be still and know that I am God," the Divine Voice says through the

psalmist. The wise Christian teacher Thomas Merton advises, "Keep still, and let [God] do some work."[2] And Buddhist sage Thich Nhat Hanh tells us the important precondition to meditation: "The first thing to do is to stop whatever else you are doing."[3] It's that simple. And that hard.

Being still is not something most of our cultural systems reward. The name of the game is productivity. We have a terrible time being still. Even in small towns. Yes, we are free from the hustle and bustle of big cities. But we still work ourselves to the bone, whether because we are forced to by economics or because we can't face the quiet emotionally. One of our highest values, after all, is hard work. Nothing wrong with that—except when we realize hard work and pressing on won't help us find our way. So we learn to be still, have a seat, and look around for signs of wisdom and guidance.

Many of us, rural towns and institutions as well as individuals, have to get to that low point when we admit, to borrow the language of Alcoholics Anonymous, that "our lives [or organizations] have become unmanageable." The old tricks and tools aren't working anymore. And the old guard is keeping out the new ideas and new leaders we need. We can't "budget cut" or "bake sale" our way out of this. Whatever wisdom we need will come only after admitting our limitations, acknowledging our lostness, and sitting still long enough to let the wisdom reveal itself. Indiana essayist Scott Russell Sanders observes, "When the pain of leaving behind what we know outweighs the pain of embracing it, or when the power we face is overwhelming and neither flight nor fight will save us, there may be salvation in sitting still."[4]

Salvation by sitting still sounds absurd to most modern ears. When we get lost, we look at each other and demand, "Don't just sit there, do something!" Quakers like to joke that our faith inspires a different motto: "Don't just do something, sit there!"

Of course, we will have to "do something" at some point if we are to find the path again, but what's needed is not frantic, desperate action. Instead, we will take wise, deliberate steps based on what we discovered when we chose to STOP. Sanders's "saving still-ness," then, is not so much passivity as receptivity. He clarifies, "By sitting still I do not mean the paralysis of dread, like that of a rabbit frozen beneath the dive of a hawk. I mean something like reverence, a respectful waiting, a deep attentiveness to forces much greater than our own."[5]

SEATED BY JESUS

There's a detail in our gospel story that perplexed me for a long time. We are told that Jesus had the people divide into groups, which we've unpacked, but then he has them sit down. What's curious is the additional detail about Jesus instructing them to sit down "in the green grass." I initially assumed this was a throwaway detail. Where else would they sit? But as I continued to reflect on the phrase in the context of the larger narrative, I began to wonder if there was more meaning to it.

One possibility is that the phrase is an allusion to the shepherd-ing role of God revealed in Jesus. As the Divine Shepherd guides, restores, and feeds the sheep as they "lie down in green pastures" (Ps 23:2), so Jesus guided, restored, and fed that group of people who were, after all, like "sheep without a shepherd." Yes, this is a nice metaphor. But maybe it is more than a metaphor. Maybe there is something about sitting down on the ground, "on the green grass," that settles and centers us and opens us to the abundance of God. Perhaps sitting down, getting in touch with the earth, helps us make the shift from a posture of restlessness and competition to a posture of receptivity and cooperation.

When I looked closer at other gospel stories, I noticed that the gospels talk often about Jesus himself sitting down. He would sit by the lake and sit in the boat with his disciples. He sat down with "sinners" in open table fellowship. He sat down to teach. He praised Mary for sitting with him as a disciple, unlike Martha, who busied herself in anxiety. He also invited others to sit down. They sat down in mutuality, friendship, and discipleship. Maybe there is an element of convention in all this sitting—it wasn't particularly unusual for a teacher, or a disciple, to take a seat. But I think it's more. Something happens when we sit down. We lower our defenses. We soften our social hierarchies. We calm our breathing. We signal that we are prepared to rest, to feast, to listen, to share, to stay awhile. When we sit down on the ground, we feel like children again—children of God and children of the earth. And we literally get in touch with the earth from which we came and to which we will return.

The Jewish tradition that shaped Jesus provided stories like the creation narratives of Genesis in which the human being was formed from the earth. In these stories, God is lord of both cosmos and compost. And human beings are made in both the *imago Dei* (image of God) and the *imago terre* (image of the earth). The Hebrew reveals a wordplay in the words for "human" and "ground," *adam* and *adamah*. To be human is to be literally an "earth creature" or "groundling." The Creator formed the first human by shaping earth and breathing life into them. We need both earth and spirit to be whole human beings. We reconnect with our origin and recall the abundance of the Creator when we sit down on the ground in the green grass.

Contemporary scientists and scholars confirm the power and importance of grounding ourselves in the earth. Journalist Richard Louv broke ground with his popular book *Last Child in the Woods*, in which he proposed that North American children (and adults) are suffering from "nature-deficit disorder."[6] In the 1980s, ecologist Edward O. Wilson put forth the "biophilia hypothesis,"[7] which argues that human beings have an innate drive to seek connection with natural places and the community of creation. More recently, journalist Florence Williams traveled around the world and reviewed various studies to uncover how connection to nature makes us happier, healthier, more empathetic, and more creative.[8] These studies and stories—and their new language—inspired new practices. Two common practices are "grounding" or "earthing" one's body by placing bare feet on the ground and the practice of "forest bathing," popularized in Japan, during which individuals soak up the forest atmosphere by walking slowly in a wooded area and soaking in the serenity using all their senses.

These discoveries and practices confirm the ancient biblical wisdom of Genesis and Jesus. If the contemporary biosocial lingo sounds a little strange to you, remember the life and leadership of Jesus. Nearly all of Jesus's parables were agrarian, and I don't think they were only the product of his time. Parables about computers and satellites wouldn't have the same impact. There is something about the earth and natural processes that teach us about God's kingdom better than anything else. Jesus created these parables from a place of connection to nature, which he experienced as full of God's presence and activity. Australian theologian Denis Edwards remarks, "The parables reflect a close observation and delight in the natural world as the place of God. They could arise only in a person who looks on creation with contemplative and loving eyes."[9] Similarly, Benedictine abbot John Klassen notes, "The parables showed that Jesus assumed the worth of the created universe.... The natural world is the stage where the reign of God is enacted, the place where faith in God with all of its dimensions is lived out."[10]

Shaped by the creation stories of his tradition and his intimate experiences of God in the natural world, Jesus naturally taught truths about the divine wisdom and presence that permeates the earth. Perhaps Jesus knew that being grounded in the earth helps us recover a sense of abundance in the universe. Connection to the community of creation helps us see that God's world is full and free and fruitful. When Jesus wanted to teach his disciples about abundance in contrast to anxiety and fear, what did he talk about? He pointed them to nature:

> Therefore I tell you, do not worry about your life, what you will eat or drink; or about your body, what you will wear. Is not life more than food, and the body more than clothes? Look at the

birds of the air; they do not sow or reap or store away in barns, and yet your heavenly Father feeds them. Are you not much more valuable than they? Can any one of you by worrying add a single hour to your life?

And why do you worry about clothes? See how the flowers of the field grow. They do not labor or spin. Yet I tell you that not even Solomon in all his splendor was dressed like one of these. If that is how God clothes the grass of the field, which is here today and tomorrow is thrown into the fire, will he not much more clothe you—you of little faith? So do not worry, saying, "What shall we eat?" or "What shall we drink?" or "What shall we wear?" For the pagans run after all these things, and your heavenly Father knows that you need them. But seek first his kingdom and his righteousness, and all these things will be given to you as well. Therefore do not worry about tomorrow, for tomorrow will worry about itself. Each day has enough trouble of its own. (Matt 6:25–34)

Jesus knew that the birds, flowers, and other creatures could illustrate the reality of abundance better than any book. Being amid the wonders of creation opens within us the possibility that the kingdom is near and what we need is here. Walking within the miracle of the earth and its fullness awakens in us the sense that perhaps miracles are not so rare. We are a part of a larger communion that Wendell Berry calls the "Great Economy."[11] Parker Palmer observed the unique way that nature evokes within us an awareness of the ecology of abundance: "Here is a summertime truth: abundance is a communal act, the joint creation of an incredibly complex ecology in which each part functions on behalf of the whole and, in return, is sustained by the whole. Community not only creates abundance— community is abundance. If we could learn that equation from the world of nature, the human world might be transformed."[12] Jesus was indeed after human transformation, so it is no wonder that he invited his disciples to contemplate the wisdom of the natural world.

DOWN TO EARTH

Jesus's instruction to ground ourselves in the divine presence and wisdom within the natural world is a reminder of where God's activity is taking place. So much God-talk relates to God sitting on a throne in heaven, up in the sky. But Jesus's teachings remind us that God is moving about in the world around us and in the earth beneath our feet. Indeed, as Paul Tillich said, "God is the Ground of Being." Theologian Sallie McFague went so far as to suggest that the earth is "God's Body,"[13] through which God reaches and touches us and through which God is reached and touched. According to Genesis, as well as the discoveries of contemporary science, God created not out of the sky but through the earth. The poet John O'Donohue said that the land is the "firstborn of creation,"[14] which bears the memory of God and the history of life.

Authentic spiritual growth is always "down to earth" and not about getting so "heavenly minded" that we miss the divine presence all around us. There is something spiritually and physically healing about abiding as a grounded human being, rooted in the earth and the world that God gave us as our home. So often it is only after we have taken off our shoes that we realize we are walking on holy ground. It is when we are in touch with the earth that we realize why Jesus taught us to pray for God's reign "on earth as it is in heaven," not to fly away to heaven. When we recognize the vastness of creation and the overflowing bounty of God's provision, we recover a sense of abundance, and the systems of anxiety and fear lose their power.

In the feeding story of Mark 6, the disciples respond to the situation in contradiction to what Jesus had taught them. They were full of anxiety and worry about the dominating questions Jesus mentioned: "What shall we eat?" and "What shall we drink?" Reacting from the assumption of scarcity, they saw the needs and demands of the people before them and immediately forgot Jesus's wisdom. They certainly did not stop to "smell the roses" or "consider the lilies." With his personal practice and wisdom teaching in mind, we see the significance of Jesus's instruction to sit down in the green grass. Perhaps it was a way of grounding the community, reminding them of the abundance in God's world, settling them into a posture of peace and receptivity.

Recall also the story of Jesus's visit to the home of Mary and Martha in Luke 10. The two women responded to Jesus's presence in different ways. Martha busied herself with housework and hospitality—not bad things—but she was moving about the house and not being present with her guest. She was acting from the assumption of scarcity and the spirit of anxiety. She was worrying about "What shall we eat?" and "What shall we drink?" And she demanded that Jesus come to her defense. Martha was disappointed, however, when Jesus sided with her sister Mary. Why? Because Mary released her anxiety and was present to what and who was with her in the moment. How did she do this? She "*sat* at the Lord's feet, listening." Sitting down puts us in a posture to be attentive and responsive to who is with us and what is happening—perhaps something wondrous that we do not want to miss, that we will miss if we are running around in anxiety.

In some ways, the posture of attending to nature and grounding in the earth is easier in small towns and rural places. We have more room to breathe, more fields and forests to explore, more grass on which children can run, and less light pollution to hide the stars. The immediacy of nature and agriculture keeps the Creator's work before us. But even in our spacious and scenic homelands, we can become distracted or fall into the disciples' temptation of scarcity and anxiety. Our lives can fill with busyness and our minds fill with fear as quickly as those of folks in the city. We still need to be reminded to sit down in the green grass, pay attention to nature's wisdom, sit down at the table, and open ourselves to the abundance hidden all around us—in God's good universe. Ordinary leaders who seek to serve in the manner of Christ can commit to grounding themselves in the earth, in their place, and in the divine presence all around. They can take up the practice of sitting down to teach and talk with people, to be still and trust the Creator, to eat and celebrate with neighbors and sinners.

GROUNDING WITH GUESTS

In the spirit of reorientation, we can also learn to see our small towns and rural regions in light of what Kathleen Norris calls a "spiritual geography."[15] The country context might be just what many urban and suburban folks need. Many people are feeling breathless from the hurry and hustle of the urban or suburban lifestyle, the realities of traffic jams and lack of solitude. I remember getting stuck behind a tractor when I first moved back to Ohio. After working in Portland, Oregon, and routinely sitting in stop-and-go traffic, encountering a single tractor every few months isn't so bad. "I can handle this," I thought, breathing a breath of gratitude for the smoothness and spaciousness of my new commuting routine.

Because of their nearness to nature and sometimes isolated location, rural regions are often home to camping and retreat places: state parks, campgrounds, spiritual retreat centers, monastic communities, bed-and-breakfasts, and the like. These places are important economic assets, to be sure. They can be destinations for folks going on a family vacation or gathering for a family reunion or celebrating a lovely wedding. A town in my county draws scores of visitors and campers for skeet shooting competitions. But what if we also viewed these places as spaces for spiritual renewal? Circling back to the hospitality practice, what are ways our venues and visits can become opportunities for urban and suburban folks to reconnect with the earth and regain a sense of wholeness in their connection to creation and their common Creator? What value could we add by making these spaces where folks could breathe, be still, take a seat, and feel grounded again?

I like the work Mark and Margaret Yackel-Juleen are doing at Shalom Hill Farm in southwestern Minnesota. As a child and teen,

Mark was not a person one would expect to become a spokesperson for rural life and spiritual well-being. He grew up in the Minneapolis – St. Paul area. After seminary, however, his first call was to two Lutheran congregations in rural Minnesota. It was there that his education on rural life began. At one point, a congregant was showing him around town and took him on a tour of the local countryside. Looking at the fields, Mark was familiar with the corn crop but had to ask what the low green plants were. "Beans," the congregant answered. Mark was amazed. "A whole field of green beans?" "No," the man answered, "soybeans."

Mark also tells the story of driving home from a council meeting one night and seeing bright lights out in a field. A farmer was harvesting corn, driving a combine with its headlights on. Yackel-Juleen recalls with humor, "I thought it was a UFO—lights shining down, dust kicking up. I was expecting the car to stall and to have a close encounter. That's how much I didn't know."

His education continued as he served rural churches whose parishioners were hit hard by the farm and financial crisis of the 1980s. It wasn't long before he realized how little city folks knew about rural life, not least seminarians who would go on to serve in small towns. In his own denomination, the Evangelical Lutheran Church in America, about 70 percent of seminary graduates would end up serving in a rural parish. Over time, both Mark and Margaret began to catch a vision for a space where seminarians and pastors could come to learn about rural life and rural-flavored spirituality— and where urban and suburban folks could go to catch their breath and reconnect to the land.[16]

Mark and Margaret were able to purchase some land from Margaret's family, and they began creating Shalom Hill Farm. As their property was developed, their mission was also clarified. The farm exists to "educate and advocate on behalf of small-town and rural culture, community, ministry, God's creation, the common good, and provide a place of retreat and renewal for groups and individuals."[17] In addition to individual retreats and group gatherings, they offer programs such as the Annual Pitchfork and Hay retreat, where a guest speaker offers reflections on a theological topic, and STaR (Small Town and Rural) Ministry 101 and 102. They also offer workshops on creation care and a weekend experience called Common Ground Rural Immersion, in which guests experience things like:

- eating (or cooking) a hearty breakfast with farm-fresh eggs
- helping with farm chores, such as gathering eggs or feeding animals
- exploring rural justice issues through study and discussion
- discussing diversity issues with immigrants who are new to Southwest Minnesota
- breaking down stereotypes
- gathering under a starlit sky around a bonfire for singing or worship
- meeting a local youth group (church, 4-H, FFA)
- experiencing the often breathtaking prairie wind
- doing service projects like painting buildings or gardening
- experiencing rural hospitality and small-town life
- sharing stories unique to their own lives[18]

As our country seems to grow increasingly disconnected and divided, ordinary leaders can learn to see our unique geography as an asset for spiritual growth. We can provide space, like Shalom Hill Farm, where guests can be civically informed and spiritually formed.

WILD CHURCHES

Even as I propose ways rural leaders can welcome outsiders for spiritual refreshment and ecological reconnection, I don't want to suggest that rural folks themselves don't need grounding practices. While common features of rural landscapes have the potential to keep us connected to our place, it's not hard for us to stay glued to our devices and distractions and to live in the same default divided way that many nonrural folks live. We also need the healing and wisdom that comes from time outdoors and "on the green grass."

My wife, Ashlyn, and I practice grounding by regularly spending time outside, whether we're sharing a Sunday afternoon picnic on the grass, reading a book on a hammock secured between two trees, or taking a hike at a local state park. We are continually amazed at the restorative power of these simple practices. I should note, though, that different kinds of grounding practices might fit better in different seasons of life, and some fit better with different personalities. We laugh when we recall a particular outing at nearby Mohican State Park, where a heavy rainstorm hit halfway through our hike to a waterfall. I grew increasingly grumpy as we pressed on, my whole body, already damp with sweat from the humidity, getting soaked from the pouring rain. I just wanted to go home. Ashlyn, on the other hand, was serene and joyous. She got happier as we went along, embracing the showers like a heavenly baptism, and broke into tears when we finally reached the waterfall. I was crying too, but for different reasons.

Okay, so maybe I wasn't crying, but the point remains that different outdoor practices are more fitting for different people in different seasons. While there's something particularly impactful about literally sitting on the earth in a grounding or earthing practice, there are many ways to stay connected to the Creator through the community of creation. Maybe it's hiking to waterfalls. Maybe it's bird-watching. Maybe it's gardening. Maybe it's landscaping. When I was in seminary, I spent so much time in my mind or considering things of the spirit that the most grounding thing I did every day was feeding our chickens. They didn't care about my ecclesiology or eschatology; they wanted literal food and water. Every day. They did a "dance" while waiting for me to feed them, as if with their choreographed moves inside their coop they could summon their sleepy caretaker.

Some folks where I live stay grounded in the earth and connected with their Creator through the practices of hunting and fishing. And you know what? I don't think there's anything wrong with that. While it's possible to participate in those practices in ways that are irresponsible and irreverent, most folks I know do them in a respectful way that could almost be called a civic-spiritual practice. For some of my urban friends, this may sound bizarre, but the truth is that some of the most knowledgeable and careful conservationists I know are hunters and fishers.

In most rural towns, everyone, from teachers to pastors, knows that events during hunting season can be expected to have lower attendance. In my hometown, kids would miss school to hunt during deer season. For some families it was a multigenerational sacred pastime—maybe even more important than the county fair (we didn't even bother starting the school year until after fair week). This scheduling conflict can be frustrating for families and organizations trying to organize events and meetings. But one church in Woodville, Texas, has fully embraced this reality of rural life. The Church in the Country has chosen to embrace its rural setting, as you might have guessed by the name. Instead of trying to imitate a city megachurch or play the role of the kind of quaint country church where people can't bring their whole selves, they have chosen to strategically contextualize their church as one "with a country state of mind."[19] The church building is designed to look and feel like a Bass Pro Shop. Country chic abounds, and the worship music is a stylized mix of contemporary worship and bluegrass.

One particularly notable locally flavored element of their church life is how they've managed to transform their lowest-attended Sunday service into their highest. How? Camo Sunday. One Sunday every November, when a lot of folks in that part of Texas head to the woods to hunt, is designated Camo Sunday. On that Sunday, the congregation meets at 11:45 for a free community lunch. Hungry hunters are particularly welcomed to join them for lunch after a long morning in the field. During lunch, they might hear a short message from the pastor or a few minutes of stand-up from a comedian, after which there will be a big giveaway of hunting gear of all kinds. Most important, though, is that everyone is invited to wear their camo.

Maybe hunting isn't your thing. That's okay. But if you scoff at Camo Sunday, I wonder if it has just as much to do with elitism as it does with ethics. Why not acknowledge a common heritage and practice in your faith community and perhaps make it less about gun culture and more about being grounded in place, community, and stewardship? Why not meet folks where they are and learn from each other about how to stay grounded in this chaotic, anxious age?

If Camo Sunday doesn't fit your place or principles, there's good news. Congregations can help their community stay grounded in plenty of other ways. How about Earth Day Sunday? Share facts about the local ecosystem and watershed. Reflect on the biblical importance of the earth and the spirituality of experiencing God in the natural world. Highlight the moral imperative to steward the earth, especially in light of disturbing patterns of climate disruption. Ask people to share special memories they have of being outdoors, maybe at specific local places.

Many churches already have Harvest Sunday or some kind of harvest party or potluck. These are great reminders of the earth's bounty and God's generosity. Maybe place a thanksgiving altar in the sanctuary or fellowship hall. Have a produce swap-or-share table. My childhood church recently hosted Farmer Appreciation Sunday, when local farmers drove their tractors and farm equipment to church and showed them off to the parishioners. The kids got to climb up and into the tractors. During the service, the farmers were called to the front to receive a blessing and a prayer. On such a day, worship planners could invite a couple farmers to sit down for a discussion up front on that Sunday, with the pastor interviewing them about misconceptions regarding farming, how they got into farming, and how farming connects to their faith. Families with "century farms" could be honored. An award or recognition could be given to someone in the community who has labored for great sustainability in farming or the community's common life.

Organizations such as Catholic Rural Life have great resources for congregations seeking to ground their life and faith through liturgy and practice. They suggest celebrating Rural Life Sunday and commemorating days such as the Feast of Saint Francis, when many churches do a "blessing of the animals," or of Saint Isidore, the patron saint of farmers.[20] The possibilities are endless, but the important thing is to find ways to connect worship with the local place and people. Stained glass is lovely, but don't let the set-apart space of the sanctuary distract from the beauty and brokenness visible outside the windows. Whether we host a yoga group, outdoor services, special celebration Sundays, or a local food potluck, we offer windows into the possibilities of a grounded life in right relationship with the earth and its Creator.

Of course, many ways to practice grounding don't require traditional religious structures. Ashlyn and I did a series of gatherings in our local state park called Outdoor Church. We met in one of the park's pavilions on three Sunday afternoons for a time of dialogue, worship, and reflective hiking. We chose an element from nature—earth/soil, wind/breath, and water—as the theme for each Sunday. The element was matched with a biblical passage that we explored based on the assumption that Scripture and nature are God's "two books." After a couple worship songs and a short message, we provided a question or practice for folks to take with them as they walked somewhere in the park. Then we came back together to reflect on our experiences.

Each week we invited folks into this twin way of experiencing the divine by reading a quote by Wendell Berry:

> I don't think it is enough appreciated how much an outdoor book the Bible is. . . . It is best read and understood outdoors, and the farther outdoors the better. Or that has been my experience of it. Passages that within walls seem improbable or incredible, outdoors seem merely natural. This is because outdoors we are confronted everywhere with wonders; we

see that the miraculous is not extraordinary but the common
mode of existence. It is our daily bread.[21]

Berry's critical observation informs our practice of grounding.
Some things about Scripture and the divine work in the world are
nearly impossible to understand while sitting indoors. But when we
go outside and engage Scripture as an outdoor book, we begin to see
a whole new range of possibilities. In Berry's words, the miraculous
doesn't seem quite as "extraordinary." Here's another reminder of
why Jesus taught his disciples to contemplate the birds, the flowers,
and the natural world to understand the abundance of God's loving
reign.

We had a blast and received a lot of positive feedback about
these gatherings. Folks talked about how life-giving this way of spiritual practice was for them. They also talked about how surprisingly
rare it was for them to spend an hour outdoors, even though they
lived out in the country. It was a special opportunity for us all to
become grounded during a time when many of us were experiencing a lot of chaos, conflict, and change.

It turns out, not surprisingly, that Outdoor Church wasn't all
that original. Of course, many American Indian tribes have practiced a more grounded, ecologically aware spirituality for many
hundreds of years. I twice had the privilege of experiencing the
sweat lodge ceremony under the guidance of a Cherokee Christian
man. They were both profound experiences. No other practice has
made me feel more connected to the earth than I did during those
hours in complete darkness and extreme heat, sitting shirtless and
shoeless in a symbolic tent, praying, listening, sharing—soaking in
the Indigenous ceremony and spiritual tradition that places us all in
a great web of interconnected relationships.

Even beyond the Native American–based expressions of faith,
a network of spiritual community groups and congregations were
practicing a more grounded yet wild spirituality. It's called the Wild
Church Network and brings together groups from across North

America and beyond who are offering Christ-centered and earth-based expressions of faith community. Their website compares these emerging and multiplying groups to mushrooms: "Popping up all over the land, like wild mushrooms after a spring rain, Wild Church communities are responding to a call from deep within to change the way we relate to the natural world, moving 'from a collection of objects, to a communion of subjects' (Thomas Berry)."[22]

The mushroom analogy is a lovely word picture, and it reminds me of something historian and activist Rebecca Solnit wrote about in her book *Hope in the Dark*. She talks about how, after a good rain, mushrooms pop up from the earth as if they came out of nowhere. However, "Many come from a sometimes vast underground fungus that remains invisible and largely unknown," she explains. "What we call mushrooms, mycologists call the fruiting body of the larger, less visible fungus. Uprisings and revolutions are often considered to be spontaneous, but it is the less visible long-term organizing and groundwork—or underground work—that often laid the foundation."[23] This dynamic is another part of the power in our practice of grounding. Staying grounded not only allows us to calm our mind, center our soul, and connect our body with the body of God, but it also puts us in a position whereby we can more easily notice the hidden and holy actions that combine with a larger root system. This root system, perhaps in the darkest and most surprising of time, will pop up and bear fruit.

EARTH WITNESS

One of the most common and iconic images of the Buddha is the "earth witness" Buddha, sometimes called the *Bhumi-sparsha mudra*, meaning "gesture of touching the earth" posture. It depicts Buddha sitting in meditation with his left hand, palm open, in his lap while his right hand is touching the ground. It comes from a story about Siddhartha Gautama as he endured the demonic temptations in the moments before his enlightenment.

It is said that Siddhartha was sitting under the Bodhi tree, nearing enlightenment, when the demon Mara attacked him with a host of temptations, seductions, and insinuations, imploring an army of demons to disrupt his meditation. The last attack Mara attempted was the suggestion that Siddhartha had no right to occupy such a "seat" of enlightenment. "Who do you call as a witness?" Mara demanded. In response, Siddhartha extended his hand to gently touch the earth and replied, "I call the earth as my witness." The earth began to shake in affirmation and responded, "I am his witness!" Mara fled in defeat. And it is said that when the morning star rose in the sky, Siddhartha realized enlightenment and became the Buddha.[24]

While we can draw many messages of wisdom from this story, it reminds me of the importance of remaining grounded in trying times. In times of trouble and temptation, we can react in so many unhealthy and unhelpful ways. We can respond in kind; we can give in to hate or give ourselves to overwork. We can turn into ourselves in avoidance and denial. We can cry out to the heavens, demanding divine intervention and an immediate fix. But we also have the choice to sit and center, gently touching the earth and remembering that we are children of the earth and children of God, even while we open our other hand in receptivity, trusting that the wisdom, help, and resources we need will come. Our rural regions and small towns need ordinary leaders who can remain grounded in our age of distraction and domination. Only grounded leaders can access the inner resources required for skillful leadership and guide others to the resources they need for renewal.

CHAPTER NINE

THE PRACTICE OF GRATITUDE

Taking the five loaves and two fish and looking up to heaven, he gave thanks.

Mark 6:41

IN AN EARLIER CHAPTER, WE talked about family dinner tables and the ritual and relational patterns around the table that shape our lives. One of the rituals that was consistent and nonnegotiable in my household was saying grace before the meal. We would have self-serve meals from time to time—every Sunday evening, for example. At those meals we were encouraged to "pray to ourselves," which meant to pray *by* yourself or *within* yourself. But whenever we had a meal together, we said grace before we ate a single bite.

As the "head of the household," Dad led the prayer almost every time. His prayers were not lengthy, but they were heartfelt and tender. He typically began with something like "Father, we pause and thank you . . ." While we may have some theological differences, it would be hard for me to improve on this tender, thankful beginning. "Father . . ." My dad and I both relate to God as a Divine Parent who is loving, attentive, and caring. "We pause . . ." We both believe in the importance of taking time for prayer, reflection, and recognizing

God's presence and activity in our lives. "We thank you . . ." We both believe the first and foremost response to divine goodness and grace in the world should be gratitude. Neither of us could say it better than Meister Eckhart: "If the only prayer you ever say in your life is 'thank you,' that would suffice."[1]

I've heard hundreds of premeal prayers, spontaneous or memorized, some deeper than others. I remember liking one I learned as a kid: "Good food, good meat. Good God, let's eat!" And another classic, kid-friendly prayer I remember was: "God is great. God is good. Let us thank him for our food. Amen." My Catholic friends recited a prayer before meals that I've come to appreciate more over the years: "Bless us, O Lord, and these thy gifts which we are about to receive from thy bounty, through Christ, our Lord. Amen."

Though unique, all of these prayers have elements in common. They assume and address a good and generous God. They name the food, drink, and guests "gifts" from this Creator. And they reflect, to use the language from this book, an "assumption of abundance."

We call this ritual "saying *grace*" for a reason. The Greek word *charis* is translated as both "grace" and "gift." When we "say grace" before a meal, we are affirming the grace at the heart of the universe and the many ways we experience that grace in "these thy gifts," including the gifts of life-sustaining food, drink, and community. We cannot separate gratitude from grace. Indeed, as theologian Karl Barth wrote, "Grace and gratitude belong together like heaven and earth. Grace evokes gratitude like the voice an echo. Gratitude follows grace like thunder [follows] lightning."[2]

This connection between grace and gratitude orients our attention to "the Giver of all good gifts" (Jas 1:17) and the abundant world that exists under God's loving reign. In her book *Grateful: The Transformative Power of Giving Thanks*, Diana Butler Bass describes this orientation beautifully: "The universe is a gift. Life is a gift. Air, light, soil, and water are gifts. Friendship, love, sex, and family are gifts. We live on a gifted planet. Everything we need is here, with us."[3] The practice of gratitude changes the way we view our community and the wider world. Indeed, we don't just *say* grace, we learn to *see* grace. Everywhere. Because this is a gifted planet, continually created by a generous God who is the Giver of many good gifts. "To be grateful is to recognize the love of God in everything he has given us," wrote Thomas Merton, "and he has given us everything. Every breath we draw is a gift of his love, every moment of existence is a grace, for it brings with it immense graces from him."[4] What a world-view! If we really do dwell on a gifted planet and receive every breath and every moment by the love of God, that changes everything. We can breathe easier, live simpler, share more freely, and pray more joyfully. Merton goes on to say, "Gratitude therefore takes nothing for granted, is never unresponsive, is constantly awakening to new wonder and to praise the goodness of God. For the grateful person knows that God is good, not by hearsay but by experience. And that is what makes all the difference." If we were to live with that world-view, it really would make all the difference, both for our own mental health and for the life of the world.

GRATITUDE IN EVERYTHING

I like Merton's description of gratitude as dynamic. It's not a static "thank you," like a forced thanks to an aunt who gave you another ugly sweater for Christmas. Instead, it's an orientation of attentive-responsive thanksgiving that is "constantly awakening to new wonder." In other words, saying grace for the basics of life nurtures within us a practice of seeing grace in ever new ways and places. Gratitude is always expanding. G. K. Chesterton reflected, "You say grace before meals. All right. But I say grace before the concert and the opera, and grace before the play and pantomime, and grace before I open a book, and grace before painting, swimming, fencing, boxing, walking, playing, dancing and grace before I dip the pen in the ink."[5]

There's nothing wrong with maintaining a ritual of saying grace before a meal, of course. But that baseline practice should be expanding as we learn to see grace in the everyday and ordinary events of life. The structured practice can give way to a spontaneous expression of gratitude. We find ourselves whispering thank you as we watch our son stepping up to the plate for his Little League game. We can't help but say thank you when a grand sunset catches us by surprise. We even let out a silent thank you when a longtime friend comes to visit us in the hospital. We are sick but we are not alone. There is still grace in the world; we notice and cherish it.

Gratitude keeps growing until, in Merton's words, we learn to "see the love of God in everything." I want to stop here and make sure you don't hear me saying "everything is God's will" or even "everything that happens to you is a gift from God." The apostle Paul, for example, instructs us to "give thanks *in* all things" not *for* all things (1 Thess 5:18). And he says, "*in* all things God works for the good" (Rom 8:28) not "God sends all things for our good." Genuinely evil things happen in the world. If we believe that Jesus reveals the heart of God to us, we should not attribute these evils to God's hand. We live in an interrelated universe with many actors and factors. Sometimes things happen that are not good and not God. We don't force positive interpretations on others. We shouldn't pressure a rape survivor, for example, to proclaim their rape was actually a gift because God let it happen so she could help other rape victims. No, this is not the heart of God. But we can learn to witness grace in all circumstances. We can train our eyes to see the goodness and generosity of God that is always responsive to our suffering, always engaging with our life reality, always drawing us toward healing and transformation, always weaving together our beautiful and broken lives into something redemptive. We can acknowledge suffering while still finding gifts and graces in every moment, discovering "the love of God in everything."

GRATITUDE AS SOCIAL ACT

The reality of grace is so expansive that it trains us to see divine goodness in all directions. We look *up* to our Creator in gratitude, yes, but also *back* to our ancestors and *around* us to the workers and innovators who bring us many of the gifts we enjoy today, as well as to the great community of creation upon which we depend. "Suddenly all my ancestors are behind me," author Linda Hogan witnesses. "Be still, they say. Watch and listen. You are the result of the love of thousands."[6] When we recognize our interdependence with "the love of thousands," we can't help but feel gratitude rise within us. It not only impacts how we see God but also how we see our neighbors, nature, and our place in the world. "I argue that gratitude is not a transaction of debt and duty," submits Diana Butler Bass. "Rather, gratitude is a spiritual awareness and a social structure of gift and response."[7] The practice of gratitude opens our eyes to see the gifts before us and the abundance around us. And it moves us into a life of free responsiveness and responsibility toward the Giver and givers of good gifts.

Most Buddhists are not theists, but they still "say grace" in the sense that they reverently remember their interdependence with the broader community of neighbor, nature, and ancestor. One meal chant comes to mind often, helping me to gather up all the givers and gifts that go into even a simple meal. Sometimes called the Meal Gatha, it begins, "Innumerable labors brought us this food. May we know how it comes to us."[8]

Rural folks who garden or farm, or enjoy farmer friendships, should especially be able to relate to that first line. "Innumerable labors" indeed. Most of us have no idea. While the "farm to table" journey is becoming shorter in some cases, most of the time it's a massive undertaking, requiring farmers and farm workers, truckers and distributors, and grocery stores, stockers, and clerks. In gratitude, we remember them. We seek to use our consumer "vote" wisely and justly. We pray for their well-being.

When we study Jesus's life and ministry, we find ample evidence that he was a leader with a grace-based worldview. He knew that life was a gift from God. He knew the interdependence of the community of creation. He saw the abundance of God in the world. He embodied a spirit of compassion that comes from knowing our relatedness. Our gospel story in Mark 6 is no different. Jesus gathered up all the gifts that surfaced in that sacred space. He called them forth and collected them. And he lifted the gifts to God in gratitude.

We are told that Jesus said a "blessing." Typically, we think of this as praying a blessing over the food. I've known folks who are superstitious about this; if we don't pray a blessing over the food, we may be poisoned and get sick. While there may have been an element of blessing the food when Jesus prayed, the common Jewish practice of that time was actually to bless God. A contemporary blessing for a meal of bread (likely similar to one Jesus would use) goes something like this: "Blessed are You, Lord our God, Sovereign of the universe, who brings forth bread from the earth."[9] A good grounding prayer!

GRATITUDE AND TRANSFORMATION

In a sense, Jesus was transforming a common meal into a Eucharistic banquet as he took, blessed, broke, and shared the bread with everyone gathered. *Eucharist* comes from the Greek meaning "thanksgiving," and while denominations disagree about what exactly happens, all Christians see the bread differently after the blessing and thanksgiving than we did before. Though we acknowledge there is something special about the Lord's Supper practiced in common worship, perhaps we should also recognize there is something sacramental about sitting down and sharing a meal with others in any setting. After all, Jesus taught that whenever two or more gather in his name, he is present there (Matt 18:20). If it's true of two, it has to be true for over five thousand!

I believe that anytime we practice gathering our resources, lifting them up, and giving thanks, we see them differently. We see them through the lens of gift and gratitude. Gratitude transforms our way of seeing people, places, and things. Before giving thanks, we look at what we have as products to be sold, purchased, or consumed. After giving thanks we look at what we have as gifts to be received, cherished, and stewarded. Before giving thanks, we look at what we have as few and less. After giving thanks we look at what we have as bounty and blessing. What begins as a few loaves and fish becomes enough, more than enough—abundance. This is part of the transformation that happened through the leadership of Jesus in the story. He transformed restlessness into presence, a massive crowd into a cluster of communities, and a few pieces of food stuff into a feast for all. Biblical scholar Walter Brueggemann summarizes, "Jesus conducted a Eucharist, a gratitude. He demonstrated that the world is filled with abundance and freighted with generosity. If bread is broken and shared, there is enough for all. Jesus is engaged in the sacramental, subversive reordering of public reality."[10]

In the next chapter, we will go deeper into how Jesus engaged in that "sacramental, subversive reordering," but for now let's note the transformation Jesus facilitated by inserting gratitude into a situation of scarcity. It reminds us that gratitude is not only a private, individual self-care practice but also a public practice that has power to transform our perceptions and redirect our actions.

GRATITUDE AS RESISTANCE

Gratitude is in style. Everyone from new age gurus to neurologists are touting its many benefits for human well-being. While this trend is positive, it means we can easily dismiss gratitude as shallow. Some see it as a practice for the privileged, who count their coins and list their blessings at the expense of awareness of and advocacy for the underprivileged. Others point out that it can be a form of denial, allowing us to ignore our issues or injustices by focusing only on the positive. These are legitimate critiques. However, gratitude can also be empowering. In a time of devastation and despair, it allows us to reframe our perspectives on power and provision. When we notice goodness, truth, and beauty, even while we are surrounded by evil, lies, and ugliness, we insist that another world is possible. Domination and violence are not the only tools for changing the world, and they are not the only story about what is unfolding in the world. The practice of giving thanks reminds us that the ultimate Source and Provider is not the market, the government, or human ingenuity but the Creator. When we turn our attention to the gifts around us, we cultivate our awareness of the One who "brings forth bread from the earth" and, as the psalmist puts it, the One who "owns the cattle on a thousand hills" (Ps 50:10). From this sense of sufficiency, we are freed from the fear that drives violence, hoarding, and isolation. The author and monk Brother David Steindl-Rast put it this way:

> Violence springs from the root of fear—fear that there may not be enough for all, fear of others as potential competitors, fear of foreigners and strangers. But the grateful person is fearless. Thereby she cuts off the very root of violence. Out of a sense-of-enough she is willing to share and thereby tends to eliminate the unjust distribution of wealth that creates the climate for violence. Fearlessly, she welcomes the new and strange, finds herself enriched by differences, and celebrates variety.[11]

Gratitude allows us to release fear and take up courage and compassion. In a culture of violent competition, this is no small thing. In fact, I agree with Diana Butler Bass when she says, "Gratitude is defiance of sorts, the defiance of kindness in the face of anger, of connection in the face of division, and hope in the face of fear. Gratitude does not acquiesce to evil—it resists evil."[12] In a world that often feels like it's overflowing with resentment and contempt, cultivating gratitude and its fruit of kindness and collaboration becomes a socially and spiritually revolutionary act.

Furthermore, gratitude is a necessary act because without gratitude we can't see grace, we miss the kin-dom's appearance, and we neglect the gifts and givers. "Resentment and gratitude cannot coexist," Henri Nouwen reminds us, "since resentment blocks the perception and experience of life as a gift."[13] God doesn't withhold gifts from ungrateful children. But when we don't recognize them as gifts, we can't receive them from the Giver because our hands are clenched, prepared to take and protect rather than receive and share.

GRATITUDE IN MY TOWN

Rural people are often grateful people. We try to notice the simple joys of life and not take them for granted. We sing and tell stories about gifts like family life, good food, summertime, faith, freedom, and time spent with friends outdoors. This is a strength to claim as we recover abundance in our homes, faith communities, and towns. We remind the world to slow down, take it in, and count blessings. "Don't blink," Kenny Chesney reminds us. "You're gonna miss this," Trace Adkins says. Country and community pride is a form of gratitude. "This is my town," we say, grateful that we are fortunate enough to know this place and these people. Nothing wrong with that. In fact, I think our country would benefit from a little more pride of place. But there is a shallow version of this gratitude, much like there is a narrow version of hospitality. And this shallow version has a shadow side.

"This is my town" sounds lovely when it's shared with affection and welcome to guests. But those same words can take on a decidedly different tone when they are said to close the door and build a wall: "This is *my* town." It's not yours. It's not open for business. It's not open for immigrants. It's not open to new folks and new ideas. Gratitude that is closed off to surprise and novelty is no gratitude at all. Brother Steindl-Rast writes that surprise is the gate of gratitude: "In moments of surprise we catch at least a glimpse of the joy to which gratefulness opens the door. More than that—in moments of surprise we already have a foot in the door."[14] Without openness to surprise, we miss out on the joy and peace that gratitude brings. And we miss out on the communal transformation that collective gratitude initiates. After all, without surprise there is no miracle. There's nothing new under the sun. Without surprise, there is no multiplication, there is only subtraction. Small-town scarcity becomes a self-fulfilling prophecy.

GRATITUDE AND THE ECONOMY OF MERCY

Believe it or not, I was a team captain for my high school varsity basketball team. I was kind of a big deal. Granted, I went to a small Christian school in small-town Ohio, but still . . . Being a team captain came with privileges; we got to go out first for the pregame warm up while the crowd went wild for us. And our pregame uniform was a bit different from the rest of the team's, so people knew how cool and talented we were. But it also came with some responsibilities. Being a Christian school, one of those responsibilities was to lead the team in prayer. Often the coach would lead the prayer before the game, and a team captain would lead the prayer afterward. Understand that these were typically not victory prayers—again, small Christian school. One of my few "claims to fame" is that I once got to play against LeBron James. Of course, that name didn't mean anything at the time. But even then, he was quite good. And his team was quite good. As I recall, we scored eight or ten points the whole game, and they were approaching triple digits. So the postgame prayer was often an attempt to salvage team morale as we licked our wounds and got ready to change our clothes.

One evening after the game, our coach asked me to pray. I was feeling exhausted and defeated, and nothing was immediately coming to mind for a way to rally the troops to fight another day. However, I had been reading a book called *Wild at Heart* that was all the rage in the evangelical world at the time. It put forth a vision of masculinity that embraced the wildness and strength of the masculine soul as God's good design. It pointed to manly men like William Wallace from the movie *Braveheart* as the archetypal image of biblical masculinity. With the cry of "Freeeeeedom!" rising in my masculine heart, I determined, in the seconds between "Will you pray?" and "Dear Lord," that I could revive the team with a prayer inspired by *Wild at Heart*. What came out? "Dear Lord, thank you that we are not women . . ."

While my prayer slipup was more about nervousness and misguided theology than about male superiority or self-importance, sometimes exercises in gratitude devolve in a similar fashion. We thank God for how great we are or how great we have it or how we are going to be made great again. Or more subtly, we thank God that we have a cushy job and good food and nice clothes when so many do not. And there's nothing wrong with that so long as it's not a practice in setting ourselves above or against others.

Jesus even speaks directly about this error in a parable about two men who visit the temple to pray (Luke 18). One prays loudly and proudly, "God, I thank you that I am not like other people— robbers, evildoers, adulterers—or even like this tax collector. I fast twice a week and give a tenth of all I get." His prayer of "gratitude" was nothing more than an exercise in image management and self-justification. The other man, by contrast, prays humbly and quietly, "God, have mercy on me, a sinner." Authentic gratitude inspires humility because it reminds us that we live in an economy of mercy. We are what we are and we have what we have through the generosity and grace of others, and ultimately the goodness of God. We look back and take notice of all the "givers" that made the "good gifts" possible. And, though we worked hard to get them, and get here, we are ultimately the beneficiaries of mercy.

GRATITUDE AS LEADERSHIP

In the middle of a hangry and anxious crowd and coleaders driven by scarcity and competition, Jesus gave thanks. It was a public, prayerful, and prophetic act that shifted the atmosphere. This is a critical practice for ordinary leaders in small towns and rural regions. Practicing gratitude in our personal life is important, to be sure, but it's also an important act of community leadership. And it has many similarities with the practice of inventory. It's about shifting the attention and energies of the group toward what is present and possible rather than what is absent and improbable.

Ordinary leaders know that gratitude is a skillful leadership move. When we have a meeting and the group spirals down into scarcity thinking, we redirect the energy by asking the group to consider where there is life, energy, and possibility. Marketing strategist Ryan Holiday points out, "Focusing exclusively on what is in our power magnifies and enhances our power. But every ounce of energy directed at things we can't actually influence is wasted, self-indulgent, and self-destructive."[15] Small-town and rural folks can easily get stuck on what we can't do and the resources we don't have. Indeed, there are real limitations, frustrations, and pains. But sometimes when we shift our energy and focus, an unexpected transformation occurs. It turns out that we didn't even know what to be grateful for. Things we thought were problems are actually opportunities in disguise.

Consider the folks in Ogallala, Nebraska, who worked for decades to rid their fields of pesky milkweed. They had little success. A few farmers, however, set about reframing the persistent weed. What if they started harvesting it instead of trying to eliminate it? What if the thing they previously saw as a liability was actually an asset? It turns out that Ralph Waldo Emerson was right: a weed really is "a plant whose virtues are yet to be discovered." They began to harvest the milkweed and extract the fibers, which are and made into a comfortable and hypoallergenic product called Ogallala down and used to fill pillows. The venture turned out to be quite profitable. Oil from the seeds is also used as a balm for soothing muscles. Not only that, since milkweed is the sole food source for the monarch butterfly caterpillar, the company has worked to protect patches of wild milkweed habitat for the monarch's migration and encouraged other private landowners to do the same.[16]

GATHERING THE GIFTS

Ordinary leaders find ways to imitate Jesus by calling forth and collecting the resources, gathering the group's gifts. If we don't make them center stage, other folks are always ready to put something else in the middle and focus people's attention on it. Good leaders center the group around exercises of group gratitude. What are you grateful for? What has been going well? Where is there life and energy?

Once we have the gifts and resources in front of us, we pause to acknowledge and honor what has emerged by God's grace. Then we are positioned to ask, "What is up here that we need more of?" After all, as anti-hunger activist Lynne Twist says, "What we appreciate, appreciates."[17] How can we combine and connect these assets to create something new? How can we honor what we have? How can we expand on this beginning?

Don't worry; we don't avoid the difficult or the painful, either. We name the elephant in the room, but we don't let it take center stage. That space is for the gifts, the assets, the offering. That's the grateful space. When something is really blocking or dividing us, we name it, we grieve it, we express it. But again, we don't let it dominate. We ask, as entrepreneur Michael Hyatt reminds us, "What does this make possible?"[18] Where is the profitable milkweed in our field that we now see as only a nasty weed getting in our way?

If your organization or group is faith based, learn from Jesus. Lift up your problem or possibility to God. Take some time as a team to gather your gifts (figuratively speaking, though there may also be ways to do so in a physical, symbolic way), considering together what relevant wisdom and resources are already available. Give thanks and place them in Divine Hands. Bless God for what's alive, working, and good, and ask God to bless them in surprising and abundant ways. Ask God to guide you on how to steward, share, spend, or invest those gifts. Then listen. And invite others in the group to listen. Give them specific contemplative practices to help them listen for the holy whisper, and choose a time to come back and discuss what they heard.

GRATITUDE AND RESILIENCE

When I moved to Kansas for college, I lived about fifteen minutes from a small town of about twelve hundred called Greensburg. I visited there soon after moving, but there wasn't much to see. Why? Not because it was a small town in rural Kansas but because the town had been almost entirely destroyed by a violent tornado that ripped through the region at 200 miles per hour not long before I moved there. Many rebuilding efforts were taking place; I swung a hammer for a few houses with some other guys on a couple of Saturdays. What I wasn't fully aware of were the discussions and debates taking place among town residents and council members about the recovery and rebuilding process.

After a contentious series of public meetings and proposals, the town agreed to a unique approach to rebuilding. They would not rebuild a replica of the town as it had been before the tornado. No, they were going to rebuild in an unexpected way that would inspire other communities toward sustainability, resilience, and innovation. In the words of then-governor Kathleen Sebelius, they were going to put the "green" in "Greensburg." The town now runs 100 percent on wind energy. They designed and engineered the whole town to incorporate green standards and best practices.[19] I got to see the town progress as the plan unfolded, a truly remarkable sight—and an unexpected one for rural southwestern Kansas.

The rebuilding plan went well but not perfectly. They had to change some designs and move a couple small wind turbines to adapt to their particular microclimate and microculture. Local holdouts opposed the projects from beginning to end. But what I witnessed in this remarkable transformation was a community of resilient folks who survived a life-threatening, life-altering tornado, came together to rebuild better than ever, and turned the very thing that threatened them—wind—into an incredible energy source. Through the process they stayed grateful—for their survival, for each other, and for a hopeful future. And they reinvested their assets—their name, their prairie principles, their resilience and strength, their experience as stewards of the land, and their neighborly ethic—to create something inspiring and enduring.

I want to emphasize the link between gratitude and resilience. This may seem like a surprising or strange connection to make, but researchers have discovered a strong linkage. Researcher Robert Emmons tells us that focusing on gratitude in times of suffering and challenge may seem inappropriate, but it's actually an essential practice. "In fact, it is precisely under crisis conditions when we have the most to gain by a grateful perspective on life," Emmons argues. "In the face of demoralization, gratitude has the power to energize. In the face of brokenness, gratitude has the power to heal. In the face of despair, gratitude has the power to bring hope."[20] This is the spirit that prevailed in Greensburg, Kansas. An NPR story about Greensburg quoted the mayor-elect Bob Dixson: "It's sad that the tragedy of the storm came through and wiped us out, but that presented us with a golden opportunity." It adds something surprising: "Amazingly, many people here speak with gratitude about the storm that crushed the town. Greensburg had dwindled for decades, and the storm offered a fresh start."[21]

My point is not to idealize Greensburg or to suggest devastating natural disasters should be met with smiles and thanksgiving. But the scientific consensus suggests that climate disruption is only going to increase and severe weather events are going to become more common. Ordinary leaders and rural communities will need to develop robust gratitude practices, not only to support their own mental health but for the sustainability and resilience of their communities. I have a feeling that the skills that gratitude strengthens, such as managing stress, building social connections, and discovering possibilities, will become increasingly essential. Rural communities are strong, but we will need to develop strength that is shaped as much by adaptability as by endurance. Whether we are rebuilding after a storm or planning for community development, we will need to keep rural resilience in mind.

GRATITUDE INTERVENTIONS

There is an emerging trend in the world of placemaking and community health called "joyful intervention." The foundational idea is that the layout, design, and infrastructure of our towns and cities have psychological impact. Dark alleys, empty shops, drab storefronts aren't neutral features. I think of the old factory building I drive past several times a week. It used to be an economic engine for our town, employing hundreds of people, supporting families, and offering new possibilities for folks in the county. It closed decades ago, but the huge building remains. It stands as a reminder of a better economic past . . . that is long gone. The building is abandoned, dozens of windows busted out, the grass growing higher than humans. Maybe a company will be able to buy it, restore it, and use it for something else. But I sometimes wonder if it would be better just to tear it down and bulldoze it over. We are doing okay now, and it's a discouraging sight we don't need.

Not only this hulking shell but all our streetscapes and infrastructure have a psychological impact. Fortunately, some sharp and creative folks have started designing "joyful interventions." Designer Ingrid Fetell explains, "The infectious quality of joy makes its dispersion as efficient as the most prolific weed. Even the smallest efforts—a painted mural, a knit cozy around a parking meter, a single flower—can be the beginning of an upward spiral that changes a community, a neighborhood, a life."[22] Hear me, rural friends: whether you realize it or not, there are artists in your community. Some have been begging to carry out a local project for years, others have been far too shy to make themselves known. But they are there. And their presence and gifts are essential to your town and region's well-being.

These joyful interventions are worth the investment and sure to inspire gratitude. But I would like to adapt the idea and apply it in the form of "gratitude interventions." These may involve art installations, but they may also just involve the way we use our words, our meetings, our parties, our calendars. If you grew up in an era anywhere close to mine, especially if you didn't have cable television, you will be familiar with the Public Broadcasting Service (PBS) moment when they tell us how their programming was made possible. They name foundations and organizations, and last but not least "contributions to your PBS station from viewers like you." Especially in small towns, we need to make space in our events, gatherings, and meetings for the reminder, "This wouldn't be possible without the generosity and partnership of 'viewers like you'"—or more like "'neighbors like you.'" That's a gratitude intervention. It reminds us that we are appreciated and that we appreciate others. It reminds us that we are in this together. It reminds us that more is possible than we imagined when we do it together.

Another public gratitude intervention that may surprise you is a town parade. We have multiple parades every year in my hometown, but often the only one I get to is the Christmas parade. To be honest, every year I almost decide not to go. I start to think it's boring, it's cheesy, it's freezing, it's not worth the effort. But every year I decide to go. And it is freezing and it is kinda cheesy. But it's also kinda beautiful. We open up all the shops for an open house, and folks pass out hot dogs and hot chocolate. Horse-drawn carriage rides and wandering Christmas characters fill the streets. And after a couple hours of shopping and talking and warming up, the parade begins. Cue the Christmas music over the speakers. And one by one the floats drive past. The people wave, the candy flies, the creativity is admired (or mocked). And after a few floats I think that the parade must be coming to a close. We're a small town. How many bands, displays, and dignitaries could there be? But they keep coming. One by one they pass before our eyes and travel slowly across town until nearly every business and organization and church and association has been paraded and celebrated. And I'm surprised by joy. I actually feel like "what we need is here." And I'm grateful. (But still cold.)

LOVED INTO BEING

My favorite gratitude intervention has to be one that Fred Rogers (a.k.a. Mister Rogers) performed on the most unlikely of occasions: the Emmy Awards. Sure, lots of guys and gals say thanks when they receive their award, but often the thank-yous seem to be mostly about *their* talent, attractiveness, and achievement. Well, Mr. Rogers did things differently.

Fred climbed the stairs and stood behind the podium. And rather than focusing on himself, he turned his attention to others. Not only the others who were there in the room but also the invisible others not in the room who made the success and flourishing of those people possible. He said, "All of us have special ones who have loved us into being. Would you just take, along with me, ten seconds to think of the people who have helped you become who you are—those who have cared about you and wanted what was best for you in life? Ten seconds of time. I'll watch the time." So, the whole room hushed, and memories filled their hearts and minds. Many began to cry. And after those sacred ten seconds, Mr. Rogers said, "Whomever you've been thinking about . . . how pleased they must be to know the difference you feel they've made. You know, they're the kind of people television does well to offer our world."[23] He transformed that moment, one often defined by vanity and individual achievement, into a holy moment of intergenerational thanksgiving and openheartedness. It was a gratitude intervention.

Let me ask you this: Who has loved you into being? During a hard time in your life? In the daily grind? In the big win moments? We keep their faces and graces before us. And we use our words, written and spoken, to make known the truth that their love has not gone unnoticed. Let's not stop there. Who has loved your community into being? Who shows up, serves, contributes, risks, gives? Who is ready to love it into new ways of being if we give them a chance?

Ordinary leaders in small towns and rural regions are moved by gratitude. They notice the "innumerable labors" and the invisible helpers. They make the effort to insert gratitude interventions into our common life. And they seek to become the kind of people who love their neighbors, love their community, into being and thus become co-creators with the ever-loving God.

CHAPTER TEN

THE PRACTICE OF GENEROSITY

Here is a boy with five small barley loaves and two small fish.

John 6:9

SISTER SIMONE CAMPBELL, CATHOLIC NUN and social justice advocate, talks about how frustrated she got when reading the story of Jesus feeding the multitude, only to have the story conclude in Matthew's gospel with the summary, "And those who ate were five thousand men, *not counting women and children*" (Matt 14:21). She decided to take her outrage to God during her daily time of prayer and contemplation to find out what that was all about. What came to her was that only the men were counted because they were the only ones who thought it was a miracle! The women would never have left home for a day trip with children and brought absolutely nothing to eat or drink. The women unpacked what they brought with them and shared it with those around them.[1] Considering how oblivious I was when I took over organizing those fellowship meals and how amazed I was when we succeeded, Sister Simone's inspired interpretation may not be far off.

While Sister Simone's take on the story may have been playful as well as prayerful, there is actually a long-running debate among scholars as to what kind of miracle is being described in the story.

What manner of miracle was it? Was it a miracle of multiplication or distribution? Was it a miracle of Jesus's power or human sharing? In other words, was the point of the story that bread was transformed or that hearts were transformed?

Some scholars suggest that we miss the point if we read the story as a "miracle of multiplication." Jesus scholar John Dominic Crossan argues that the point of the story is not multiplication but distribution, and the bread is not manna from heaven but food that is already present but offered to the just hands of God-in-Christ.[2] The miracle happened when people trusted in Jesus's kingdom message and were willing to share their resources with everyone in a spirit of cooperation and community. Even William Barclay, a biblical commentary author often quoted by evangelicals, proposes, "This is a miracle in which the presence of Jesus turned a crowd of selfish men and women into a fellowship of sharers. It may be that this story represents the biggest miracle of all—one which changed not loaves and fishes, but men and women."[3]

There is no shortage of preachers and teachers who critique, or even mock, this interpretation. They argue that it diminishes the miracle's significance by forcing a natural interpretation on a super-natural event. The point of the story, they insist, is not human gen-erosity or cooperation but the divine power of Jesus Christ. If it was merely about sharing and not the miraculous power of the Messiah, then the gospel writers wouldn't have considered it so remarkable that all four of them included it. Father James Martin writes, "The idea that sharing food would have so flabbergasted Jesus' followers that all four evangelists would make room for it in their Gospels . . . is hard to fathom. Only one other miracle narrative appears in all four Gospels: the Resurrection."[4]

MORE OF A MIRACLE?

Father Martin makes a powerful point, but all the debate over the mechanics of the miracle can distract us from the meaning of the miracle. The miracle wasn't just that there was abundance;

the miracle was that the abundance was *shared*. The punch line at the end of the story points to this: they *all* ate and were satisfied. Anyone with even a cursory knowledge of economics knows that distributing resources widely enough that everyone has what they need is a not-so-minor miracle. And any parent or cook who has prepared food for more than a couple of people knows that making a meal that satisfies everyone is next to impossible.

A miracle of multiplication without the miracle of distribution wouldn't be much of a miracle at all. Capitalism can multiply money with no help from Jesus or his friends. But in the kin-dom of God that Jesus demonstrated, there is both more than enough and more than enough *for everyone*.

Would a miracle of generosity be less of a miracle than one of multiplication? I don't think so. Consider the communities living out Jesus's message in the early church. Acts tells us that the Spirit of God transformed the disparate groups into a diverse but united fellowship with a profound sense of mission. Part of the powerful prophetic witness made manifest by this community was the miracle of distributive justice:

> All the believers were one in heart and mind. No one claimed that any of their possessions was their own, but they shared everything they had. With great power the apostles continued to testify to the resurrection of the Lord Jesus. And God's grace was so powerfully at work in them all that there were no needy persons among them. For from time to time those who owned land or houses sold them, brought the money from the sales and put it at the apostles' feet, and it was distributed to anyone who had need. (Acts 4:32–35)

Empowered by the divine grace "so powerfully at work in them all," these early fellowships made sure that there was enough for everyone. If anyone at all was being left out or left behind, they would take care of them, either through economic activity (selling) or generous giving (sharing).

GENERATIVITY

God's creative grace is still "powerfully at work" through our acts of sharing and generosity today. Our sharing has the power to shape our communities. Generosity is generative. It sustains, initiates, creates. It brings new things into the world that weren't there before, whether it's a new enterprise or a new sense of hope for the future. Generosity is no less a miracle than supernatural multiplication when we see it as participation in God's ongoing creative and redemptive work in the world. It provides us an opportunity to be co-creators with God.

In order to experience and embrace this partnership with God, we need to explore the ways that money works in our small towns and rural regions. I want to acknowledge quickly that generosity is about more than money, of course. The practice of generosity invites us to cultivate a generous spirit and thus live an increasingly generous life. We share our thoughts, words, time, talents, energy. Nevertheless, while generosity is *more than* money, it is not *less than* money. And financial challenges are profoundly common in most small towns and rural regions. We need to talk about money.

Money, as Lynne Twist explains in *The Soul of Money*, is "a current, a carrier, a conduit for our intentions." Therefore, it can carry "blessed energy, possibility, and intention, or it can carry control, domination, and guilt."[5] This is close to the teachings of Jesus, who said, "Where your treasure is, there your heart will be also" (Matt 6:21). Generosity isn't something we conjure up so we can be good people. It is about entering the currents of grace at work in our lives and in the world. The flow is one of giving and receiving as we learn to become channels of divine grace in the world. When we only give, the flow dries up, and we become resentful and bitter. When we only receive, we dam the flow and keep it from reaching others as well as ourselves. When we are in the flow, we are co-creators with God in shaping and stewarding the world.

Whether or not we have named the experience, we have all felt different energies attached to money. We've all experienced gifts given to us "with strings attached." The gift doesn't feel like a gift but like a tool for manipulation or even a weapon. And we've also experienced a gift that was simple but carried with it a spirit of love, celebration, or encouragement from the giver.

There is a family, call them the Burgs, who live in my county and happen to be quite wealthy. They have lived in the region for generations, and the patriarch made his money from oil wells, farming, and several business ventures. The Burgs have given away a lot of money to local organizations and have invested heavily in local economic development. Their generosity has generated new things that didn't exist before: a new restaurant, daycare, laundry mat, campground, walking path, and more, to say nothing of the jobs, tax revenue, and morale as residents see the possibilities of growth. The Burgs' generosity has also generated things I think are less positive for the county. They use their wealth to support political candidates who support policies I believe are harmful to the region. They have enabled business and regulatory practices that pollute our fields and streams.

Most ordinary leaders in rural regions and small towns can quickly identify those "movers and shakers" or "givers and funders" who are comfortable exercising generative generosity in the community. When we consider the flow of wealth in our own communities, then, we need to be aware of two financial dimensions at the same time. We are attentive to *where* money is flowing within our region (the organizational financial flow). Who is giving? Where is the money going? What people and projects are being supported or neglected? But the second dimension is the question of *how* the money is flowing (the civic spiritual flow). What energies or expectations are attached to that money? What values are being reinforced by that money? What kind of citizen or community is being nurtured by the flow of money in our community? Think of money and wealth like a river moving through your region. Where is the water flowing, and what kinds of life is it nourishing as it goes?

AVAILABILITY

Awareness of where and how wealth is flowing is critical. But it's also important to remember that we are not passive observers of that flow. We are participants who have a part to play in moving the waters. We are partners with God in channeling resources and renewing our regions. You see, generosity enables generativity, but it requires availability. There is power in planned giving, strategic investment, and just distribution, to be sure. But the basic posture of a generous person is one of availability. We make ourselves available to God and however God chooses to show up. Jesus's example reminds us that the with-God life is an adventure of availability. Jesus's life was one of radical availability, and the miracle of Mark 6 demonstrates Jesus's readiness for the Spirit's surprises. With no room for surprise, the miracle would not have been possible.

Availability means that we manage our resources *responsibly*, to be sure, but we also release them *responsively*, leaving room for the promptings and surprises of the Spirit. Yes, we balance our budgets and plan for strategic giving, but we also learn that when hungry folks show up on our path, Jesus's way is to keep our eyes open for loaves and fishes that show up when we don't expect them. A posture of generosity means we avoid the disciples' approach— relying only on common sense and scarcity economics. We learn from the Master: Jesus discerned the moment and decided to trust in the flow of divine provision. He knew not to sell the Spirit short, and he knew that provision flows toward obedient responsiveness. He acted with a ready, responsive heart and a spirit of availability.

Writing about the context of hospitality, church historian Amy Oden states, "Ready hearts trust not so much that we will succeed in some particular outcome, but that God will do a new thing. Such readiness takes courage, gratitude, and radical openness."[6] Since God is always doing a new thing, we, as the partners of God, should be ready to do new things or give in new ways. Ordinary leaders have boundaries and clear commitments, to be sure, but they are radically available to God and the Spirit's surprises.

When I think of small-town leaders who exemplify generosity, I think of Leslie. She lives in nearby Cardington, Ohio, and I have seen her practice generosity in countless ways. Leslie's family has lived in the community for several generations, and she builds on that heritage with her unique style of business savvy, philanthropy, and spiritual awareness. After living in the city in young adulthood, Leslie moved back to Cardington with her wife and reconnected with her roots. She got involved in local development groups and took over a tax accounting practice. When she noticed the social and economic life of the community growing stagnant, Leslie made herself available by meeting with others to explore ways they could bring about renewal. She brought new ideas to existing institutions while also starting a new community Christmas event that was wildly successful. And when her business grew and moved into a new building, she transformed her old building into People Place, where local folks can learn ways to develop themselves through body work, spiritual practices, and coaching. People who are interested in these ways to wellness no longer have to travel an hour to Columbus. But even more than these excellent examples of generosity, Leslie practices generosity most often through her mindful availability. When she hears about a need in the community, she finds a creative way to meet it. When someone is struggling, she is available with a kind and sincere presence. When someone has an idea, she gives of her time and money to see if they can make it happen. When hateful political signs popped up in her community, she purchased hundreds of signs and bumper stickers, sharing the simple but critical message "love one another." The signs and stickers are now spreading across the country and even around the world.

Leslie may sound like a charismatic leader or activist, but anyone who knows her knows that she is quite humble. Harkening to previous practices we've discussed, Leslie is a grounded and grateful individual. And I think those characteristics are what enable her to be a generous person. Leslie always reminds me of what we can do together when ordinary leaders make themselves available to God and their neighbors. And she reminds me of how beautiful local generosity can be. It calls us to be fully present and available to our people and our place. Anything bigger can grow from that mustard seed. As Albert Camus wrote, "Real generosity toward the future lies in giving all to the present."[7]

ASK

Generosity flows from our availability, but that doesn't mean the flow is always seamless and mysterious. Availability opens our hearts, but we also have to open our mouths and learn how to ask. Nineteenth-century preacher Charles Spurgeon stated, "Whether we like it or not, asking is the rule of the kingdom."[8] He was talking about prayer, and that is an essential expression of asking, but I'm talking about "asking" in a broader sense. The flow of generosity is released when we "make an ask"—whether that's making an ask of God, of generous donors, of neglected neighbors, or even sending our requests into the world, trusting this abundant universe to send us what we need. I personally believe that God is at work and play within all these places and people, so it's all prayer in a spiritual sense. All these asks are ways that we get to co-create our communities with God by moving into the open space of possibility and agency God has left open for us. God invites us into the practices of generosity by saying, "Ask me. Ask them. Ask us. And answer." In the kingdom of God, asking and answering are closely linked. As soon as we ask, we make ourselves available to be the answer to our prayers in a way that is fitting for our roles and relationships.

As a library guy, I love the story of Margaret Elysia Garcia I read in *YES!* magazine.[9] Margaret moved with her family from Los Angeles to Greenville, California, a small town of about eleven hundred residents in the rural Indian Valley. Her daughter started seventh grade at a local charter school that shared buildings with the local public school, and Margaret was horrified to find out that the school library had been defunct for years. In fact, there hadn't been a librarian at the school since 1997. Even if the library had been open to the students, it wouldn't have added much value, since the dust-gathering shelves were filled with outdated books and pulp fiction. The collection included very little current literature or books by people of color.

Being an ordinary leader, she grew increasingly discontent with the neglected and pitiful state of the library and set her mind to do something about it. She got permission from the principals of both schools to solicit book donations. Unfortunately, she was up against some big barriers. For many years, Indian Valley had been supported by struggling ranching and logging industries, but as they failed, unemployment had risen above 10 percent. The economic decline was evident to local teachers, who saw two-thirds of their students qualifying for free or reduced-price lunch. For Margaret, though, the situation only fueled her motivation. How could families in the region escape poverty and revitalize their community without quality education, including access to diverse literature to support robust literacy? "It's a scary place for a mind to atrophy," she concluded.

I don't know what Margaret's personal religious views are, but I believe she did a very Jesus-like thing. She asked! She asked locals and nonlocals, everyone in her network, to consider donating to her cause: "Just one book. A real book. Something literary or fun—something that speaks to your truth, their [students'] truths. Something that teaches them something about the world and makes them feel less alone." Having made her ask, she released it to the online world and went to bed. When she woke up the next morning, she was greeted by thousands of responses, including shares from best-selling authors.

Within a few days, books began to arrive. As donations poured in, Margaret had to ask for help again, this time from local parents and retired neighbors who could record the donations and create a database. Somewhere around fifteen thousand titles were sent to this tiny school in a tiny town. Not only has this flood of generosity impacted the schools, which now have an overflowing, bustling library, it has also impacted the surrounding community. Folks were inspired by the kindness of folks around the world who chose to care and to give. It also awakened new interest in reading, so people often stop Garcia at the grocery store to ask for book recommendations. New book groups have formed, and authors have agreed to hold online video chats and presentations for the students.

Hope returned to Greenville and Indian Valley because one woman cared enough to face a problem and was courageous enough to ask others to partner with her on a project of renewal. Of course, the town faces other challenges. But maybe the energy and community created by the collaborative project will provide the momentum and optimism needed to tackle other problems and imagine new pathways forward.

Margaret's story is an inspiring illustration of generosity. It reminds us of the possibilities that emerge when even a single ordinary leader steps up. And it reminds us that we never know what will happen when we risk the ask.

PRACTICE MUTUAL AID

Jesus knew that asking evokes generosity and sometimes you have to "ask around." Sometimes you have to go around the systems and ask the people directly, trusting that God will make a way where there seems to be no way. Sometimes the miracle happens by mutual aid.

Movements of mutual aid often form during times of crisis. When communities of people are marginalized by the systems and structures of society, they are forced to create their own means of subsistence and support. Jesus and early Christ-centered communities demonstrated that it was possible to survive and thrive "in the wilderness"—not only in a literal sense, being in a rural setting, but also in the sense of being isolated and excluded from power structures, no matter the geographic locale. They showed that a person didn't have to compromise with the corrupt and unjust systems in the Roman Empire to live an abundant life.

Later groups, such as the Quakers and Anabaptists, had to create their own systems of mutual aid when they were persecuted and excluded from the political and religious systems of their day. Many Mennonite communities have maintained their close-knit networks even after they gained more political acceptance. They formed cooperatives, commonly owned farms, and mutual aid structures that upheld their families and fellowships during trying times. For them, mutual aid was not only a pragmatic necessity; it was also a spiritual and ethical practice. It was living in the Jesus way of community, mutuality, and service, rather than the world's way of individualism, consumerism, and competition. The Church of Jesus Christ of Latter-day Saints (LDS) developed mutual aid and common ownership practices when they fled persecution and settled in the Utah desert. Those networks enabled the saints to survive and thrive, somehow creating abundance in the wilderness. And they developed into a massive, private social welfare system based in Salt Lake City that serves hundreds of thousands of people.[10]

Mutual aid groups and networks of reciprocal generosity have persisted, inside and outside religious communities, across history. The recent COVID-19 pandemic has provoked a new wave of mutual aid manifestations, not due to persecution but out of practical necessity (and, some would argue, political failure). The small town of Athens, Ohio, for example, launched a variety of assistance programs for local residents and businesses. The nonprofit group Rural Action created the "Athens County Response Fund," which collected $11,000 in a week of online fundraising. Rural Action partnered with other organizations—from the county government to local small business associations and foundations—to distribute the money to individuals, organizations, and businesses who needed the funds. A graduate assistant at the local Ohio University started a "Student Emergency Fund" for students who were encountering unexpected travel and housing costs or wage loss due to the pandemic. Additionally, the Ohio University Inn offered free peanut butter and jelly sandwiches to K–12 children with no questions asked. A local pizza shop and a pub provided free lunches to school children using public library facilities. A group of local citizens looked at all these great things popping up but still saw needs in the area, so they started the Mutual Aid Southeast Ohio group online. This group helped connect area residents with special skills and resources to other local residents who needed those goods and services. They began to connect people with medical supplies and tools and groceries. They matched high-risk folks who couldn't leave their house with less at-risk folks who could run errands or deliver food.[11]

I saw similar services popping up in my county. Online groups provided support and assistance. "Blessing boxes" where food could be donated or taken were placed in each township. The food pantry got creative about ways to safely continue providing access to food for those who needed it, and a local camp and retreat center became a distribution point for the "farms to families" food box program. A local writer put up a "little free library" in town, and the local quilters guild went wild making cloth masks and donating them wherever there was a need. Teachers organized drive-by, socially distanced greeting times with their students so they could offer a friendly hello and make sure kids got their free lunches.

These kinds of local innovation, kindness, and generosity were common across North America and beyond. People taking care of people. Neighbors looking out for neighbors. Networks of local folks formed on social media to practice mutual aid, a movement that in Canada took on the name "caremonger groups" (in contrast to fear-mongering or scaremongering).[12] Witnessing and learning about these expressions of creativity and kindness was encouraging to me when crosscurrents of selfishness, fear, and ignorance seemed so common. These innovations also revealed what could really be possible if we had the will and shared commitment to make them happen. I could almost hear the living Christ calling and convicting us, luring us toward a vision in which we join to create more inclusive, resilient, collaborative communities.

Generosity doesn't exclude the realm of economic exchange, however. Even the idealized descriptions of common life described in Acts include examples of buying and selling in addition to giving and receiving. And an interesting note about the famous parable about the "Good Samaritan" is that the Samaritan man was probably traveling for commercial reasons when he came upon the injured man, so he used the money he made from his business to pay for the injured person's healing and recovery. Entrepreneurs and business folks are critical kinds of ordinary leaders that we need if we are to recover abundance in our small towns and rural regions. We should not discount their role in renewal, since their financial acumen and market savvy might help release new streams of generosity or bring into view opportunities that were previously unseen or untapped.

In their book *Switch: How to Change Things When Change Is Hard*, Dan and Chip Heath tell about a group of teenagers in Howard, South Dakota, a town of about eight hundred people in a county of just over twenty-two hundred people (the numbers were a bit higher in 1995 when this story took place).[13] These high schoolers were tired of seeing their hometown decline and wanted to revive it. Many of the factors that could help revive their economy—such as entrepreneurship, investment, and immigration—were mostly out of their control. But spending was something folks had some power over, so the students surveyed one thousand registered voters in Miner County about their spending habits.

What they found was that most of them were driving about an hour to Sioux Falls to do most of their shopping. Those of us who live in small towns and rural regions may not be shocked to hear this. The students were probably not shocked either. But when they started to do the math, they realized the economic impact this was having on their town's economy. It was devastating for a declining economy. But redirecting that money to their local economy could give their community a considerable boost. The power was right there hiding in the problem. If each adult would spend just 10 percent more of their disposable income at local businesses, the county economy would gain about seven million dollars. "They had found their first rallying cry," the Heaths report. "Let's keep Miner dollars in Miner County."

So the high school class made a presentation to the community. They didn't know exactly what to expect, but they shared their findings and made the call to action. Based on the feedback they received and the observations they made, they could tell that their presentation made an impact. People were spending more consciously and locally. But they weren't prepared for the numbers released by the South Dakota Department of Revenue. After one year, spending in Miner County had increased by 15.6 million dollars, almost double what they had proposed.

Of course, the county didn't transform into a booming, thriving region overnight. Miner County still has its challenges. As with other stories in this book, this is not a "happily ever after" saga so much as a three-steps-forward-two-steps-back account. But the story reminds us of the critical role youth play in small towns and about the power of ordinary leaders who ask questions, propose solutions, and put forth a call to action. And it reminds us of what is possible when we look at our community with a sense of possibility and positivity, as a place worthy of investment. In fact, other small towns paid attention to this story and put it into action. About one hundred miles away in Miller, South Dakota, local leaders were inspired to start their own buy-local campaign focused on Christmas shopping. In Marion, Ohio, a town about twenty minutes from where I live, local leaders launched a Marion Made campaign and organized buy-local events, including a "Think Local First—Marion

County" Facebook page that specifically mentions the story of the high schoolers in Miner County, South Dakota. What would be possible if your residents shifted only 10 percent of their spending to local businesses?

Buying local isn't just a trend. It's a practical, tangible practice that helps us nurture a sense of ownership and possibility by investing in our local community. Remember that business about "where your treasure is, there your heart will be also"? If you say you care about your small town or rural region, put your money where your mouth is, and your heart will follow. Ordinary leaders aren't waiting for "white knights"[14] from big corporations to move into town and save them. We are inviting people into partnership to renew and revitalize our own communities. We are being the change we want to see and calling others to join us in a spirit of generosity. This generosity looks like charitable and spontaneous giving. It also looks like robust economics that invests in entrepreneurship, innovation, ownership, and local markets.

DON'T DIS-COUNT

Big checks and community-wide movements are thrilling. But our feeding miracle story reminds us that generosity isn't limited to high-dollar "gifts." There is no minimum donation requirement. The version of our story in John's gospel demonstrates this by introducing a character who isn't included in the other versions. As in the other versions, Jesus refuses the "salvation by relocation" solution of the disciples. And, as in the other versions, Jesus answers the disciples' scarcity with a call to accept responsibility and discover the hidden abundance. But instead of hearing about a simple inventory of food collected from "the crowd," we are met with a specific gift from a specific person.

We learn about this specific person because of a specific disciple: Andrew. While the disciples as a group are spiraling into a whirlwind of scarcity thinking and anxiety, Andrew decides to "speak up"

(John 6:8). What does he say? "Here's a boy." He brings the little guy to Jesus and introduces them: "Jesus, meet boy. Boy, meet Jesus." He connects them. Now, it's possible that the boy came to Andrew, and Andrew just happened to be the one who brought him to Jesus. But details like that are rarely incidental in the gospels. And this role of connecting and introducing seemed to be Andrew's modus operandi. Both in the gospels and in the longer narrative of church history, Andrew is known for connecting, introducing, drawing in. The Greek Orthodox Church calls St. Andrew the *Protokletos*—the "first called." He was the first one called to discipleship as Jesus began his ministry. After Andrew spent some time in Jesus's presence, he left the scene, and the "first thing" he did was seek out his brother Simon Peter and tell him about his encounter. What next? The text says, "And he brought him to Jesus" (John 1:42). Peter, of course, became a more prominent figure among the disciples, but Andrew was also in Jesus's inner circle. Maybe he was happy to be a more "behind the scenes" person who found people and introduced them to Jesus, confident their lives would be changed and their mission would become much bigger.

Our small towns and rural regions are in great need of ordinary leaders who are "Andrews." We need folks who are skilled at making connections with people and resources. They are quiet evangelists who have a way of drawing people into causes and communities without making a big fuss about it. You want these people on your side. They are loyal and resourceful and relational. They will introduce you to just the right person, and you will wonder, "How in the world do you know all these people?" They will help you gain access to a grant or a giver and you will exclaim, "I didn't even know this existed!" And they will bring you people who need care and compassion, and you will confess, "I didn't even notice this person until you brought us together."

Now, having praised the great *Protokletos*, I have to add that he's not the perfect leader either. While Andrew does speak up and bring the boy to Jesus, it's not clear that he does so with much faith that the introduction will make a difference. As the other disciples highlighted the large size of the crowd and the isolated location, Andrew focuses on the smallness of both the boy and his food. John's gospel also adds the detail that the bread is made from barley, commonly used among the poor. Tiny fish were often paired with bread only as a kind of relish to add a little bit of flavor. So Andrew, while noble, isn't exactly brimming with positivity and possibility. He is saying to Jesus, in essence, "There's good news, and there's bad news. Good news is that I found this child who has food. Bad news is that it's just a little lad with a little loaf. And it's not great food, either." No wonder he concludes with the rhetorical question, "How far will they go among so many?" (John 6:9).

The gift and the child may have been small, but they were not insignificant. On the contrary, the encounter was a game changer. Generosity begets generosity. Acts of generosity, however small they may seem (even with mixed motives—some scholars suggest the boy had brought the food to peddle)—generates a flow of giving within others. We don't know for sure whether the little guy's act of generosity unleashed the generosity of the whole group, but we know that often happens with giving. And we know that the boy's action was noteworthy and consequential enough that it was included in John's version of the event.

As I noted at the beginning of the chapter, the story itself tells us that crowd included five thousand men, specifically "not counting women and children." But what if the miracle wouldn't have been possible without the women and children? What if the miracle would have been stalled without them, as the powerful patriarchs got together but failed to find a solution because their thinking was limited to the conventional means and methods of their patriarchal society? What if, instead of a miracle occurring—to be told in all four gospels—the miracle was thwarted and became a footnote in the spirit of Matthew 13:58: "And [Jesus] did not do many miracles there because of their lack of faith." Maybe it would go something like: "Jesus did not do any feeding miracle there because of their lack of faith—their limited imagination about who can contribute and who counts in the kingdom."

When we consider that the crowd may have been fed because of the mothers who packed provisions and turned them over to Christ and the community or because of a boy who unleashed a wave of generosity, we realize that the very people left out of the count may have been the very members who made the miracle possible. It was the dis-counted members of the group who made their resources and relationships count the most.

This turnabout would certainly fit the spirit of Jesus's life and ministry. He had a habit of taking people from the margins and putting them in the middle, of making the "least of these" the most important for the moment. Jesus challenged his audience to recognize women as full and faithful disciples, asking piercingly on one particular occasion, "Do you see this woman?" (Luke 7:44). He condemned the gatekeeping efforts of his disciples to keep children from coming to him, turning the tables as he "called a little child to him, and placed the child among them" (Matt 18:2), reminding them that in the coming peaceable kingdom, "A little child shall lead them" (Isa 11:6). Jesus wanted to make sure we count women and children, and he wants us to remember that their life and gifts count for his kingdom. I like to think that Andrew, however clumsily and with faltering faith, was trying also to move the marginalized to the middle.

The story's witness raises the questions: Who is getting discounted in our communities? Who are we forgetting to count and account for? The story prods us to remember, based on Jesus's example, that these folks may actually be game changers. They may have the gifts and make the contributions that release a wave of generosity and make new things possible. Scan the "crowd" of your community and look for those who have been ignored or overlooked. And then look inward. Perhaps you have been discounting your own contributions. Maybe you need to be reminded that your own acts of generosity, no matter how small they may seem, really are important in the eyes of God and for the flourishing of your community. They matter. You matter.

I have a suspicion. Maybe we miss the point with all the debate about whether the miracle among the multitude was a miracle of multiplication or distribution, whether bread or hearts were changed. Maybe when we "seek first" that Commonwealth of God, we can have our bread and share it too. Maybe "all these things" are added as well. Call it wishful thinking or prophetic imagination, but I suspect that, in Jesus's economy, we witness the miracles of distribution *and* multiplication. We receive new bread *and* new hearts. And I think that kingdom is one worthy of our investment, using every form of generosity. Who knows what manner of miracle may take place in our homes, communities, and regions when ordinary leaders show the way by risking those investments.

CHAPTER ELEVEN

THE PRACTICE OF SOLIDARITY

They all *ate and were satisfied.*

Mark 6:42

WORKING AT A PUBLIC LIBRARY provides me an up-close and personal seat from which to view the struggles and gifts of the people in my community. Sometimes this view is painful. Sometimes it's beautiful. It's almost always interesting. You see, the "public" part in "public library" means it's open to everyone. That's the glory (and the challenge) of my work. The lady who openly espoused communism and is seeking her dream job of working at a morgue has a place at the library. The gun-obsessed gentleman who leads a local private militia also has a place. The strung-out young adult who has nowhere to go during the day also has a place, as does the elderly religious lady who only checks out Amish romance novels. Everyone is welcome in the library, so long as they are willing to follow a few basic rules that show respect for other patrons and the mission of the library. Most people love this about the library. But not everyone.

One year, during the month of June, the youth services librarian decided to put up a pride month display. It included a poster from the American Library Association and a few books that had LGBTQ characters in them or addressed topics relevant to queer experience. The display was simple and subtle, and you would hardly notice it if you weren't looking for it. Well, just the "right" person noticed it. Her name, we'll say, is Kara. Kara is a very outspoken conservative activist who campaigned for the complete abolition of abortion, forced her way into school board meetings to troll the school leadership (even though her children are homeschooled), and showed up to a private gathering for a district political candidate and videotaped herself being forced to leave (the candidate was a conservative Republican, but she still believed he was corrupt). While I disagreed with some of Kara's views, I didn't have any particular ill-will toward her. She was a friendly person most of the time; we would chat as she checked out a book or movie. Kara brought her kids to story time and summer reading programming. She was also passionate about reforming the foster care system, and Ohio's system does indeed need to be reformed. But my experience with her would be transformed after she discovered the gay pride display.

First, she shared her concern with the youth services librarian, who listened politely and explained that she put up the display simply to make sure all the youth knew they were welcome in the library. She wanted the library to be a safe space for everyone. Since Kara's direct appeal did not work, she went over the librarian's head to the director. The director listened politely and took the matter to the library board. The board meets monthly, at the same time and same place every month. Meetings are open to the public, and the minutes are posted on the website for anyone to read. I know because I put them there every month. So these meetings are not secret. Kara attended the next board meeting ready with her impeccable logic and impeachable family values. She also brought her cell phone, which she stealthily laid down on the table where she could record both audio and video of everything that was said during that meeting. A few passionate words were exchanged, but nothing major happened at this top-secret/open-to-the-public meeting. Kara made generous use of slippery-slope arguments and well-worn dehumanizing comparisons between sex offenders and LGBTQ individuals.

When Kara didn't get the response from the board that she hoped for, she shared her outrage on social media and with all her conservative activist connections. This is where it really got fun for the staff. We started getting emails and phone calls from these folks. These phone calls were not from curious patrons asking for more information nor were they calls from concerned community members; they were threatening calls from activists demanding that we immediately take down the display. If we didn't, one angry voicemail informed us, they would organize a campaign to shut down any attempt to pass a library levy. Apparently, gay-positive books sitting on a shelf is so offputting and outrageous that they would rather have the library die a slow death from lack of funds—information democracy, community resources, and children's programming be damned. Talk about cancel culture.

As wild as it was to experience such passionate activism at a small-town library, the highlight for me wasn't the phone calls and secret recordings and references to networks of demonic forces and liberal conspiracies. It wasn't even Kara's suggestion that we were encouraging children to look at gay sex manuals. No, for me it was how proud I was of our director and board. They listened to Kara's concerns, but they never asked the youth services librarian to take down the display. Didn't even hint that she should do it. They stood by her.

Thank God for those progressive activist librarians, right? Wrong. Our director is a devout Catholic and a self-described "constitutional conservative." Rush Limbaugh and Glenn Beck blast from her computer all day long. She, along with probably half the board of directors, are fairly traditional Christian people. I don't know their exact beliefs on same-sex marriage, but I know they certainly have no leftist allegiances or aspirations to move forward any "homosexual agenda."

So why did they stand with our youth services librarian? Because they believe the library should be a place for everyone. Everyone.

Libraries are anti-censorship. They are antidiscrimination. And that democratic, egalitarian ethic unites librarians regardless of whatever political leanings they may have.

Another favorite story of mine from working at the library comes from an older woman named Sherri who is a regular patron. Like my wife, Sherri is from Tennessee, and they both have that sassy, sweet, sharp Appalachian charm. She gives me a hard time, always threatening to tell my boss or practice corporal punishment on me if I make a mistake. I give it back from time to time. I like to tell her that she has a $150 fine so she won't be able to check out season 211 of *Grey's Anatomy*. She usually has a comeback. But the thing she always has is a story. One particular story has stuck with me.

Sherri frequently talks about her kids, one of whom is gay and lives in Atlanta. Well, before he moved away, they attended a nearby church every Sunday. Sherri and her son liked the church well enough and enjoyed listening to the preacher's sermons—that is, except when he would get to preaching about sexual immorality. Specifically, the sexual immorality of "homosexual behavior." It's degrading, he said, and sinful, and the homosexuals are tearing down our country. One particular Sunday, Momma Sherri had had enough. She looked over and saw her son crying. She couldn't handle seeing her son beaten up by a sermon. So, whether it was her southern sass, momma bear spirit, or the Holy Ghost, she spoke her mind to the preacher. When she told me this, I responded, "Oh, wow, so after the service, you pulled him aside and told him you were upset?" "No!" she corrected. "I stood up, right then and there, and told him that was enough. I told him everyone was a sinner, and I could name some of his sins. No one had any right to judge. And besides that, God loves everyone. God loves gay folks just as much as straight folks. Jesus told us to love our neighbors and love everyone. So move on!" All of my theological training pales in comparison to Momma Sherri's sermonette. I can't really talk much about religion in a public library, so instead of saying amen, I said, "You go, girl." And she replied, "You betcha, honey," as if to say "Amen and amen." Or maybe "May it be so."

You see, to Sherri and to the library, "Y'all" means "all." All. No exceptions. Everyone deserves to be respected and have a space to explore and learn. Everyone is loved and cherished by God.

For Jesus, "y'all" means "all." It's right there in the story. "Did you get enough to eat?" I've been asked that question hundreds, maybe thousands, of times by my mother. It's clearly answered in the text: "They all ate and were satisfied." We can easily pass by this summary sentence as a nice conclusion to a nice story. But it's packed full of meaning. "All" brings together the diverse dimensions of this event. It points to the wonder and wideness of the miracle. It indicates divine power and possibility: Jesus and all the friends he pulled in were able to do the job to the fullest. The word also captures the compassionate and inclusive nature of the miracle. It was, after all, as the gospel of John emphasizes, a sign pointing to the kingdom, a kingdom that breaks down the dividing walls created by both Greco-Roman society and the religious systems of Judaism. At this miracle meal, Jesus did no means testing and demanded no citizenship requirement or proof of insurance. More relevant to his context, Jesus did nothing to differentiate between those ritually compliant and pure and those who were not. He did nothing to distinguish among people according to any of the usual identity and status markers. Jesus offered them a new center, a new identity, that would allow them to maintain their diversity while deepening their unity. The meal initiated them into a new way of being in the world. Jesus called it the kingdom of God. The apostle Paul called it life "in Christ."

All ate. And all were satisfied. The Greek verb translated "satisfied" is *chortazo*, which means completely full and deeply satisfied. An alternative translation would be "And everyone ate, as much as they wanted." They didn't just get enough food to barely keep them alive or even to tide them over until they got home. They ate until they couldn't eat any more. They were given a taste of things to come, abundant life in the loving reign of God—and in the big family of God. The word for "satisfied" is the same one used by Jesus in the Sermon on the Mount where he promises, "Blessed are those who hunger and thirst for righteous for they will be *filled*" (Matt 5:6). This promise of deep satisfaction reminds us that God is aware of our hungers, knows what we need, and provides the right kind of nourishment to satisfy our hunger.

THE KINGDOM OF GOD IS LIKE A POTLUCK

This invitation is not only an invitation to feast. It's also an invitation to participate. Jesus models this invitation in the gospel story. One faithful reading of this story attends not only to the feeding *of* the five thousand but the feeding *with* the five thousand. Sometimes we simply need to sit with Christ and let him host and feed us. But the vision of the kingdom calls us not simply to worship Jesus as a powerful provider but also to follow Jesus by learning and practicing his kingdom way. So Jesus is playfully and prophetically teaching the disciples, as well as the larger group, how to recover abundance. He invites the disciples to take inventory and draw out the resources from the crowd. He welcomes the contributions offered by the boy. And he sends the disciples out into the crowd to create community and serve food. Whether you view the miracle as one of multiplication, generosity, distribution, or some other methodology, it's clear that Jesus did not perform it on his own, as a solo demonstration of his supreme power.

You see, the kingdom of heaven is like a potluck. I've been to dozens, probably even hundreds, of potlucks. There's nothing quite so sacred and satisfying as a potluck at a local church in a small town. In one sense, the potluck is a quintessential American feast. But on the other hand, it's radically communitarian. Truth be told, Marx would be proud—you know: from each according to their ability, to each according to their need.

Some people can bring only a little bit of something. A dark secret I carry is that I've shown up at potlucks empty-handed. In my defense, I was young and hungry. At least I know I'm not alone in my failure. Some people aren't much into cooking or don't have time, so they pick up some brownies from the grocery store or a bucket of chicken at the fast food drive-through. Other folks are willing to bring a dish but haven't done much cooking and are a little timid, so they might put together a veggie tray. Some folks bring a special dish because, if they don't, they might not get anything to eat because they're vegan or gluten-free or allergic to peanuts. At the far end of the spectrum, fortunately, are those who bring their signature dish, possibly something passed down from previous generations: homemade mac and cheese, classic green bean casserole, irresistible deviled eggs, or a mildly spicy chili. (Okay, I'm getting too hungry.) The point is that everyone is invited, if not expected, to bring something. That's why my Indiana friends call it a "pitch-in."

In their book *Practicing the King's Economy*, Michael Rhodes, Robby Holt, and Brian Fikkert combine their expertise in congregational ministry and community development to propose that the kingdom economy of Jesus is like a potluck. They tell the story of a church in Cincinnati, Ohio, that ran a soup kitchen. The leadership group realized that, though they had been serving food for years, they weren't really building relationships with the people who came. So they began getting to know the guests better. And they began inquiring about their gifts and skills, interests and dreams. What they found amazed them. The folks they were feeding were plumbers, musicians, artists, teachers, carpenters, and caregivers. And over half of the people they were making soup for listed cooking as one of their talents! So the congregants began inviting the soup kitchen guests to transition from passive recipients to active contributors to the meal and the community. Most were happy to oblige and step into this more dignifying and empowering role.

Of course, soup kitchens aren't bad. Sometimes we do need to simply receive, and sometimes we do need to step into the role of charitable giver. But if we are learning the way of Jesus, not to mention the wisdom of sustainable economic and community development, we are called to transition from a soup kitchen to a potluck relationship. "A soup kitchen divides us up into haves and have-nots," explain Rhodes, Holt, and Fikkert. "At a potluck, every single person both gives and receives. Food comes from everyone and goes to everyone. Everyone gets fed and everyone brings a plate."[1]

CHARITY AND SOLIDARITY

The potluck principle points us toward a distinction that's important for ordinary leaders in small towns and rural regions to understand: the difference between charity and solidarity. Charity is seen in the soup kitchen, where one person has resources and the other doesn't, so the one with soup gives some of it to the one with only an empty bowl. The service sounds nice, but it nurtures a spirit of separateness and an imbalance of power and value between the two parties. Solidarity, on the other hand, is more like a potluck. Everyone needs to eat, and everyone has a role in creating the meal. Better yet, everyone comes together to create a more just and inclusive food system so that everyone can eat and be satisfied. Solidarity is about joining together to create systems, relationships, and opportunities that make the feeding of the five thousand a common and communal occurrence.

In Christian faith, the concept of solidarity was developed in the twentieth century by a collection of priests, theologians, and social-change agents seeking to find freedom from poverty and oppression in their own communities. They were reading the Bible in "base communities," small groups of local folks, often in rural parishes across Latin America, and they were developing a new way of understanding Jesus's message that spoke to their context. Unfortunately, many of these political and spiritual leaders had seen and felt the negative impacts of Western paternalism on their own people. These leaders, then, worked from a framework of liberation theology, which invited the people to "drink from their own wells" and emphasized solidarity over charity. Uruguayan journalist Eduardo Galeano summarizes this philosophy clearly: "I don't believe in charity. I believe in solidarity. Charity is so vertical. It goes from the top to the bottom. Solidarity is horizontal. It respects the other person. I have a lot to learn from other people."[2] Indigenous Australian artist and activist Lilla Watson speaks to this horizonal solidarity when she declares, "If you have come here to help me, you are wasting your time. But if you have come because your liberation is bound up with mine, then let us work together."[3]

Solidarity doesn't mean *sameness*. It doesn't mean we pretend we are color and class blind, erasing history and singing kumbaya together. But we do learn to recognize our *relatedness*, accepting that we are linked in what Martin Luther King Jr. called "an inescapable network of mutuality."[4]

I still think there is a role for charity, however—to meet immediate, emergency needs, for example. But too often, in small towns and rural regions, we don't question the motives or methods of someone's charity because, quite frankly, we need it so much. Sometimes we feel so much lack and loss that we are grateful for any gift of any kind. It's important for ordinary leaders to remember that there are times, as the instructive book title reminds us, "when helping hurts."[5] We can become more aware of the impact our helping has without discouraging people from being generous. It's important to keep generosity and solidarity in close relationship, ensuring that our generosity builds up our community and brings us together rather than unwittingly separating and disempowering. Charity is best practiced in a spirit of solidarity, and when properly practiced, it can actually nurture solidarity. Often, however, doing so requires first recognizing our relatedness and being willing to confront systemic issues as well as individual needs. And that involves asking hard questions and having hard conversations.

WHAT THE SOCIALISTS WANT YOU TO THINK

Brazilian archbishop Hélder Câmara named a challenge that often accompanies solidarity: "When I give food to the poor, they call me a saint. When I ask why the poor have no food, they call me a communist."[6] I don't think I've ever been called a communist, but I'll never forget the time I was called a socialist by a small-town mayor. When I lived in Kansas, I occasionally stopped by the local "hardware store" (read "general store") to get a pop on a hot day or grab some basics like milk and bread because I didn't feel like making the drive to the nearest grocery store. One morning, I stopped in before class, and several local farmers were sitting around a table in a corner of the store, drinking coffee. They often came by the hardware store in the morning to grab a cup of hot coffee and get caught up on local gossip, check on their neighbors, and complain about the woes of society. There actually was a coffee shop in town, understand, but that one sold fair-trade coffee and gifts from various international ministries, so it was referred to as "Obama's coffee shop."

One person in the hardware store was standing. He was the only non-farmer hanging out by the table that morning and happened to be a candidate for the town mayor. I selected a few items and proceeded to pay at the counter when the gentleman walked up to me and introduced himself, informing me of the office for which he was running.

At first I was a bit annoyed; I wanted to get in and out. I had things to do and people to see. But then I realized this was an opportunity. The town water had become unsafe to drink due to dangerously high levels of nitrate pollution from farming operations. To get drinkable water, community members either had to buy bottled water or go to the fire station, where they could fill their own bottles with clean water. I referred to this water station as "the village well." To be honest, I thought the system was ridiculous and was disappointed that there seemed to be little political will to do anything about it. But perhaps there was something being done that I wasn't aware of; perhaps the mayoral candidate would have some insight.

"I do have a concern," I admitted to the promising politician. "It's about the water. Seems like there are safety issues that need addressed. Little ones and pregnant mothers are using the water, and it's unsafe. Everyone has to fend for themselves to get access to a basic resource of the community."

He interrupted me with a heavy sigh and a pregnant pause. Was he preparing to empathize and console, even if he was without adequate answers? To share his five-step solution to the problem? To inform me about a committee meeting or stakeholder discussions happening in the near future? Nope. He wanted to set me straight: "That's what the socialists want you to think."

I stood there in stunned silence. For a moment, I wondered if he had the same convictions about public roads and police, but I decided to move on. I grabbed my caffeinated beverage and breakfast bar and went to class. I was late, and for no good reason.

Thankfully, after I moved, a task force was put together and a more forward-thinking, community-minded mayor spearheaded a plan. A water treatment system was installed. But I'm aware that many people think the mayoral candidate's attitude is the epitome of how rural folks relate to government. Taxes bad, freedom good. Public bad, private good. Godless communists vs. Christian capitalists. Interestingly enough, some highly rural states like Kansas and Oklahoma have a history of progressivism and populism. You've probably heard of "bleeding Kansas," the violent confrontations that took place in the late 1850s when Kansas was a battleground between proslavery and antislavery advocates. You probably have not heard that in the late nineteenth and early twentieth century Kansas was a hub of socialist organizing. And you probably aren't aware that Oklahoma was the site of a socialist uprising called the Green Corn Rebellion in which a group of white, Seminole, Creek, and African American farmers and organizers came together to resist economic exploitation and the injustices in military draft practices.[7]

It amazes me that in less than a century, the heartland could go from a hub of radical communitarian movements to a region of radical individualism. Kansans went from joining across racial divides to stand up for justice and fairness to suggesting everyone is on their own to find clean water.

I'm not saying that we need a socialist revolution in the heartland. I believe there's a lot of rural real estate between Karl Marx and Ayn Rand. There's a space of solidarity where we may debate the means and methods of solving problems and distributing resources, but we agree that none of us is whole until all of us are whole. Whether we tax polluters, build water treatment infrastructure, subsidize water access, or rally nonprofits to distribute water to households (or all of the above), we agree that providing clean water for all is our shared task and ethical imperative. Call it socialism or sainthood, liberation theology or small-town neighborliness, it's the call of all who seek to follow Jesus.

Half the battle is won when we can stop debating "if" and get to work on "how." And if we are clear on our relationship and responsibility, we can find the resources. Ordinary leaders cultivate that relationship, call us to that responsibility, and bring stakeholders together to find those resources. And we keep working together until we can say that "everyone ate and was satisfied." Or that "everyone drank and showered and the whole town had clean water."

KINSHIP AND KINGDOM

Solidarity means moving beyond the radical individualism of our culture and learning the ethics of kinship. The practice of solidarity teaches us that Jesus's *kingdom* is indeed the *kin-dom* of God. If we are to recover abundance in our communities and realize the loving reign of God in the world, that effort is going to take all of us. This kin-dom vision calls us to affirm the close bonds that develop naturally in many small towns. But it also calls us to expand and extend those relational ties to reach new folks and do justice in new ways. To borrow language from an earlier chapter, the kin-dom of God requires that we cultivate both bonding and bridging social capital.

In some ways, small towns and rural regions are great at this kinship ethic. Most of us place high value on family and taking care of those who are literally our kin. We pride ourselves on knowing everyone in town. We know family names and who's related to whom. We know the ex-husband of the hairdresser and where the dentist lives. We know which kids are considered riffraff, which ones have neglectful parents, and which star pupils are headed off to a good college. So often our small towns have a familial and familiar feel to them. When you're here, you're family. And yet, like family, we have plenty of long-standing feuds that tear us apart, sometimes lasting generations. And, also like family, we can develop closed family systems that are hard to break into. A local woman told me about a time when someone asked if she was new to the area. "Well, my husband and I have lived here for twenty-nine years," she responded. "And my husband has had a dental practice in town for about fifteen years."

"Oh, okay," replied the inquirer, "so you *are* new then."

But the kin-dom vision Jesus calls us to is one that expands our relatedness beyond our biological families and into a spirit of kinship with our siblings in the faith, our neighbors, our fellow citizens, and even, Jesus insists, our enemies. The circle of kinship is ever-expanding, ever-widening. The apostle Paul referred to his early disciples as *adelphoi*, "brothers" and "sisters." Whatever economic, ethnic, or political differences they had, they were made kin in Christ.

Bringing forth the kin-dom means confronting those times and ways when we have not been our brother's or sister's keeper. The disciples illustrate this wonderfully (and painfully) when they tell Jesus to send the hungry seekers away so they can figure it out and fight it out somewhere else. The same Greek imperative word *apoluo*, "send them away," is also used in the New Testament for the practice of divorce. It means to actively set aside a covenant of kinship and to be loosed from the responsibilities of relatedness. Reflecting from both his Choctaw and Christian heritage of kinship theology, Episcopal priest Steven Charleston frames sin as the violation of this kinship relationship with our Creator, with our fellow human beings, and with Creation itself: "Racism destroys kinship. Sexism destroys kinship. Classism destroys kinship. Homophobia destroys kinship. When human beings exile other human beings from the circle of life, they are breaking the hoop of the human nation, tearing apart what God has created. The sin of humanity is not a lifetime stain inherited from mythic ancestors who disobeyed a rule, but a daily choice made by all of us in the here and now, in living relationships that embody our kinship."[8]

If we violate our kinship by "daily choices," then repairing those relationships will require new daily choices. If those sins are often sins of omission, then kinship calls us to counteract actions of neglect with actions of intentional inclusion. If the violations are actions of targeted harm, then we are called to counteract them with actions of personalized repair. For example, some of the conversations I've tried to have with members of my community are about why we don't have very many people of color in our village. For many, it's simply a demographic fact of life. We are rural and small, and black folks, generally speaking, tend to live in the city. But we are within commuting distance of the thriving, growing, and diverse city of Columbus. I'm sure there are demographic and geographic factors, but I think there are also social factors. I'm ashamed to admit that it was only a decade ago that a young white man was indicted for leaving a burned cross in the yard of a local black family, marked with the words: "The KKK will make you pay." Many in the community condemned the crime but believed it was a "prank" rather than an act of targeted racist violence. If my county is to become a place where people of color want to live and make a living, we will need more than economic development. We will also need to develop a spirit of solidarity through specific acts of repair and welcome. Of course, there are deep historical wounds that we can't heal by ourselves, but ordinary leaders *call out* neighbors when necessary and *call them in* to act like neighbors.

The COVID-19 pandemic brought out the worst and the best in our small towns and rural regions. I saw this in my hometown. Some people got caught up in the "China virus" fever and took out their anxiety on a Chinese family who ran the local Chinese restaurant. The owners were receiving ignorant and hateful comments, even threats, from local residents. Between the nastiness and the public health risks, the family decided to close the restaurant. After several months of the restaurant being closed and questions about whether the owners still lived locally, most folks assumed the place was gone for good. But after about a year of being closed, we learned that the restaurant would soon be reopening. And an ordinary leader who is passionate about supporting small businesses in our county decided to make sure the reopening would reflect the best in our community. He turned the reopening into an opportunity for solidarity. He asked people to go buy some food, take it home, and leave the owners with kind words and cards. The Chinese family was showered with support. Words and letters had been used to bully and dehumanize the restaurant owners; they were also used to express welcome and support.

As important as intentional and specific actions are to the practice of solidarity, it's important to remember that solidarity is not just about *acting*. It's also about *listening*. It calls us to listen for the divine through the variety of voices that make up our community. And we especially need to listen to those whose voices are often ignored or drowned out. Their stories help us see who we really are and who we can become. Take the story of Ayaz Virji, a doctor who answered the call to serve when he found out there was a severe shortage of doctors in rural America.[9] The Virji family moved from Harrisburg, Pennsylvania, to Dawson, Minnesota, a town of about fifteen hundred people. It took some time to adjust, but the family settled in and appreciated the best things about small towns that many of us can relate to: folks looking out for one another, walking to work and not sitting in traffic, a slower pace of life, knowing our neighbors by name. Ayaz liked practicing medicine in a small town because he could move away from the "turnstile medicine" of the city (get through as many patients as quickly as possible) to what he calls "dignified medicine," in which he can get to know the patient in a more holistic way over a longer period of time. His wife opened a salon and spa, which thrived.

Everything was going well except for one thing. You see, Ayaz happens to be Indian. And he happens to be Muslim. This didn't seem to be a problem for the first two or three years of living in Dawson. Residents were grateful to have a skillful doctor in their small town and appreciated the family's kindness and contributions to the community. Then came the 2016 election. The family noticed a change in tone among some people in the community. Hateful words and symbols were written on the sidewalk in front of their house. Their children no longer felt safe in school. When Ayaz found out that the majority of the town voted for Donald Trump, he was outraged. He simply couldn't imagine how his neighbors could support someone who so brazenly scapegoated Muslims, talking about creating a registry of Muslims and calling Islam a "cancer." Trump's rhetoric was clearly influencing folks in Dawson, and Ayaz was infuriated that the fearmongering was working, dividing the community and making his family feel unsafe in their own community. He was ready to move.

Before he had the chance to move, though, Ayaz was approached by Pastor Mandy, a local Lutheran pastoral intern. She was an ordinary leader who wanted to practice solidarity by listening to and lifting up the voice of her marginalized neighbor. So Mandy asked Ayaz to give a talk at a community gathering. This gathering would be a time to reflect on how to love our neighbors, and part of that reflecting would be Ayaz giving a talk on misconceptions about Islam. He was initially reluctant, and some people even actively discouraged him from doing it. But after his strongest emotions began to cool, something like a calling emerged: "A calming. A call for justice. For explanation. For truth. Resulting in this talk. This necessary talk."[10]

The speech, as you can imagine, was not without controversy, but it opened the eyes of many. And it made such a big splash in their small county that he began receiving invitations from all around the country to share his experiences and knowledge.

Eventually, his speech was turned into a book, *Love Thy Neighbor: A Muslim Doctor's Struggle for Home in Rural America*. Ayaz's speech in Dawson, his talks around the country, and now the book are reaching folks around the world, carrying a message of solidarity. He puts a name and face on the religion of Islam and in the process provides a new way of seeing the religion of Christianity. He helps us see the beauty and brokenness, the strength and vulnerability, of small rural communities in the United States. And we get a picture of the possibilities of life together when we live into our best values of faith, inclusion, respect, and compassion. Ayaz's story may seem like an unusual situation, but there are folks like him in our small towns and rural regions across the country. We will be challenged and enriched if we take the time to listen to their stories and honor their perspectives.

FAMILY QUARRELS

The practice of solidarity isn't limited to big challenges like racial reconciliation. As important as these social justice dramas and traumas are to confront, the reality is that small towns and rural regions have plenty of other forces dividing us. Three relationships are frequently strained in our contexts: intergenerational relationships, inter-congregational relationships, and rural–urban relationships. These relationship conflicts often feel like family quarrels because the kinship is close but too quickly becomes rivalrous. Nevertheless, restoring right relationship between these groups is essential to rural renewal.

First is the relationship between generations. Anyone who lives in a small town or rural region has witnessed or experienced the conflict between the "old guard" and the emerging generation. Many rural folks claim to want nothing more than a new generation of leaders. They are exhausted. And they are concerned for the future of their town. But at the same time, they are afraid that the emerging generation isn't ready to take the reins—that the younger generation is too idealistic or inexperienced, and therefore letting them lead runs the risks of ruining what previous generations have built. They are afraid to let go. And, of course, ego gets in the way as well.

On the other side, ordinary leaders who are ready to take the reins too often undervalue the wisdom and experience of the "old guard." The previous generation doesn't have all the answers, of course, but they at least understand the world as it has been. We can't get from "here" to "there" without knowing where "here" is— and what "here" is. Both generations need to learn how to listen, learn, and lead together. The surviving and thriving of our community are at stake. To build a better future will take all of us. And it will take a delicate dance of learning when to step up and step back, leading and following, sticking with what we know and risking new moves. Wherever you find yourself in those movements, it's important to reflect on your role as an ordinary leader. How are you relating to the previous or emerging generation? How can that relationship be repaired, strengthened, or leveraged? What pathways to leadership exist in your community? Are they "secret" and exclusive or clear and open? What would be possible if leaders from different generations worked together in solidarity?

Just as we need intergenerational solidarity, we also need intercongregational solidarity. It's an absurd feature of too many small towns and rural regions that our churches and congregations are characterized by competition instead of collaboration. It's a classic case of the scarcity mentality. We are all competing for the limited number of people in our community who might join a faith community. But this is an issue only if we believe our purpose is constant numerical growth rather than learning and exploring new metrics, based on an abundance mentality, that enable us to do the "math of mission."[11]

Leadership guru Patrick Lencioni describes this issue as the problem of "silos." Silos are those barriers between departments that are upheld by turf warfare, ineffective policies and procedures, and rivalry that result in "causing people who are supposed to be on the same team to work against one another."[12] Similarly, small church pastor Karl Vaters calls this lack of cooperation the number-one reason for small church stagnancy and ineffective ministry. "We're not working together," he admonishes. "Because of our limited resources, it's critical for small churches to tear down the silo walls between churches and work together to advance the kingdom of God."[13] I couldn't agree more. For example, my county has a dozen food pantries. On one hand, this is great! Many congregations and other organizations care about food insecurity in our county. And having pantries located in different townships ensures everyone in need has access. On the other hand, I wonder how we are limiting ourselves by our food pantry silos. I wonder what would happen if we learned to share our resources, volunteers, wisdom, and networks. I have a feeling that possibilities for new outreach and better outcomes would open up if we cooperated in some of our programs. Ordinary leaders are always looking for these connections because they understand the power of partnership. And they are nurturing new expressions of solidarity because they know we are stronger and better together.

The third rivalrous relationship is the rural–urban relationship. Much has been made of these cultural divides, but it's important to name a basic yet often-forgotten truth: urban folks need rural folks. And rural folks need urban folks. Our best shot at thriving is through collaboration around issues of mutual interest. This project of strengthening rural–urban solidarity is daunting and, at times, perplexing. But it's critical. Economist and social critic E. M. Schumacher went so far as to say, "To restore a proper balance between city and rural life is perhaps the greatest task in front of modern man."[14] He insists that the health of one is tied to the health of the other, like the health of body and mind are tied to one another. The reality is that rural regions are still the primary places of food and fiber production, so the destruction of rural places and people leads to the destruction of urban places and people. Speaking specifically to the realities of America's "heartland," sociologists Patrick Carr and Maria Kefalas came to this same conclusion after their study of "brain drain" in Iowa:

What is happening in many small towns—devastating loss of educated and talented young people, the aging of the population, and the erosion of the local community—has repercussions far beyond their boundaries. Put simply, the health of the small towns that are dotted across the Heartland matters because, without them, the country couldn't function, in the same way that a body cannot function without a heart. . . . We should care because the Heartland is the place where our food comes from, it is the place that helps elect our presidents . . . and it is the place that sends more than its fair share of young men and women to fight for this country. The future of many towns that gives the Heartland its shape and its sinews is of vital importance, and we believe that ignoring their hollowing out will be detrimental in the short and long terms.[15]

You probably already believe this. But remember that solidarity and interdependence mean it goes both ways. Small towns and rural communities need cities too. The hard truth is that my own small town would be struggling much more if we didn't have the relative proximity of Columbus, which increases our property values, generates jobs for our families, and brings tourists and consumers to our shops. It's also a hub for cultural creativity, diversity, and a marketplace of ideas that both challenges and enriches us. Ordinary leaders will almost surely face resistance when they start promoting rural–urban partnership, but strengthening this solidarity is sure to unleash new opportunities and make our communities more sustainable and stronger. We can maintain our unique, rural identity *and* appreciate and benefit from our cities.

Whether the issue is racism, classism, or separation by silos, many forces pull us apart. So Christ is always at work calling us back together and calling us forward to the kin-dom. Underneath many of these divisions is a powerful pull called "contempt." It pulls us apart and pulls us away from our relatedness and our responsibility. It is the rejection of our kinship and the opposite of solidarity.

The concept of contempt was popularized recently by relationship researcher John Gottman. Gottman found that while there are many enemies to a successful marriage, the ultimate indicator of impending divorce is contempt. It's more toxic than simple frustration or negativity. It's not just about having passionate arguments or being annoyed at your partner's habits. In marriage, it is a belief that we are better than our partner and they are no longer worth our time. It is "poisonous to a relationship because it conveys disgust and superiority, especially moral, ethical, or characterological."[16] When contempt takes over in a relationship, partners can't remember a single positive quality about one another. There is no admiration or curiosity. There is only disgust and disregard of a partner who we think has become utterly unworthy of respect or attention.

Economist and social critic Arthur Brooks took this concept of contempt and applied it to contemporary politics and the societal bonds of Americans. He contends that contempt is making us unhappy as people and incapable of making political progress. His research reveals significant common ground on public policy and a weariness with our divisions, but something keeps us from coming together and moving forward. Brooks argues that the main reason for our stagnation and division is this spirit of contempt.

So, what can we do about it? Brooks asks us to remember who benefits from our ongoing contempt for one another. Powerful people, whom he calls "rhetorical dope peddlers," gain by making money and winning elections. While we might enjoy feeling superior to "the other side," and although believing they are simply deviant and stupid is convenient, such perspectives don't ultimately make us feel better or solve the problems that desperately need to be addressed in our nation. Brooks also invites us to make a commitment: "Each of us can make a commitment never to treat others with contempt, even if we believe they deserve it." Instead, we engage in authentic dialogues and debates. We don't "send them away" in an anti-kinship divorce but stay in relationship and maintain responsibility. Brooks admits that this approach may sound like an appeal to benevolence alone, but in actuality it has other benefits. "This might sound like a call for magnanimity, but it is just as much an appeal to self-interest. Contempt makes persuasion impossible—no one has ever been hated into agreement, after all—so its expression is either petty self-indulgence or cheap virtue signaling, neither of which wins converts."[17]

If we are committed to recovering abundance for ourselves and our communities, we simply don't have time for contempt. It's cheap and easy and common, but just as it's the primary predictor of divorce, it may well be the primary predictor of decline. We do well to develop a contempt for contempt, to borrow from Francis de Sales.[18] The kin-dom of God and the possibilities of renewal call us to a conversion—from contempt to kinship. The turn is going to take all of us. If we are willing to welcome all to the table and respect the plate they offer, the banquet of God's kingdom is possible. We can all eat and be satisfied.

CHAPTER TWELVE

THE PRACTICE
OF MEMORY

Gather the pieces that are left over. Let nothing be wasted.

John 6:12

WHEN I WAS GROWING UP, we often had leftovers after a meal. We would carefully stow the food in plastic containers and place them in the fridge before we did the dishes. These remnants would be packed for lunch the next day, saved for a midnight snack (which, in the Midwest, is 8:00 p.m.), or perhaps repurposed in a casserole or soup. The preservation and consumption of leftovers was an ethical imperative for our family, and I remember learning when I was twelve years old that it was an imperative for others, too. That's when I read in a library book about a ritual prayer in Islam asking for forgiveness for throwing away food. Apparently, food waste is kind of a big deal for Muslims. Food is never to be wasted. It is to be saved and eaten by the family, given to the poor, or, if worse comes to worst, fed to animals. This little snippet about prayer and food waste stuck with me because it made sense in light of our household leftovers ethic.

As a young adult I had dinner with a family who prepared a gigantic meal of quality, delicious food—a veritable feast of many colors containing all the major food groups. Afterward, they took all the food that wasn't eaten and dumped it into the trash. Right out of the pot and pan. Not after a couple weeks of shamefully dancing around its presence in the fridge. Not after a couple feeble attempts to warm it up for lunch. Not with a self-justifying whisper that at least we are composting. I almost tossed my cookies. Inconceivable!

Morally upright though my parents may have been for their leftover heroics, I have to admit my fidelity to their ways was lukewarm for many years. I never, ever, immediately threw leftovers away. But in spite of their influence, I've let too many containers become petri dishes. And too many times I've opted for a drive-through fix or tasty homemade dish when there were perfectly good food remnants waiting in the fridge. I'm happy to report, however, that my attitude toward leftovers has greatly improved over the past few years. I've grown fond of them now—without all the heavy moral baggage of my boyhood days. No need to compare myself to starving kids in [insert name of developing world nation]. My appreciation for leftovers is mostly shame-free. Instead, I praise leftovers for three reasons.

First, leftovers prolong the pleasure of a good meal. I don't often leave a restaurant with a to-go box, but when I do I carry it like an ancient warrior carrying the spoils of war. If I leave a restaurant with a box, it means either I've practiced self-discipline and not eaten the whole thing, or the feast was so abundant that I couldn't consume it all in one meal. Either is a reason to celebrate. For me, there's nothing as satisfying as turning those leftovers into a snack while taking in a favorite show with my honey.

Second, leftovers ease the effort required for the next meal. One way of looking at life is as a series of decisions about what to make for the next meal, especially if we are trying to eat "right"—avoiding fast food or highly processed food or single-serve meals designed for single men. Leftovers ease this burden by providing semi-fresh food that can easily be packed and eaten on a lunch break.

Third, leftovers evoke memories. When I'm putting away the taco meat and beans after a fiesta with friends, I'm thinking about the joy and comradery we shared at the meal, and I'm grateful we get to host these kinds of experiences with people we care about. When I'm spreading mayonnaise on my turkey sandwich, I'm also remembering the Thanksgiving dinner we all experienced a couple days before. Sometimes we are so hungry and busy at mealtime that we don't actually taste our food; it's only in eating the leftovers that we remember how tasty or filling it really was. In fact, some foods are actually better as leftovers, after they've had some time sitting in the refrigerator or after they are reheated. There's actually scientific research that confirms this; foods continue to undergo transformation long after they are fresh. Likewise, it's often only after the fact, in our reflection and remembering, that we really taste the full meaning and significance of the occasion.

In our gospel text, it would seem logical to end the story after everyone is full and happy. We might expect: "They all ate and were satisfied. And they all lived happily ever after in the kingdom of God." But that's not what happened. Jesus keeps the story going by telling the disciples to clean up: "Gather the pieces that are left over. Let nothing be wasted" (John 6:12). Jesus was concerned about the leftovers. Why is this detail included? Why is Jesus's call to gather the leftovers included in these sacred stories?

It's possible the meaning is straightforward. Like my parents and many faithful Muslims, Jesus viewed preserving leftovers as a moral imperative. Both frugal and faithful, Jesus wasn't about to leave leftover half-eaten bread and fish strewn about the countryside. A miracle of divine superabundance is no reason to be wasteful. Maybe those leftovers were part of the provision for the next day. Leaving them on the ground to rot would be tantamount to rejecting a gift and neglecting divine provision. It would also mean leaving a mess, which isn't very neighborly. And besides: waste not, want not. In this reading, Jesus's instruction had a moral and practical purpose.

Some scholars read Jesus's final instruction as a parable representing God's call to gather up all the scattered people who have
been left out and left behind. Jesus was calling his followers to join
him in the great mission of God to reach out to the lost and restore
them to the family and kingdom of God. In his book *God's Country:
Faith, Hope, and the Future of the Rural Church*, Mennonite pastor
Brad Roth points out that the "sign" in John's gospel is both multiplication and gathering. The specific number of baskets filled with
leftovers is the giveaway for Roth. He says, "The key is the number of
baskets: twelve, a number signaling that we're talking about God's
whole people. There are twelve tribes and twelve apostles."[1] What
I like is how Roth takes this symbolism and draws from it a message for small towns and rural churches. Gathering up all the fragments reminds us that God is present and active in all places and
wants to include everyone and every place in that great renewal of
all things. So, the bread, often a sacramental sign for Christ or the
body of Christ, points beyond itself to God's desire for the church's
wholeness. When Jesus instructed the disciples to gather up the leftovers, he was essentially saying, "Let none be left behind or ignored
or disparaged. Let none be lost. Gather up all the fragments into
the kingdom." Roth clarifies the implications of this interpretation:
"Without the rural church, some fragment would be lost."[2] Rural
people are important, and rural churches are important parts of the
body of Christ. In this reading, gathering leftovers has a missional
purpose.

I like this interpretation, but in light of our focus on civic-
spiritual practices, I wonder if there's yet another layer. Maybe gathering up the leftovers had a spiritual purpose. Of course, the practical
and missional readings are also spiritual, but this reading suggests
that Jesus was doing something internally formative within the disciples. Maybe Jesus really wanted his slow-to-learn disciples to truly
grasp the meaning of the miracle. So he gives them a final practice
to engage after the crowds head out (presumably). Often, we recognize only in those moments after an event the true significance of

what happened and who was gathered. As they load the dishwasher, the hosts remember how one of their friends came out of his shell when they were playing the board game. The night after the retreat ends, a person remembers an important insight while journaling. Only after three days of rest does the newly married couple feel the full rush of gratitude for their special day and all the special people who celebrated with them. To paraphrase John Dewey, we do not learn from experience; we learn from reflecting on experience.[3] Additionally, we learn from embodying what we learned in practical and relational ways. So maybe Jesus wanted the disciples to take a little time to reflect, remember, and let the meaning of the miracle sink in.

In the Hebrew Bible, we learn that the people of Israel were commanded to keep a jar full of manna and carry it with them alongside the covenant tablets. Perpetual, preserved leftovers! Why carry this jar across the desert? The passage tells us: "Moses said, 'This is what the Lord has commanded: "Take an omer of manna and keep it for the generations to come, so they can see the bread I gave you to eat in the wilderness when I brought you out of Egypt"'" (Exod 16:32). It was intended to be an enduring physical reminder of God's faithfulness and creative provision. Even in rural places, even in the wilderness. You see, our story isn't about the first time God fed the multitude. Not even close. God has actually made a habit of it. We just forget.

Jump ahead two chapters later in the gospel of Mark and you will find that the disciples forgot. In Mark 8 we are told that "another large crowd gathered." And Jesus sets the disciples up again: "I have compassion for these people; they have already been with me three days and have nothing to eat. If I send them home hungry, they will collapse on the way, because some of them have come a long distance." Sound familiar? Once again, we have a large crowd gathering. Once again, Jesus has compassion on these folks and indicates that he wants them to host them. Hey, great! They can do this! They learned from Jesus the last time how to call forth the abundance of the people and the place and to manifest God's commonwealth. Shouldn't be a problem. Except . . . the pattern repeats itself.

"His disciples answered, 'But where in this remote place can anyone get enough bread to feed them?'" (Mark 8:4). The disciples went right back into that scarcity thinking. The food is not enough. The place is not enough. We are not enough. God is not enough. In my sanctified imagination, I picture Jesus sighing or lifting up his face and asking heaven for patience. But the text doesn't tell us that. We only know that Jesus went back to his favorite strategy of answering a question with a question. Once again, he calls his disciples to be available to the moment, look more closely for the kingdom, and take an inventory of what is present and possible. Same song and dance: "How many loaves do you have?"

The rest, as they say, is history. Again. The people sat down, food was collected and lifted up with gratitude and blessing, and the disciples distributed the food until everyone ate and was satisfied. With leftovers again! Only four thousand were fed this time, but still. How many miracles does it take?

REMEMBERING THE FUTURE

Looking down on the disciples is fun. But if we laugh at them, we should laugh out of familiarity. We are also disciples of little faith, of short memory. This is problematic. Our bad memory limits our sense of possibility. If it's never been done, we reason, it's pretty unlikely that we could do it now. Using our text, if Jesus had never facilitated a miracle among the multitude, there would be no reason to believe it was possible. But Jesus, the great inaugurator and instigator of the kingdom, opened up new possibilities. When we witness these wonders personally, we begin to believe that miracles are possible IRL (in real life). The world looks different afterward; it's the same world, but we view it with new hope for healing and transformation.

Neuroscientists actually have a term for this interplay between memory and possibility. It's called "future memory." It means, in essence, that our vision of what is possible is based on what we've heard or seen in the past. Memory scientist and Nobel laureate Eric Kandel puts it this way: "We are who we are because of what we learn and what we remember."[4] In other words, memory isn't neutral, it's formational. Applying this principle to spiritual growth, pastor and spiritual director Casey Tygrett posits, "Without memory, there is no formation, whether those memories are joyful and treasured, ambiguous and circumstantial, or traumatic. We are God's memory-made beings."[5] For better or worse, our memories make us who we are.

Jesus provided a miracle-shaped moment and a memory that transformed the trajectory of the people who experienced it. Of course, that great meal miracle was about getting food to hungry people. That would be enough. But based on the wider witness of Jesus's life and ministry, I have a feeling it was about more than that. Jesus was orchestrating an experience that disciples and seekers alike could look back to and be continually shaped by.

Miracles challenge us to learn new stories—about ourselves, our neighbors, and the God-world relationship. Theology professor James Bryan Smith is right: "Our stories are running our lives—in ways we may not even be aware of."[6] Ordinary leaders are open to God's new words and works, so they don't run away when God "breaks the script" with a strategic surprise. And ordinary leaders learn to tell the new story in word and deed.

MULTIPLYING THE MIRACLE

When our future-memory embraces both the possibilities and responsibilities of God's kingdom, we once again experience the miracle of multiplication. Perhaps the miracle of old was the multiplication of fish and bread. May it be so today. But the miracle after the miracle is also the multiplication of miracle workers. If Jesus (with his companions) could feed twenty thousand, let's say (counting women and children this time), what world-shaking possibilities are available if those twenty thousand each learned how to feed thousands of others? Jesus didn't just come to do miracles; he came to make miracle makers. Empowered by those defining moments and future-shaping memories, the multitude could go forth and multiply the miracles in their own families and villages. In other words, Jesus was saying, "*Do* try this at home. I've shown you how to recover abundance. Go and do likewise."

We don't know how the experience shaped everyone who witnessed the miracle. Perhaps miracles came about because members of the multitude returned home as new creations in Christ. I believe they did. But we also know from the example of the disciples how easy it is to forget. We need to be reminded. So we keep telling the stories, remembering those holy moments, and gathering the leftovers. Perhaps that is why Jesus gave his disciples a ritual of remembrance.

In the Lord's Supper, we re-member and re-collect the script-breaking stories of Jesus. We recall his death, yes, but also his life, and allow those memories to re-call us to continue his ministry. When Jesus said, "Do this in remembrance of me," the Greek word for "remember" is *anamnesis*, which literally means "against amnesia." It is a refusal to forget. When we eat at the Lord's table, we are refusing to forget God's redemptive work across history, the example of Jesus, and the promises of divine presence. This kind of remembering is bringing the past into the present and letting it speak to us.

When I lived in Oregon, I heard about a nearby inclusive Catholic church that was led by a female priest. Naturally, I was curious. And I heard that they practiced an open table, welcoming all, Catholic or not, for the Eucharist. At that time, I was hungry for liturgy, so I sometimes attended Catholic churches in the area. But I always felt let down, if not a bit pained, to reach the climax of the mass and not be able to go up and receive the Eucharist because I'm not Catholic. So I was excited to visit this inclusive church one evening.

A small but friendly group gathered for worship that night. The liturgy was rich and historical, but also inclusive. And the point came in the service when we were invited to "take and eat" the Eucharist. When the priest invited the gathered to the table, she looked right at me and said, "*All* are welcome to the table." Feeling spiritually tender and hungry, I slipped out from the pew and made my way to the line. One by one, each member of the faithful approached the presiding priest as she gently raised the bread and offered, "The body of Christ. Take and eat." As I prepared myself to receive the elements, I assumed the priest would offer the same words to me. But she didn't. Instead, she dipped the bread into the wine, raised it, placed it before me, and looked me in the eyes. She smiled and said, "*You* are the body of Christ." It was a defining moment. The set-apart space, the directly spoken words of identity, and the taste of the bread and juice combined to make it an unforgettable and formative memory.

Memories, moments, meals, miracles—all these things combine in a type of holy alchemy to mark our minds with a sense of belonging and calling. In Christ, we know who we are, whose we are, what we are, and why we are. We are children of the Holy One and siblings at the table of Christ. We are wonder workers and co-creators in the world. We are the body of Christ, fully fed and called to become bread for others.

COMMUNITIES OF MEMORY

Rural communities are communities of memory. Of course, all communities are communities of memory, in some sense. But many small towns and rural regions have a vibrant sense of memory and story. When I moved back to my hometown, I was reminded of how rural folks tend to value family names more than city and suburban folks do. If your neighborhood is an urban melting pot or a newly developed suburban cul de sac, I suppose someone's last name doesn't convey much meaning. But for many folks in rural towns with deep histories and foundational families whose descendants still run the town, a name means an awful lot. In my county, the ancient Hebrew wisdom remains relevant: "A good name is more desirable than great riches; to be esteemed is better than silver or gold" (Prov 22:1). Your last name is an asset if it's still respected; thankfully, the "Henry" name I bear is still in good shape. Before they know anything about me as an individual, there are folks who "know" me because I am Don and Sandy's son or Charles and Edna's grandkid, and so forth. (Sadly, if your name has baggage or stigma attached to it, you will struggle to do well in this town.)

I have a coworker at the library who illustrates this family name principle every time someone new comes into the library. She looks at their library card application and tries to understand their essence based on their tribal affiliation via last name. She's not afraid to ask clarifying questions: Are you related to [name]? Do you know [name]? It's kind of funny to see what happens when she can't make a connection to some long-standing family in the area and is thus unable to place them in a correct category. If she were a computer, her screen would read "Does not compute!" as she shoots out sparks and smoke.

This way of being a memory-shaped community can be silly. It can even be harmful. It can make finding a place in our community hard for new people. But it's also a reminder that we are not purely individuals. No one is an island. No one is completely self-made and self-sufficient. For better or worse, our ancestors live on in us. In the language of Christian theology, we remain related to our ancestors through the communion of saints. In Christ, we are present to them, and they are present to us.

This connection with ancestors among rural folks is not so much an existential, mystical communion as one that is felt and embodied in the ordinary ventures of life. A farmer feels the presence of his ancestors as he farms the land that his grandfather farmed for fifty years. A young mother feels the presence of her mother as she holds her baby in her arms for the first time, wishing her mom were still around to spoil him. A parishioner feels connected to his great-grandparents while worshipping in a local congregation, feeling that the space is still filled with their prayers and songs.

Wendell Berry reminds us that in the sharing of place, work, and love, we often experience our membership with one another and our communion with those who came before us. Re-membering the dead and honoring their memory with our lives is a testimony of wholeness and unity when so many cultural forces are breaking common bonds, dividing us up into convenient categories, and tearing apart what God has joined together.

THE PAST IS PRIORITY

Before we get into how this orientation can be problematic, let's first acknowledge this past-orientation as a rural reality and acknowledge that it runs counter to the future-oriented, forward-focused, ahistorical tendencies of our society. In our country, especially within urban and suburban centers, we tend to view the present in relation to a far-stretching future. In contrast, small towns and rural regions tend to approach the present in relation to a deep, historical past. Perhaps this rootedness is a necessary corrective to current cultural trends that fetishize change and accept uncritically the relentless march of technological advance. While rural communities are tempted to get stuck in the past, many urban and suburban communities are tempted to "backslide into the future," as poet Paul Valery put it.[7] They go with the flow of dominant "progressive" forces, too often disregarding the witness and wisdom of our ancestors and the lessons of history.

Reverend Anthony Pappas tells about a rural parish where he was serving as a pastor. As he began his ministry there, he implemented some new programs and put forward a fresh vision for the congregation. Wheels were put in motion to foster growth and new life. He was excited, but he also began to notice that the congregants didn't share his enthusiasm. They weren't resistant, really. They were generally positive. But they weren't eager to pull together and exert themselves for a bold new vision. Pastor Pappas was perplexed until a conversation with a deacon led to a paradigm-shifting realization:

"It was the 'good ol' days' not a 'bright new tomorrow' that motivated them," he shared in *Entering the World of the Small Church*.
"I was heading in the wrong direction. They were energized, not to
create a new future, but to restore the good of the past. Yesterday,
not tomorrow, attracted their interest and concern."[8]

In a world obsessed with "bright new tomorrows," this mindset can be experienced as "backward" and staying "stuck in the
past." But what if it's just different? What if focusing on the past
and focusing on the future both have pros and cons, strengths and
weaknesses, promises and pitfalls? Small church researcher Carl
Dudley seems to think they do. He agrees with Pappas when he says,
"Conserving the relationship between people, place, and happening is the contribution of many small churches to the pilgrimages
of church members. Small churches are not against change. They
simply feel that conserving the past is a priority."[9]

I recently read a story about a school in the small town of Sen-
eca, Illinois, that came up with a great idea to preserve local history
and provide quality education for its students. It took place during
the COVID-19 pandemic when many schools were struggling to
keep kids safe and learning at the same time. As is often the case,
necessity was the mother of invention. But it all started with a local
kid and FFA member named Levi who noticed something when
he was working as a groundskeeper at Mt. Calvary Cemetery. He
noticed that many of the oldest tombstones were so dirty and dilap-
idated that people couldn't read them. Levi mentioned this to his
dad, a local teacher, FFA advisor, and self-described "history geek."
His dad decided this could be a great opportunity for a socially distanced but interactive and service-oriented educational experience.
"Extreme Makeover: Gravestone Edition" was born.

When the students all met at the cemetery, many of them were
skeptical. But Levi's dad, "Mr. Maierhofer," was passionate about the
project. And it didn't take long for the students to get into it, once
they witnessed how the chemical cleaning process transformed the
black gravestones to gray, then to white. They also started to grow

interested in the stories of the deceased. Each student selected a name or family to research, mostly using Ancestory.com. After they gathered their information and stories, they gave an oral presentation to their classmates while standing next to the tombstone. They learned about all kinds of folks who had inhabited their community in earlier times: German immigrants, a child who died while his father was fighting in the Civil War, brothers who fought in World War I, a woman who lived to be 105 years old, and a professional baseball player. They also learned from who *wasn't* there. There were very few farmers buried in town, they discovered. Most farmers, especially the earliest pioneers, had family burial plots on their farmland.

This project benefited everyone involved. It provided an innovative way for teachers and the school to fulfill their responsibilities safely and work within their mission. It benefited the community through the volunteer hours in the cemetery and the new knowledge and history the students uncovered. And all the students—both new students who were learning about the area and students who have multigenerational roots in the community but may not be in touch with their history—made new connections with their community's history.

The story is a great example of local innovation that honors the past while supporting the present generation. But I also see the project as a kind of metaphor for ordinary leadership in small towns and rural regions. We clean the tombstones, we tend the stones, but not because we are obsessed with the past or enamored with the dead. We tend and keep these memorials because we want to make sure their stories are told, their years and names respected, and the present and future of our community to benefit from their examples.

I had a church history professor in college who used to say, "If history doesn't matter, then you don't matter." It was a startling reminder that one day we will be reduced to a name and length of time, like the etchings on those tombstones. Maybe our ashes will be scattered or buried in a field like those old farmers. But if the lives of our ancestors don't matter, then ours won't either. Ordinary leaders keep alive the respect for the dignity of every life as part of the story we are telling together. In the project of recovering abundance, we need storytellers and memory keepers who work to uncover all our stories and histories. It's nice to know where we came from, but it's also critical for our wholeness as communities and our sense of direction moving forward.

SITTING TILL BEDTIME

Wendell Berry talks about a tradition in his rural corner of the country called "sitting till bedtime." In this practice, neighbors gathered at someone's home after a hard day's work and "told each other stories . . . that they had all heard before." Berry recalls, "Sometimes they told stories about each other, about themselves, living again in their own memories and thus keeping their memories alive."[10] This practice of "sitting till bedtime," often done informally around the table or beside the fire, preserved the community's history and family heritage. It promoted humor and humility while also passing on wisdom about how to live well in their place.

I had never heard of this practice until I read about it in Berry's essay "The Work of Local Culture." But I think I experienced something similar growing up. My parents liked to have friends over for snacks, games, laughter, and catching up (and maybe a little gossip). I specifically remember our neighbors, the Harveys, coming over. They would walk over after dinner with a huge paper bag of popcorn and sit down at my parents' dinner table for a couple games of "up and down the river." Both the Henrys and the Harveys had histories in Holiness Quakerism, so they grew up playing with Rook cards (allowed as an alternative to standard playing cards, which were associated with gambling). "Up and down the river" used Rook cards but did require a "bid" (not to be confused with a "bet"). The bidding happened before any cards were played, and it involved everyone simultaneously and rhythmically pounding three times on the table before indicating their bid using their fingers. As a child with a bedtime, I would lie in bed, upstairs in my room, listening to this pounding and the occasional outburst of laughter, and wishing I could be downstairs where the Quaker-appropriate fun was taking place. When I was a little older, I got to join the game. And I learned that there was more to those evenings than noisy bids and laughter. In between hands, stories were told and retold, jokes tested, concerns confessed, and news passed on. I think it was our version of "sitting till bedtime."

As I recall those visits, I am grateful that I had those experiences of neighborliness. It taught me that entertainment doesn't require phones and televisions but can be enjoyed around the table with friends and family. It taught me the value and utility of storytelling and local knowledge. And it taught me that we have both the privilege and responsibility to know, care for, and enjoy our neighbors.

Our communities include good folks who keep local memories alive in more formal ways, too. God bless all our local historical societies. And we can thank groups like the American Legion and VFW who keep before us the stories and sacrifices of local veterans. And don't get me started on how important libraries are to our community well-being. When you think about local history and storytelling, someone probably comes to mind. Don't undervalue them. Get to know them. Give them opportunities to tell those stories and uncover that history. If it's a bit dry, partner with them to make that history more interactive and engaging. Work together to see what can be drawn from these wells that will nourish our work today.

Ordinary leaders are memory keepers, storytellers, and historians. We remember the miracle and praise the leftovers. We gather up everything and include everyone so that nothing is lost—so that no one is lost. In doing so, we work toward a future for our communities in which "hope and history rhyme," to borrow from Irish poet Seamus Heaney.[11]

PITFALLS IN A COMMUNITY OF MEMORY

Though memory provides many positive possibilities, it also hides many pitfalls. It's not enough to remember. We have to remember rightly. Memory, neuroscientists tell us, is malleable. That is, we have the power to shape it, even as it has the power to shape us. It's more than the ability to store information in our brain; it's an active process that is constantly remaking our connections between past experiences and our dreams and fears for the future. Remembering rightly, then, means not only trying to gather all the information but facing the fullness of our history and framing it in a way that leads to redemptive possibilities. I'm borrowing, in part, from Miroslav Volf and his book *The End of Memory*, in which he talks about "right remembering" as both truthful remembering and redemptive remembering. This is a practice of remembering that doesn't ignore injustice or fixate on wrongs but remembers in light of the "meta-memories" of God's promises and purposes.[12]

Icons and Idols

One way we fail to remember rightly is by turning icons into idols. What's the difference? An icon is something that represents and symbolizes something or someone; it points beyond itself to a higher or truer reality. An icon becomes an idol when people mistake the symbol for the reality; it becomes the object of worship. The use of icons—paintings, pictures, statues, sculptures, and the like—to aid the worshipper in religious devotion as they reflect on the Reality to which the icon points has a rich history. When the worshipper focuses on the icon as the ultimate concern rather than seeing *through* it like a window to the divine, it has become an idol. This occurs in spiritual practice and also in civic practice. Let me illustrate.

In my hometown we have an icon that locals often call "the monument." Shaped like a miniature version of the Washington Monument and more formally known as "the victory shaft," it is over one hundred years old and a great source of pride for residents of the county. It was gifted to us in 1919 by the federal government after county residents outpaced all the eighty-seven counties in Ohio in War Savings Stamp purchases during a special drive that year. Morrow County actually had the highest per capita rate of War Bond and Stamp purchases in the whole country earlier in 1919. The dedication of the monument was a huge event attended by thousands of people from all around. Then-Senator Warren G. Harding (who had roots in the region) gave a speech praising our people, especially farmers, noting that 25 percent of those who went to war were farmers. He also thanked farmers for taking responsibility to feed both their neighbors and our allies across the sea. After the unveiling of the shaft, citizens were able to walk up and see the names of local men who died in the war and read the inscription: "Dedicated in honor of all Morrow County men and women who wore the uniform of their country and served under the colors during the World War of 1917–1918 and to the Memory of those who relinquished all that Liberty might not perish."

It's quite the symbol of community pride and a monument to local history and sacrifice. But since that original dedication in 1919, most of the folks who wanted to read the names and inscriptions for themselves had to risk life and limb to do so. You see, this great monument was placed right in the middle of the four-way intersection of the town square. It makes some symbolic sense, I suppose, but it created a somewhat narrow and rather confusing roundabout. Out-of-towners have an especially hard time navigating around the monument. Every few months I get word that a trucker, driving through town, couldn't make the sharp turn and got stuck on the concrete base around the shaft. It's only a matter of time before a truck flips completely over or damages the shaft itself.

Because of these risks, every few years the idea is put forward that we should . . . move the monument. As soon as this is mentioned, all hell breaks loose. Name calling commences. Facebook arguments run wild. Impassioned speeches are given about liberal snowflakes and the general breakdown of society. Accusations are made about dishonoring veterans. All because a few folks want to learn what it would take to move the monument just up the street to the veterans' memorial. Imagine the military monument in the veterans' memorial—where people could actually read it and experience it outside of their car!

I'm exaggerating, of course (though only a little). And the truth is, I don't have strong feelings about the monument or where it should be located. But I do have the humble opinion that this icon has turned into an idol. How do I know? The outsize reaction to questions or suggestions of change is a pretty good indicator. When an icon has become untouchable, it has most likely turned into an idol. People almost treat our monument like the biblical Ark of the Covenant: touch it, and you will be struck down.

It bothers me that folks get so worked up about the symbol but seem to be complacent about the reality. I'd love for folks to be energized about what the symbol represents, about the spirit and possibilities of our county. It tells a story about people who have civic pride and patriotism, who value service and sacrifice. It tells a story about people who are able to come together for a common cause and the common good. It tells a story about people who are willing to give their hard-earned money to a cause they believe is important. The monument functions better as an icon, which we see through to the spirit and possibilities of our community.

Monuments are often reflections of our memories. They represent what we want to remember and how we want to remember them. Monuments, as I'm sure you know, are the subject of heated debates in our country. Small towns and rural regions are important to this debate. Some of these monuments need to be recognized as symbols of a failure to remember rightly and be taken down. Some, though, simply need to be dethroned. They should be converted from idols to icons, through which we can recall our history, confront our darkness, and rise to our possibilities. When we change the way we relate to these symbols and stories, the monuments can be tools for right remembering.

Selective Memory

Another way we fail to remember rightly is by practicing selective memory. To some extent, all memory is selective memory. We filter out information that isn't relevant to the needs of the moment. But sometimes, individually and collectively, we also filter out information that is inconvenient, painful, or indicting. In the chapter on organizing, I told you about the vigil we led in our hometown. As we planned the gathering and heard responses about it afterward, a common refrain was that while racism may be a problem somewhere else, it was not a problem in our sweet little town. How did people know? They found proof in our history. Early Quaker settlers in the county were conductors on the Underground Railroad, and some were active abolitionists, so we solved these problems a long time ago. There is indeed a lot of rich history among Friends, Presbyterians, and others in our county seeking justice and healing for those impacted by racism. I love this history; I don't think it's known widely enough by local folks. And I think we should bring it up and build on it for our current context. But a lot has happened in the last couple hundred years, and not all of it has been admirable. Recall the burning cross story from the last chapter.

Ordinary leaders in small towns and rural regions call forth the best and beautiful in their community's history. But they aren't afraid of inconvenient truths, either. As ministers are charged to recall the "whole counsel of God" in Scripture, ordinary leaders recall the whole counsel of memory from our history—the good and bad, the beautiful and ugly—because we aren't just history keepers, we are history shapers. We aren't just memory keepers, we are memory makers. So we need the full picture to guide our movements. We need the whole story to best go about advancing the story. Selective memory doesn't serve us as we seek to find our way forward and recover the possibilities of abundant life for our people and place. The eighteenth-century rabbi Baal Shem Tov said it well: "Forgetfulness leads to exile, while remembrance is the secret of redemption."[13]

Nostalgia

A third way we fail to remember rightly is when we get stuck in nostalgia. Nostalgia is the belief that all of our best days are in the past. It is a form of selective memory in which we generalize the past as positive and the present as negative. It's a common problem, and it's apparently an old problem. The teacher in Ecclesiastes had to advise, "Do not say, 'Why were the old days better than these?' For it is not wise to ask such questions" (Eccl 7:10).

Like many things, in small doses nostalgia isn't such a bad thing. There's nothing wrong with a little bit of sentimentality and reminiscing about the "good ol' days." We all remember times as a child or honeymooner or new parent and think, "Those were the days." The problem is when we forget that the "good ol' days" weren't always good. Even more, the problem is when we forget that there are "good *new* days" to come, which we can't experience and engage if we are stuck in the past. Psychiatrist Gordon Livingston pointed out that nostalgia is often the enemy of hope.[14] It tricks us into believing that our best days are behind us, sapping our energy and trapping it in the past. But when we have a realistic sense of history, we see that now as in the past, a mix of challenge and opportunity lies before us, available as we co-create the future.

The dark side of nostalgia is not just its power to limit our future, however; it's the power it holds to keep us inescapably attached to the past. A similar concept in addiction studies is called "euphoric recall." When someone has an addiction to drugs and alcohol, for example, their brain has been rewired against right remembering. They tend to remember their past life with the substance in euphoric terms. Life with drugs and alcohol was so much easier—so happy and functional. They don't remember the isolation and illness and lack of dignity and autonomy.

Since in small towns and rural regions we tend to orient ourselves to the past, we are especially susceptible to the temptations of nostalgia and euphoric recall. Sometimes we believe that salvation for the now is a recreation of the old. We will get a new industrial factory to move in so we can replace the old. A new mining or oil and gas company will come in and make us great again. A strong conservative leader who looks like us will restore things to the way we were. Our towns were small when we shared the same values and religions and skin color . . . In our euphoric recall, though, we forget the secrets of domestic abuse that hid behind "spouses staying together." We forget the segregating systems that were enforced by our "shared values." We forget the "bust" that inevitably follows the "boom" created by outside corporations. And we don't realize how easily that strong leader can exploit our enduring divisions and keep us moving into the future by peddling false promises.

PLANTING AND PRESERVING SEEDS

A fascinating gentleman with a long beard farms a piece of land near Industry, Maine, in the state's western foothills. His name is Will Bonsall, and his farm has had a fascinating mission for decades. Apart from helping the seventy-year-old live with as much sustainability and self-sufficiency as possible, the place is dedicated to the Scatterseed Project, which is dedicated to "collecting, preserving, and sharing our horticulture heritage." So Bonsall and his apprentices preserve seeds from an incredibly diverse array of plants. For example, he had seeds for over eleven hundred varieties of peas. His farm is a seed bank of sorts. It's called "scatterseed" because he doesn't want to simply build up a collection for its own sake but to "scatter" these riches to the world by making them available to the general public. Bonsall's operation is unique in another way: he preserves seeds not only by storing and sharing them but by planting them. This keeps them alive, adapting, and evolving. Will is concerned about conservation, no doubt. He preserves the thousands of varieties not because they are all particularly productive or useful for many people in many places but because he values diversity and he's aware that some may have future utility, even if they don't seem important right now. We don't know what kinds of social and eco-logical conditions will emerge in the coming years, especially with climate disruption at work in the world. So this seed collection is an insurance policy of sorts.[15]

Seed saving and swapping is a great skill, and Bonsall is under-taking a massive, and massively important, project with his appren-tices. But I also think ordinary leaders like us in small towns and rural regions can learn a lot of leadership lessons from this work. Preserving the memories, histories, and stories of our communities is like a Maine farmer collecting and saving seeds (this is practically a parable of Jesus). We gather and keep them because their diver-sity is beautiful and because we don't know exactly how or when they will prove themselves valuable. But these stories and memories don't have to be stored in the dark recesses of our historical societ-ies and libraries (as amazing and critical as those institutions are). No, we honor and preserve them by planting them and scattering them. We use them, invest them, apply them, share them, experi-ment with them.

This memory work may change over time; the process may be practiced differently between generations. As Bonsall demonstrated, it's a dynamic, innovative process that unfolds as we preserve the original forms and cultivate new varieties. As church historian Jaro-slav Pelikan said about the difference between tradition and tradi-tionalism, it's not the dead faith of the living but the living faith of the dead.[16] In keeping and cultivating these seeds, we discover that what we've saved is saving us. In our storehouse are seeds of hope, seeds of wisdom, seeds of liberation, seeds for abundance.

LEGACY WORK

Since the practice of memory is an organic process of keeping and cultivating life, it calls us to confront the painful truths about the end of life. Any conversation about growth and multiplication turns us toward death. Whether we're talking about horticulture, social change, or spiritual formation, the ancient principle taught by Jesus remains: "Very truly I tell you, unless a kernel of wheat falls to the ground and dies, it remains only a single seed. But if it dies, it produces many seeds" (John 12:24).

Often, this experience of dying involves ordinary leaders and rural communities surrendering our nostalgia or narrow dreams or the need to control. It means letting go of our attachment to previous manifestations and forms so we can be open to the varieties of life growing in the present. We cannot receive, or construct, the "New Jerusalem" until we grieve and release the Old Jerusalem. Death is a very real but metaphorical process. However, the hard truth is that some of our churches, organizations, and even towns will die. How does this fit into the narrative of recovering abundance? What kind of work and worship can ordinary leaders facilitate in such scenarios?

I believe a good portion of struggling congregations can find new life as they reclaim their gifts, imagine new uses for their space and resources, and embrace the advantages of being a small church. But revitalization isn't for everyone. For those who discern their path is death, ordinary leaders step in to guide the group toward a meaningful and fruitful death. As rural pastor Brad Roth notes, we can be guided by ancient wisdom that calls us to *Ars moriendi*, "the art of dying."[17] The process can be dignified with grief, wisdom, companionship, and heartfelt planning. It doesn't have to be a slow descent into failure.

Author Kathleen Norris, writing about her experiences living in North Dakota, notes that folks in rural regions are forced to reckon with the death of cherished institutions as decline and decay take over their towns. This can lead us to despair, but it can also teach us deep and healing truths. She suggests this: "Maybe the desert wisdom of the Dakotas can teach us to love anyway, to love what is dying, in the face of death, and not pretend that things are other than they are."[18] Loving something as you are letting it go isn't easy. But we can find solace in the reality of resurrection. The seed has to die, but, as Jesus taught, it becomes "many seeds."

Churches, for example, are closing their doors all across rural America. Too often these endings are painful, dysfunctional, and chaotic. Death is messy. But as professor and church planter Ed Stetzer argues, nonprofit and denominational leaders can make this process easier and more dignified when they step in to provide a kind of "hospice care" for these congregations. Stetzer asks the readers of *Christianity Today*, "Why not make the death of your church a strategic decision rather than an unfortunate accident?"[19] It's a good question for ordinary leaders in declining churches that do not have the resources for revitalization.

What we need is here, to be sure. But what we need may be to lay down a congregation that has lived a good life and find a way to reinvest its gifts in a new ministry or project. Brad Roth proposes, "In the most simple and concrete terms, churches can glorify God in their dissolution by how they treat each other and what they do with their assets. Congregations can catch a resurrection vision by committing their remaining funds and sometimes their building to the ongoing mission of the church, such as through new church plants or revitalization efforts."[20] When we live into this "resurrection vision," we are still participating in the processes of Recovering Abundance and can certainly integrate practices such as inventory, generosity, and gratitude as we plan our legacy.

Organizations and projects such as the Church Legacy Initiative companion congregations through this process. They cherish the history of the congregation, discern the meaning of its mission over the years, and determine how that mission and history can find new life after death, whether by carrying out "bucket list" projects, making generous gifts to other organizations and ministries, or donating the building to a new church plant. Pastor Cate Noellert calls this "legacy work," which "is about coming in before [churches] get down to the bitter end and offering them a better end—the idea of finishing well and finishing strong and doing that with more care, with more empowerment—giving them the chance to close of their own accord and leave a legacy for the future."[21]

Whether we're talking about an individual, a business, a church, or a town, we all have a life cycle. We carry the memories of the life we have lived and the lives we have touched. We want to be remembered, and the way we are present at the end of our life is often a factor in *how* we are remembered. So we accept our inheritance, fully engage our best years, and plan our legacy. Whether the path is revitalization or resurrection, ordinary leaders have a sacred role to play as we partner with God to make "all things," even our small towns and rural communities, "new."

THE GROWING EDGE

These experiences of death and resurrection provide a glimpse into the ecology of renewal taking place in our communities—within us, around us, beyond us. Howard Thurman's dynamic description of this mystery is worth quoting in full:

> All around us worlds are dying and new worlds are being born; all around us life is dying and life is being born. The fruit ripens on the tree, the roots are silently at work in the darkness of the earth against a time when there shall be new lives, fresh blossoms, green fruit. Such is the growing edge! It is the extra breath from the exhausted lung, the one more thing to try when all else has failed, the upward reach of life when weariness closes in upon all endeavor. This is the basis of hope in moments of despair, the incentive to carry on when times are out of joint and men have lost their reason, the source of confidence when worlds crash and dreams whiten into ash. The birth of a child— life's most dramatic answer to death—this is the growing edge incarnate. Look well to the growing edge![22]

I love Thurman's image of the birth of a child as an answer to death. It's a beautiful sentence and a fascinating take on Christmas, and I say, "Bring on the babies!" But it's not just about babies. It's also

about the birth of new ideas, new visions, new businesses, new ministries, new partnerships. And in the midst of death and decline,
there's new life being born all over the place in our small towns and
rural regions.

You and I have the privilege of participating in this birthing
process. The practices we've explored will help us through the pain
and promise of this process. When we stay put and keep training in
the practices of abundant life, we become co-creators with the Holy
One, our midwife and guide. Sikh activist Valerie Kaur asks a powerful question about America that I think also speaks to small-town
and rural churches: "So the mother in me asks what if? What if this
darkness is not the darkness of the tomb, but the darkness of the
womb? What if our America is not dead but a country that is waiting to be born? What if the story of America is one long labor?"[23]

Ordinary leaders, the process is messy, the way takes practice,
but this is the divine invitation:

Look well to the growing edge; we need you, so don't get stuck
or stagnant.

Don't forget to breathe and push, because we are in the
midst of a long labor of renewal. Eat up and gather the leftovers; we've got a long but rewarding journey ahead.

Save your seeds of story and memory; you'll need them to
tell a new story.

NOTES

INTRODUCTION

1   J. D. Vance, *Hillbilly Elegy: A Memoir of a Family and Culture in Crisis* (New York: Harper, 2016), 195.
2   Ivan Illich, quoted in Patrick Scriven, "Telling an Alternative Story," Lewis Center for Church Leadership, February 25, 2015, https://www.church leadership.com/leading-ideas/telling-an-alternative-story/.
3   Martin Buber, quoted in Parker Palmer, *The Active Life: A Spirituality of Work, Creativity, and Caring* (San Francisco: HarperCollins, 1991), 36.
4   Chimamanda Ngozi Adichie, "The Danger of a Single Story," filmed July 2009 at TEDGlobal 2009 in Oxford, UK, video, 18:33, http://www.ted.com/talks /chimamanda_adichie_the_danger_of_a_single_story.
5   Wendell Berry, *It All Turns on Affection: The Jefferson Lecture and Other Essays* (Berkeley, CA: Counterpoint, 2012).
6   Thich Nhat Hanh, *Touching Peace: Practicing the Art of Mindful Living* (Berkeley, CA: Parallax Press, 1992), 1.

CHAPTER ONE

1   C. S. Lewis, *The Weight of Glory* (New York: HarperCollins, 1949), 161.
2   Emilie Griffin, *Wilderness Time: A Guide for Spiritual Retreat* (San Francisco: HarperCollins, 1997), 1.
3   Dallas Willard, quoted in Ruth Haley Barton, *Invitation to Retreat: The Gift and Necessity of Time Away with God* (Downers Grove, IL: InterVarsity Press, 2018), 1.
4   Belden Lane, *The Solace of Fierce Landscapes: Exploring Desert and Mountain Spirituality* (New York: Oxford University Press, 1998).
5   "About," Oasis Ranch and Retreat Center, accessed April 28, 2021, https://tinyurl.com/kymctvxn.

6   Philip Zaleski, *The Recollected Heart: A Guide to Making a Contemplative Weekend Retreat* (Notre Dame, IN: Ave Maria Press, 2009), 11.

7   Mark Batterson, *The Circle Maker: Praying Circles around Your Biggest Dreams and Greatest Fears* (Grand Rapids, MI: Zondervan, 2016), 31.

8   Ron Heifetz and Marty Linsky, *Leadership on the Line: Staying Alive through the Dangers of Leading* (Boston: Harvard Business School Press, 2002).

9   Edwin Friedman, *A Failure of Nerve: Leadership in the Age of the Quick Fix* (New York: Church Publishing, 2007), 33.

10 Friedman, *A Failure of Nerve*, 33.

11 Cal Newport, *Deep Work: Rules for Focused Success in a Distracted World* (New York: Grand Central Publishing, 2016), 277.

12 David Brooks, quoted in Newport, *Deep Work*, 277.

13 Madeleine L'Engle, *A Circle of Quiet* (San Francisco: HarperOne, 1972), 4.

14 Wallace J. Nichols, *Blue Mind: The Surprising Science That Shows How Being Near, In, On, or Under Water Can Make You Happier, Healthier, and Better at What You Do* (New York: Little, Brown, 2014), 142.

15 Nichols, *Blue Mind*, 6.

16 Beth Booram and David Booram, *When Faith Becomes Sight: Opening Your Eyes to God's Presence All Around You* (Downers Grove, IL: InterVarsity Press, 2019), 207.

17 Richard Rohr, *Adam's Return: The Five Promises of Male Initiation* (New York: Crossroad, 2004), 37.

CHAPTER TWO

1   Flora Slosson Wuellner, *Enter by the Gate: Jesus' 7 Guidelines When Making Hard Choices* (Nashville: Upper Room Books, 2004), 78.

2   Wuellner, *Enter by the Gate*, 70.

3   Henri Nouwen, *Out of Solitude: Three Meditations on the Christian Life* (Notre Dame, IN: Ave Maria Press, 2004), 56.

4   "Verge of a Miracle," by Rich Mullins, track 6 on *Rich Mullins*, Reunion, 1986.

5   Marcus Borg, *Meeting Jesus Again for the First Time: The Historical Jesus and the Heart of Contemporary Faith* (New York: HarperOne, 1995), 48.

6   Richard Rohr, "Our Foundational Commitment," accessed April 28, 2021, https://cac.org/our-foundational-commitment-2020-01-05/.

7   Parker Palmer, *The Active Life: A Spirituality of Work, Creativity, and Caring* (New York: Jossey-Bass, 1999), 122.

8   Thomas Kelly, *A Testament of Devotion* (New York: HarperCollins, 1941), 123.

9   Thomas Merton, *Conjectures of a Guilty Bystander* (New York: Random House, 1965), 81.

10   Kelly, *Testament of Devotion*, 99.

11   Henri Nouwen, *In the Name of Jesus: Reflections on Christian Leadership* (Chestnut Ridge, NY: Crossroad, 1989).

12   Henri Nouwen, *Life of the Beloved: Spiritual Living in a Secular World* (New York: Crossroad, 1992), 77.

13   Henri Nouwen, *The Selfless Way of Christ: Downward Mobility and the Spiritual Life* (Maryknoll, NY: Orbis Books, 2007), 50.

14   Parker Palmer, *Let Your Life Speak: Listening for the Voice of Vocation* (San Francisco: Jossey-Bass, 2000), 47.

15   Rumi, quoted in Palmer, *Let Your Life Speak*, 31.

16   Martin Buber, *The Way of Man: According to the Teaching of Hasidism* (Secaucus, NJ: Citadel Press, 1966), 15.

17   For an introduction to Ignatian spirituality, see James Martin, *The Jesuit Guide to (Almost) Everything: A Spirituality for Real Life* (New York: HarperCollins, 2010); Margaret Silf, *Inner Compass: An Invitation to Ignatian Spirituality* (Chicago: Loyola Press, 1999).

18   Paul Robb, "Conversion as a Human Experience," *Studies in the Spirituality of Jesuits* XIV (May 1982): 11–12.

19   Parker Palmer, *Healing the Heart of Democracy: The Courage to Create a Politics Worthy of the Human Spirit* (San Francisco: Jossey-Bass, 2011), 56.

20   A helpful resource for families learning the Examen practice is Dennis and Sheila Linn, *Sleeping with Bread: Holding What Gives You Life* (Mahwah, NJ: Paulist Press, 1995).

21   Abraham Heschel, *Man Is Not Alone: A Philosophy of Religion* (New York: Farrar, Straus and Giroux, 1951), 88.

22   Frederick Buechner, *Wishful Thinking: A Theological ABC* (New York: HarperCollins, 1993), 119.

23   "Millions of People in Rural Communities Face Hunger," Feeding America, accessed April 29, 2021, https://www.feedingamerica.org/hunger-in-america/rural-hunger-facts.

CHAPTER THREE

1   Patrick J. Carr and Maria J. Kefalas, *Hollowing Out the Middle: The Rural Brain Drain and What It Means for America* (Boston: Beacon Press, 2009).

2   Kevin Williamson, "If Your Town Is Failing, Just Go," *National Review*, October 6, 2015, https://www.nationalreview.com/2015/10/mobility-globalization-poverty-solution/.

3   Paul Krugman, "The Gambler's Ruin of Small Cities," *New York Times*, December 30, 2017, https://www.nytimes.com/2017/12/30/opinion/the-gamblers-ruin-of-small-cities-wonkish.html.

4 Bonnie Thurston, *The Spiritual Landscape of Mark* (Collegeville, PA: Liturgical Press, 2008).

5 *Look and See: A Portrait of Wendell Berry*, directed by Laura Dunn (Two Birds Film, 2016).

6 Parker Palmer, *The Active Life: A Spirituality of Work, Creativity, and Caring* (San Francisco: Jossey-Bass, 1990), 124.

7 For more on the desert fathers and mothers, see Christine Valters Paintner, *Desert Fathers and Mothers: Early Christian Wisdom Sayings* (Woodstock, VT: Skylight Paths, 2012); Thomas Merton, *The Wisdom of the Desert* (New York: New Directions, 1970).

8 Quoted in Jonathan Wilson-Hartgrove, *The Wisdom of Stability: Rooted Faith in a Mobile Culture* (Brewster, WA: Paraclete Press, 2010), 35.

9 Quoted in Kathleen Norris, *Dakota: A Spiritual Geography* (New York: Mariner Books, 2001), 24.

10 Wilson-Hartgrove, *The Wisdom of Stability*, 151–152.

11 Quoted in Michael Casey, *The Unexciting Life: Reflections on Benedictine Spirituality* (Petersham, MA: St. Bede's Publications, 2005), 245.

12 Kathleen Norris, *Acedia and Me: A Marriage, Monks, and a Writer's Life* (New York: Riverhead Books, 2008), 289.

13 "*Praktikos* VI.12," in *Evagrius of Pontus*, trans. Robert E. Sinkewicz (Oxford: Oxford University Press, 2003).

14 Quoted in Scott Russell Sanders, *Earth Works: Selected Essays* (Bloomington: Indiana University Press, 2012), 121–122.

15 Robert Putnam, *Bowling Alone: The Collapse and Revival of American Community, Revised & Updated* (New York: Simon & Schuster, 2001), 204.

16 Ronald Eller, *Uneven Ground: Appalachia Since 1945* (Lexington: University Press of Kentucky), 147–148.

17 Chezza Zoeller, "Featured Hero: Maria Gunnoe," One Earth, November 6, 2020, https://www.oneearth.org/featured-hero-maria-gunnoe.

18 Sarah Millhouse, "Brain Gain: Professionals Find Niche in Rural Upper Midwest," *The Daily Yonder*, May 30, 2018, https://dailyyonder.com/brain-gain-professionals-find-niche-rural-upper-midwest/2018/05/30/.

19 "Meet the Gals," Rethinking Rural, accessed July 15, 2021, http://www.rethinkingrural.org/home/the-rr-team/.

20 "Our Mission," Rethinking Rural, accessed July 15, 2021, http://www.rethinkingrural.org/home/about/.

21 "What Is STAY?" The STAY Project, accessed July 15, 2021, https://www.thestayproject.net/what-we-do.

22 Richard Florida, "Why Some Americans Won't Move, Even for a Higher Salary," *Bloomberg*, May 30, 2019, https://www.bloomberg.com/news/articles/2019-05-30/people-in-the-u-s-are-moving-homes-less-than-ever.

23   Quoted in Charles Marsh, *The Beloved Community: How Faith Shapes Social Justice from the Civil Right Movement to Today* (New York: Basic Books, 2005), 78.

CHAPTER FOUR

1   John McKnight and Peter Block, *The Abundant Community: Awakening the Power of Families and Neighborhoods* (San Francisco: Berrett-Koehler, 2010), 99.

2   Peter Block, *Community: The Structure of Belonging* (San Francisco: Berrett-Koehler, 2008), 50.

3   Block, *Community,* 121.

4   Mark Lau Branson, *Memories, Hopes, and Conversations: Appreciative Inquiry, Missional Engagement, and Congregational Care* (Lanham, MD: Rowman & Littlefield, 2016), 26.

5   Deborah Fallows, "Do You Speak Eastport?" *The Atlantic*, November 18, 2013, https://www.theatlantic.com/national/archive/2013/11/do-you-speak -eastport/281586.

6   "Oil: Boom in Ohio," *TIME*, February 21, 1964, http://content.time.com /time/subscriber/article/0,33009,870849,00.html.

7   Cornelia Butler Flora, Jan Flora, and Stephen Gasteyer, *Rural Communities: Legacy + Change* (New York: Westview Press, 2016), 15–17.

8   Patrick Strickland, "Life in the Pine Ridge Indian Reservation," *Al Jazeera*, November 2, 2016, https://www.aljazeera.com/features/2016/11/2/life -on-the-pine-ridge-native-american-reservation.

9   Araz Hachadourian and Christa Hillstrom, "6 Solutions That Support Native Sovereignty—From Tribal Schooling to Bison Herds," *Yes! Magazine*, December 19, 2016, https://www.yesmagazine.org/issue/50 -solutions/2016/12/19/6-solutions-that-support-native-sovereignty -from-tribal-schooling-to-bison-herds.

10   "Community Development," Thunder Valley CDC, accessed July 19, 2021, https://thundervalley.org/live-rez/our-programs/community-development.

11   Quoted in Marcus Borg, *The Heart of Christianity: Rediscovering a Life of Faith* (New York: HarperCollins, 2004), 179.

12   Barbara Brown Taylor, *The Seeds of Heaven: Sermons on the Gospel of Matthew* (Louisville, KY: Westminster John Knox Press, 2004), 53.

13   Walter Brueggemann, "The Trusted Creature," *The Catholic Biblical Quarterly* 31, no. 4 (1969): 484–498, http://www.jstor.org/stable/43712674.

14   Wendell Berry, *The Selected Poems of Wendell Berry* (Berkeley, CA: Counterpoint, 1998), 90.

CHAPTER FIVE

1 Susan Trollinger, *Selling the Amish: The Tourism of Nostalgia* (Baltimore: Johns Hopkins University Press, 2012), 150.

2 Gene Logsdon, *At Nature's Pace: Farming and the American Dream* (White River Junction, VT: Chelsea Green, 1994), xii.

3 Donald B. Kraybill and Steven M. Nolt, *Amish Enterprise: From Plows to Profits* (Baltimore: Johns Hopkins University Press, 2004), 25.

4 Kraybill and Nolt, *Amish Enterprise,* 26.

5 Kraybill and Nolt, *Amish Enterprise,* 27.

6 Kraybill and Nolt, *Amish Enterprise,* 14.

7 N. T. Wright, *Matthew* (Downers Grove, IL: InterVarsity Press, 2011), 64.

8 "Chesterhill Produce Auction: A Rural Appalachia Case Story," The Voinovich School of Leadership and Public Affairs, Ohio University, January 2010, https://chesterhillproduceauction.com/wp-content/uploads/2019/03/CPA-Case-Study-Jan.-2010.pdf.pdf.

9 Eugene Peterson, "A Conversation with Eugene Peterson 2007," interview by Dean Nelson, Writer's Symposium by the Sea, University of California Television, February 8, 2008, YouTube video, 29:36, https://www.youtube.com/watch?v=FaaIui7cESs.

10 "Chesterhill Produce Auction."

11 Walter Brueggemann, *The Prophetic Imagination* (Minneapolis: Fortress Press, 2001), 40.

12 Brueggemann, *Prophetic Imagination,* 4.

13 Casey Tygrett, *As I Recall: Discovering the Place of Memories in Our Spiritual Life* (Downers Grove, IL: InterVarsity Press, 2019), 152.

14 Steve Willis, *Imagining the Small Church: Celebrating a Simpler Path* (Herndon, VA: Alban Institute, 2012), 95.

15 "About Us," Partners for Sacred Places, accessed July 26, 2021, https://sacredplaces.org/about-us/.

16 "Home," Nuns & Nones, accessed July 26, 2021, https://www.nunsandnones.org/.

CHAPTER SIX

1 William D. Barns, "Oliver Hudson Kelley and the Genesis of the Grange: A Reappraisal," *Agricultural History* 41, no. 3 (1967): 229–242, http://www.jstor.org/stable/3740337.

2 Jenny Bourne, *In Essentials, Unity: An Economic History of the Grange Movement* (Athens: Ohio University Press, 2017), 14–15.

3 Thomas A. Woods, *Knights of the Plow: Oliver H. Kelley and the Origins of the Grange in Republican Ideology* (Ames: Iowa State University Press, 1991), 90.

4   "Patrons of Husbandry," Ohio History Central, accessed July 21, 2021, https://ohiohistorycentral.org/w/Patrons_of_Husbandry.

5   Thomas Burnell, "Grange," *Encyclopedia of the Great Plains*, accessed July 21, 2021, http://plainshumanities.unl.edu/encyclopedia/doc/egp.pd .025.

6   Maureen Pao, "Cesar Chavez: The Life behind a Legacy of Farm Labor Rights," *NPR*, August 12, 2016, https://www.npr.org/2016/08/02/488428577 /cesar-chavez-the-life-behind-a-legacy-of-farm-labor-rights.

7   "The History of Si Se Puede," United Farm Workers, accessed July 21, 2021, https://ufw.org/research/history/history-si-se-puede.

8   Walter Wink, *The Powers That Be: Theology for a New Millennium* (New York: Random House, 2010), 27.

9   Gary Paul Nabhan, *Jesus for Farmers and Fishes: Jesus for All Those Marginalized by Our Food System* (Minneapolis: Broadleaf Books, 2021), 5.

10 John Dominic Crossan, *God and Empire: Jesus against Rome, Then and Now* (New York: HarperCollins, 2007), 13.

11 Richard Horsley and Neil Silberman, *The Message and the Kingdom: How Jesus and Paul Ignited a Revolution and Transformed the Ancient World* (Minneapolis: Fortress Press, 2002), 55.

12 Horsley and Silberman, *The Message and the Kingdom*, 55.

13 Richard Horsley, *Jesus and the Powers: Conflict, Covenant, and the Hope of the Poor* (Minneapolis: Fortress Press, 2011), 153.

14 Horsley, *Jesus and the Powers*, 88.

15 Dennis Jacobsen, *Congregations and Community Organizing* (Minneapolis: Fortress Press, 2001), 39.

16 Martin Luther King Jr., *The Radical King*, ed. Cornel West (Boston: Beacon Press, 2015), 193.

17 J. D. Vance, *Hillbilly Elegy: A Memoir of a Family and Culture in Crisis* (New York: HarperCollins, 2016), 147.

18 Vance, *Hillbilly Elegy*, 256.

19 Charles Mackay, *Extraordinary Popular Delusions and the Madness of Crowds* (New York: L.C. Page, 1932).

20 Parker Palmer, *The Active Life: A Spirituality of Work, Creativity, and Caring* (San Francisco: Jossey-Bass, 1991), 133.

21 Palmer, *The Active Life*, 129.

22 Palmer, *The Active Life*, 130.

23 Quoted in Parker Palmer, *A Hidden Wholeness: The Journey toward an Undivided Life* (San Francisco: Jossey-Bass, 2004), 71.

24 David Garland, *Mark* (Grand Rapids: Zondervan, 2002), 152.

25 Anne Helen Petersen, "What Happened in Bethel, Ohio?" *Buzzfeed*, July 5, 2020, https://www.buzzfeednews.com/article/annehelenpetersen/bethel -ohio-black-lives-matter-protest.

26   Mason Adams, "How #NoHateInMyHoller Became the War Cry for Appalachia,"
      The Daily Yonder, August 30, 2017, https://dailyyonder.com/nohateinmyholler
      -became-war-cry-appalachia/2017/08/30/.

CHAPTER SEVEN

1   Henri Nouwen, *With Burning Hearts: A Meditation on the Eucharistic Life*
      (Maryknoll, NY: Orbis Books, 1994), 4–5.

2   John Dominic Crossan, *Jesus: A Revolutionary Biography* (San Francisco:
      HarperCollins, 1994).

3   Quoted in Christine Pohl, *Making Room: Recovering Hospitality as a Chris-
      tian Tradition* (Grand Rapids, MI: Eerdmans, 1999), 8.

4   Peter Leithart, *Blessed Are the Hungry: Meditations on the Lord's Supper*
      (Moscow, ID: Canon Press, 2000), 115.

5   "Langar: The Communal Meal," The Pluralism Project of Harvard Univer-
      sity, July 27, 2021, https://pluralism.org/langar-the-communal-meal.

6   John McKnight and Peter Block, *The Abundant Community: Awakening
      the Power of Families and Neighborhoods* (San Francisco: Berrett-Koehler,
      2010), 79.

7   Ana Maria Pineda, "Hospitality," in *Practicing Our Faith: A Way of Life for a
      Searching People,* ed. Dorothy Bass (Minneapolis: Fortress Press, 2019), 42.

8   Robert Putnam, *The Collapse and Revival of American Community* (New
      York: Simon & Schuster, 2000), 23.

9   Henri Nouwen, *Reaching Out: The Three Movements of the Spiritual Life*
      (New York: Doubleday, 1975), 69.

10   Gerhard Lohfink, *Does God Need the Church?: Toward a Theology of the Peo-
      ple of God* (Collegeville, MN: Liturgical Press, 1999), 143.

11   Priya Parker, *The Art of Gathering: How We Meet and Why It Matters* (New
      York: Riverhead Books, 2018), 75.

12   Parker, *Art of Gathering,* 74.

13   "The Rural Climate Dialogues," Voices for Rural Resilience, accessed July
      27, 2021, https://voicesforrural.org/rural-climate-dialogues.

14   Whitney Kimball Coe, quoted in Dale Mackey, "Letting 'America Be Amer-
      ica Again,'" *The Daily Yonder,* March 23, 2018, https://dailyyonder.com
      /letting-america-america/2018/03/23/.

15   Quoted in Jennifer Brown, *How to Be an Inclusive Leader: Your Role in Cre-
      ating Cultures of Belonging Where Everyone Can Thrive* (Oakland, CA: Ber-
      rett-Koehler, 2019), 90.

16   Quoted in Stephen Clark, *G. K. Chesterton: Thinking Backward, Looking
      Forward* (West Conshohocken, PA: Templeton Foundation Press, 2006),
      108.

17 Gustavo Gutiérrez, *We Drink from Our Own Wells: The Spiritual Journey of a People* (New York: Orbis, 2003), 7.

18 J. D. Vance, *Hillbilly Elegy: A Memoir of a Family and Culture in Crisis* (New York: HarperCollins, 2016), 3.

19 Quoted in David Scott, *A Revolution of Love: The Meaning of Mother Teresa* (Chicago: Loyola Press, 2001), 62.

20 Quoted in Pohl, *Making Room*, 74.

21 Ray Oldenburg, *The Great Good Place: Cafes, Coffee Shops, Bookstores, Bars, Hair Salons, and Other Hangouts at the Heart of a Community* (Cambridge, MA: Da Capo Press, 1999).

22 Brandon O'Brien, *The Strategically Small Church: Intimate, Nimble, Authentic, and Effective* (Minneapolis: Bethany House, 2010), 15.

23 Steve Willis, *Imagining the Small Church: Celebrating a Simpler Path* (Lanham, MD: Rowman & Littlefield, 2012), 66.

24 "Hikers," Presbyterian Church of the Mountain, accessed July 28, 2021, https://churchofthemountain.org/hikers/.

25 "Hikers Turn to Church of the Mountain on Appalachian Trail," Synod of the Trinity, May 20, 2015, https://www.syntrinity.org/featured/hikers-turn-to-church-of-the-mountain-on-appalachian-trail/.

CHAPTER EIGHT

1 Mark Jenkins, "So You're Lost in the Wilderness—These Tips Could Save Your Life," *The Guardian*, May 31, 2016, https://www.theguardian.com/travel/2016/may/31/wilderness-survival-outdoor-gear-life-saving-tips-hiking-camping.

2 Thomas Merton, *New Seeds of Contemplation* (Bardstown, KY: Abbey of Gethsemani, 1961), 261.

3 Thich Nhat Hanh, *How to Sit* (Berkeley, CA: Parallax Press, 2014), 6.

4 Scott Russell Sanders, *Earth Works: Selected Essays* (Bloomington: Indiana University Press, 2012), 114.

5 Sanders, *Earth Works*, 114.

6 Richard Louv, *Last Child in the Woods: Saving Our Children from Nature-Deficit Disorder* (Chapel Hill, NC: Algonquin Books, 2005).

7 Edward O. Wilson, *Biophilia* (Cambridge, MA: Harvard University Press, 1984).

8 Florence Williams, *The Nature Fix: Why Nature Makes Us Healthier, Happier, and More Creative* (New York: W. W. Norton, 2017).

9 Denis Edwards, *Ecology at the Heart of Faith: The Change of Heart That Leads to a New Way of Living on Earth* (Maryknoll, NY: Orbis Books, 2006), 51.

10   Quoted in Steven Chase, *Nature as Spiritual Practice* (Grand Rapids, MI: Eerdmans, 2011), 80.

11   Wendell Berry, *What Matters? Economics for a Renewed Commonwealth* (Berkeley, CA: Counterpoint, 2010), 118.

12   Parker Palmer, *Let Your Life Speak: Listening for the Voice of Vocation* (San Francisco: Jossey-Bass, 2000), 98.

13   Sallie McFague, *The Body of God: An Ecological Theology* (Minneapolis: Fortress Press, 1993).

14   John O'Donohue, *Four Elements: Reflections on Nature* (New York: Harmony Books, 2011), 129.

15   Kathleen Norris, *Dakota: A Spiritual Geography* (New York: Mariner, 1993).

16   Richard Siemers, "Close Encounter—'City' Pastors Learn about Farm Life," *The Land*, April 10, 2009, https://www.thelandonline.com/archives/cover -story-close-encounter-city-pastors-learn-about-farm-life/article _e855ebb1-7e64-500e-a4c4-6750467d2acf.html.

17   Shalom Hill Farm, accessed August 4, 2021, https://shalomhillfarm.org/.

18   "Educational Opportunities," Shalom Hill Farm, accessed August 4, 2021, https://shalomhillfarm.org/opportunities.

19   "Mission & Vision," Church in the Country, accessed August 4, 2021, https://churchinthecountry.com/about-us/.

20   "Rural Life Celebration," Catholic Rural Life, accessed August 4, 2021, https://catholicrurallife.org/resources/rural-life-celebration-guide/.

21   Wendell Berry, *Sex, Economy, Freedom, and Community: Eight Essays* (New York: Pantheon Books, 1993), 103.

22   "A Movement Is Emerging," Wild Church Network, accessed August 4, 2021, https://www.wildchurchnetwork.com/.

23   Rebecca Solnit, *Hope in the Dark: Untold Histories, Wild Possibilities* (Chicago: Haymarket Books, 2016), xv.

24   John McIlwaine, "Touching the Earth," Garrison Institute, February 8, 2017, https://www.garrisoninstitute.org/blog/touching-the-earth/.

CHAPTER NINE

1   Quoted in Joan Chittister, *The Breath of the Soul: Reflections on Prayer* (New London, CT: Twenty-Third Publications, 2009), 39.

2   Karl Barth, *Church Dogmatics: The Doctrine of Reconciliation, Volume 4, Part 1* (New York: T & T Clark International, 1956), 41.

3   Diana Butler Bass, *Grateful: The Transformative Power of Giving Thanks* (New York: HarperOne, 2018), xxiv.

4   Thomas Merton, *Thoughts in Solitude* (New York: Farrar, Straus and Giroux, 1999), 33.

5   Quoted in David Harden, *Placed People: Rootedness in G. K. Chesterton, C. S. Lewis, and Wendell Berry* (Eugene, OR: Pickwick, 2015), 128.

6   Linda Hogan, *Dwellings: A Spiritual History of the Living World* (New York: Touchstone, 1995), 159.

7   Butler Bass, *Grateful*, xxiv.

8   Steven Harper, "Meal Chant Stew," Gratefulness, accessed August 5, 2021, https://gratefulness.org/resource/meal-chant-stew/.

9   "Ha-Matzi-Bread," Judaism 101.

10 Walter Brueggemann, "The Liturgy of Abundance, the Myth of Scarcity," *The Christian Century*, March 24–31, 1999.

11 Interview with Jill Suttie, "Is Gratitude the Path to a Better World?," *Greater Good*, May 29, 2013, https://greatergood.berkeley.edu/article/item/is _gratitude_the_path_to_better_world.

12 Butler Bass, *Gratitude*, 185.

13 Henri Nouwen, *The Return of the Prodigal Son: A Story of Homecoming* (New York: Image Books, 1994), 85.

14 David Steindl-Rast, *Gratefulness, the Heart of Prayer: An Approach to Life in Fullness* (New York: Paulist Press, 1984), 11.

15 Ryan Holiday, *The Obstacle Is the Way: The Timeless Art of Turning Trials into Triumph* (New York: Portfolio, 2014), 44.

16 "2019 Innovation Business of the Year: Monarch Flyway," University of Nebraska Omaha, accessed August 5, 2021, https://www.unomaha.edu /nebraska-business-development-center/news/2020/03/innovation -business-of-the-year-monarch-flyway.php.

17 Lynne Twist, *The Soul of Money: Transforming Your Relationship with Money and Life* (New York: W. W. Norton, 2003), 120.

18 Michael Hyatt, "A Question That Changes Everything: How to Reframe Crisis as Opportunity," Michael Hyatt, September 17, 2012, https://michaelhyatt .com/a-question-that-changes-everything/.

19 Steve Hewitt, "How We Rebuilt Tornado-Destroyed Town," CNN, March 26, 2011, http://www.cnn.com/2011/OPINION/05/26/hewitt.rebuilding .city/index.html.

20 Robert Emmons, "How Gratitude Can Help You through Hard Times," *Greater Good*, May 13, 2013, https://greatergood.berkeley.edu/article/item /how_gratitude_can_help_you_through_hard_times.

21 "Twister Impetus for Turning Kansas Town Green," NPR, May 2, 2008, https://www.npr.org/transcripts/90118597.

22 Marisa Schulz, "Why Cities Should Tap into the Power of Joyful Interventions," Strong Towns, August 25, 2020, https://www.strongtowns.org/journal/2020 /8/21/the-art-of-joyful-interventions.

23 Grace Smuggler, "Who Loved You into Being?" Smuggling Grace, February 15, 2017, https://reneeroederer.com/2017/02/15/who-loved-you-into -being/.

CHAPTER TEN

1 "Surprising Truths: Stories of Rural America," Plenary at Earlham School of Religion Ministry of Writing Conference, November 2, 2019.

2 John Dominic Crossan, *The Power of Parable: How Fiction by Jesus Became Fiction about Jesus* (New York: HarperCollins, 2012), 227–228.

3 William Barclay, *Barclay on the Lectionary: Mark, Year B* (Edinburgh: St. Andrew Press, 2014), 206–207.

4 James Martin, *Jesus: A Pilgrimage* (New York: HarperCollins, 2014), 320.

5 Lynne Twist, *The Soul of Money: Transforming Your Relationship with Money and Life* (New York: W. W. Norton, 2003), 97.

6 Amy Oden, *God's Welcome: Hospitality for a Gospel-Hungry World* (Cleveland: Pilgrim Press, 2008), 19.

7 Albert Camus, *The Rebel*, trans. Anthony Bower (New York: Knopf, 1954), 271.

8 Quoted in Richard Foster, *Prayer: Finding the Heart's True Home* (San Francisco: HarperCollins, 1992), 179.

9 Jane Braxton Little, "A Mom's Plea for Library Books Brought in 15,000—And Transformed Her Small Town," *YES!*, September 19, 2016, https://www.yesmagazine.org/democracy/2016/09/19/a-moms-plea-for-library-books-brought-in-15000-and-transformed-her-small-town.

10 "Mormon Welfare Program," PBS, June 24, 2016, https://www.pbs.org/wnet/religionandethics/2016/06/24/mormon-welfare-program/31091/.

11 Conor Morris, "Athens County Community Springs Forth with Help for Struggling Citizens," *The Athens*, March 18, 2020, https://www.athensnews.com/news/local/athens-county-community-springs-forth-with-help-for-struggling-citizens/article_a5765b86-6948-11ea-a842-9f195ddc8ede.html.

12 Tom Gerken, "Coronavirus: Kind Canadians Start 'Caremongering' Trend," BBC, March 16, 2020, https://www.bbc.com/news/world-us-canada-51915723.

13 Chip Heath and Dan Heath, *Switch: How to Change Things When Change Is Hard* (New York: Broadway Books, 2010), 67–71.

14 Michael Shuman, *The Local Economy Solution: How Innovative, Self-Financing "Pollinator" Enterprises Can Grow Jobs and Prosperity* (White River Junction, VT: Chelsea Green, 2015), 36–38.

CHAPTER ELEVEN

1 Michael Rhodes, Robby Holt, and Brian Fikkert, *Practicing the King's Economy: Honoring Jesus in How We Work, Earn, Spend, Save, and Give* (Grand Rapids, MI: Baker Books, 2018), 87.

2 Quoted in Reta Halteman Finger, *Of Widows and Meals: Communal Meals in the Book of Acts* (Grand Rapids, MI: Eerdmans, 2008), 183.

3 Quoted in Zoltan Grossman, *Unlikely Alliances: Native Nations and White Communities Join to Defend Rural Lands* (Seattle: University of Washington Press, 2017), 30.

4 Martin Luther King Jr., *The Radical King*, ed. Cornel West (Boston: Beacon, 2015), 128.

5 Steve Corbett and Brian Fikkert, *When Helping Hurts: How to Alleviate Poverty Without Hurting the Poor . . . and Yourself* (Chicago: Moody, 2009).

6 Dom Hélder Câmara, *Essential Writings* (Maryknoll, NY: Orbis Books, 2009), 11.

7 Richard Grant, "When the Socialist Revolution Came to Oklahoma—And Was Crushed," *Smithsonian*, October 2019, https://www.smithsonianmag .com/history/socialist-revolution-oklahoma-crushed-green-corn -rebellion-180973073/.

8 Steven Charleston, *The Four Vision Quests of Jesus* (New York: Morehouse, 2015), 158.

9 Ayaz Virji, *Love Thy Neighbor: A Muslim Doctor's Struggle for Home in Rural America* (New York: Convergent Books, 2019).

10 Virji, *Love Thy Neighbor*, 16.

11 Gil Rendle, *Doing the Math of Mission: Fruits, Faithfulness, and Metrics* (Lanham, MD: Rowman & Littlefield, 2014).

12 Patrick M. Lencioni, *Silos, Politics and Turf Wars: A Leadership Fable about Destroying the Barriers That Turn Colleagues into Competitors* (San Francisco: Jossey-Bass, 2006), 175.

13 Karl Vaters, "Dismantling Ministry Silos in the Small Church," *Christianity Today*, June 2, 2015, https://www.christianitytoday.com/karl -vaters/2015/june/dismantling-ministry-silos-in-small-church.html.

14 E. F. Schumacher, *Small Is Beautiful: Economics as If People Mattered* (New York: Harper & Row, 1973), 216.

15 Patrick J. Carr and Maria J. Kefalas, *Hollowing Out the Middle: The Rural Brain Drain and What It Means for America* (Boston: Beacon Press, 2009), xi.

16 Ellie Lisitsa, "The Four Horsemen: Contempt," The Gottman Institute, May 13, 2013, https://www.gottman.com/blog/the-four-horsemen-contempt/.

17 Arthur C. Brooks, "Our Culture of Contempt," *New York Times*, March 2, 2019, https://www.nytimes.com/2019/03/02/opinion/sunday/political -polarization.html.

18 Francis de Sales, *Thy Will Be Done! Letters of Saint Francis de Sales* (Manchester, NH: Sophia Institute Press, 1995), 65.

CHAPTER TWELVE

1 Brad Roth, *God's Country: Faith, Hope, and the Future of the Rural Church* (Harrisonburg, VA: Herald Press, 2017), 33.

2 Roth, *God's Country*, 34.

3 John Dewey, *How We Think* (New York: Dover, 2003), 78.

4   Eric R. Kandel, *In Search of Memory: The Emergence of a New Science of Mind* (New York: W.W. Norton, 2006), 10.

5   Casey Tygrett, *As I Recall: Discovering the Place of Memories in Our Spiritual Life* (Downers Grove, IL: InterVarsity Press, 2019), 11.

6   James Bryan Smith, *The Magnificent Story: Uncovering a Gospel of Beauty, Goodness, and Truth* (Downers Grove, IL: InterVarsity Press, 2017), 5.

7   Lovett H. Weems, "Leadership in the Small Membership Church," Lewis Center for Church Membership, October 4, 2017, https://www.churchleadership.com/leading-ideas/leadership-and-the-small-membership-church/.

8   Anthony Pappas, *Entering the World of the Small Church* (Lanham, MD: Alban Institute, 2000), 58.

9   Quoted in Steve Willis, *Imagining the Small Church: Celebrating a Simpler Path* (Lanham, MD: Rowman & Littlefield, 2012), 36.

10 Wendell Berry, *What Matters? Economics for a Renewed Commonwealth* (Berkeley, CA: Counterpoint, 2010), 145.

11 Seamus Heaney, *The Cure of Troy: A Version of Sophocles' Philoctetes* (New York: Farrar, Straus and Giroux, 1990), 77.

12 Miroslav Volf, *The End of Memory: Remembering Rightly in a Violent World* (Grand Rapids, MI: Eerdmans, 2006), 11.

13 Quoted in Tom Vellner, "Remembrance as the Secret of Redemption," *BU Today*, April 26, 2012, https://www.bu.edu/articles/2012/remembrance-as-the-secret-of-redemption/.

14 Gordon Livingston, *Too Soon Old, Too Late Smart* (New York: Marlowe, 2004), 148–149.

15 Laura Poppick, "The Maine Farmer Saving the World's Rarest Heirloom Seeds," *Down East*, April 2020, https://downeast.com/land-wildlife/rare-heirloom-seeds/.

16 Jaroslav Pelikan, *The Vindication of Tradition* (New Haven, CT: Yale University Press, 1984), 65.

17 Roth, *God's Country*, 164.

18 Kathleen Norris, *Dakota: A Spiritual Geography* (New York: First Mariner Books, 2001), 121.

19 Ed Stetzer, "Creating a Hospice Ministry for Churches," *Christianity Today*, September 17, 2014, https://churchleaders.com/outreach-missions/outreach-missions-articles/176393-ed-stetzer-creating-a-hospice-ministry-for-churches.html.

20 Roth, *God's Country*, 176.

21 Yonat Shimron, "Legacy ministries to dying churches give congregations a way to end well," Faith and Leadership, September 5, 2017, https://faithandleadership.com/legacy-ministries-dying-churches-give-congregations-way-end-well.

22 Howard Thurman, *Meditations of the Heart* (Boston: Beacon Press, 1953), 134.

23 Valarie Kaur, *See No Stranger: A Memoir and Manifesto of Revolutionary Love* (New York: Random House, 2020), xiii.

RECOMMENDED READING

Berry, Wendell. *Jayber Crow: A Novel*. Berkeley, CA: Counterpoint Press, 2001.

Block, Peter. *Community: The Structure of Belonging*. San Francisco: Berrett-Koehler, 2008.

Chambers, Cassie. *Hill Women: Finding Family and a Way Forward in the Appalachian Mountains*. New York: Ballantine Books, 2021.

Curtice, Kaitlin B. *Native: Identity, Belonging, and Rediscovering God*. Grand Rapids, MI: Brazos Press, 2020.

Daman, Glenn. *The Forgotten Church: Why Rural Ministry Matters for Every Church in America*. Chicago: Moody, 2018.

Elsdon, Mark. *We Aren't Broke: Uncovering Hidden Resources for Mission and Ministry*. Grand Rapids, MI: Eerdmans, 2021.

Flora, Cornelia Butler, Jan L. Flora, and Stephen P. Gasteyer. *Rural Communities: Legacy + Change*. New York: Westview Press, 2016.

Kaur, Valarie. *See No Stranger: A Memoir and Manifesto of Revolutionary Love*. New York: Random House, 2020.

Macy, Joanna, and Chris Johnstone. *Active Hope: How to Face the Mess We're in without Going Crazy*. Novato, CA: New World Library, 2012.

McKnight, John, and Peter Block. *The Abundant Community: Awakening the Power of Families and Neighborhoods*. San Francisco: Berrett-Koehler, 2010.

Nabhan, Gary Paul. *Jesus for Farmers and Fishers: Justice for All Those Marginalized by Our Food System*. Minneapolis: Broadleaf Books, 2021.

Norris, Kathleen. *Dakota: A Spiritual Geography*. New York: First Mariner Books, 2001.

O'Brien, Brandon J. *Not from Around Here: What Unites Us, What Divides Us, and How We Can Move Forward*. Chicago: Moody, 2019.

Palmer, Parker. *Healing the Heart of Democracy: The Courage to Create a Politics Worthy of the Human Spirit*. San Francisco: Jossey-Bass, 2011.

Roth, Brad. *God's Country: Faith, Hope, and the Future of the Rural Church*. Harrisonburg, VA: Herald Press, 2017.

Sanders, Scott Russell. *Staying Put: Making a Home in a Restless World*. Boston: Beacon Press, 1993.

Stanton, Allen. *Reclaiming Rural: Building Thriving Rural Congregations*. Lanham, MD: Rowman & Littlefield, 2021.

Stavros, Jacqueline, and Cheri Torres. *Conversations Worth Having: Using Appreciative Inquiry to Fuel Productive and Meaningful Engagement*. San Francisco: Berrett-Koehler, 2018.

Willis, Steve. *Imagining the Small Church: Celebrating a Simpler Path*. Lanham, MD: Rowman & Littlefield, 2012.